Being Philosophical

T0314370

Other Books of Interest from St. Augustine's Press

D. Q. McInerny, *Being Ethical*

James V. Schall, *On the Principles of Taxing Beer:
And Other Brief Philosophical Essays*

James V. Schall, *At a Breezy Time of Day*

Ralph McInerny, *The Defamation of Pius XII*

Ralph McInerny, *Good Knights: Eight Stories*

Ralph McInerny, *The Soul of Wit*

Ralph McInerny, *Let's Read Latin*

Marvin R. O'Connell, *Telling Stories that Matter: Memoirs and Essays*

Rémi Brague, *Moderately Modern*

Christopher Kaczor, *O Rare Ralph McInerny*

Josef Pieper, *A Journey to Point Omega: Autobiography from 1964*

Paweł Armada, *Humanism as Realism: Three Essays Concerning the Thought of
Paul Elmer More and Irving Babbitt*

Gabriel Marcel, *Toward Another Kingdom: Two Dramas of the Darker Years*

Michael Davis, *Electras: Aeschylus, Sophocles, and Euripides*

Michael Franz (editor), *Eric Voegelin's Late Meditations and Essays:
Critical Commentary Companions*

Francisco Insa, *The Formation of Affectivity: A Christian Approach*

D. C. Schindler, *God and the City: An Essay in Political Metaphysics*

Roger Scruton, *An Intelligent Person's Guide to Modern Culture*

Roger Scruton, *The Meaning of Conservatism: Revised 3rd Edition*

Roger Scruton, *The Politics of Culture and Other Essays*

Roger Scruton, *On Hunting*

Leon J. Podles, *Losing the Good Portion:
Why Men Are Alienated from Christianity*

Allen Mendenhall, *Shouting Softly: Lines on Law, Literature, and Culture*

Being Philosophical
D. Q. McInerny

St. Augustine's Press
South Bend, Indiana

Manufactured in the United States of America.

1 2 3 4 5 6   28 27 26 25 24 23

Library of Congress Control Number: 2023945687

Paperback ISBN: 978-1-58731-077-5
Ebook ISBN: 978-1-58731-078-2

∞ The paper used in this publication meets the minimum requirements of the American National Standard for Information Sciences – Permanence of Paper for Printed Materials, ANSI Z39.48-1984.

St. Augustine's Press
www.staugustine.net

Table of Contents

Introduction   1

Chapter One — Clear and Correct Thinking: Logic   6

Chapter Two — The Material World: The Philosophy of Nature   30

Chapter Three — The Living World: Philosophical Psychology   59

Chapter Four — How Do We Know? Epistemology   90

Chapter Five — The Moral Realm: Ethics   125

Chapter Six — The Social Realm: Political Philosophy   159

Chapter Seven — Foundational Principles: Metaphysics   196

Chapter Eight — Ultimate Questions: Natural Theology   234

Introduction

Philosophy is the systematic study of whatever the human mind is capable of knowing. That covers a great deal; in fact, it covers just about everything. To be a philosopher is to be a life-long student, someone whose curiosity is unquenchable, and who is continuously asking questions. The importance of asking questions, the right questions, for philosophy is beyond dispute, but we must be always mindful of the common-sense truth that the whole purpose of posing a question is to put us on the path of finding an acceptable answer to it. Simply to ask questions, as if it were an end in itself, is little more than an exercise in mental gymnastics, is to truncate the very process of intellectual inquiry. A question not ordered toward answers would be like stopping at inhalation, the first half of the vital exercise of breathing; if we do not follow it with exhalation the body will promptly put up a protest. The kind of answers the philosopher is most interested in serve, at a very basic level, to explain *what* things are and then, penetrating more deeply, *why* things are. The second question is concerned with origins. What accounts for the most rudimentary bit of knowledge we can know about anything is the fact that it exists.

The philosopher takes truth with the utmost seriousness. It is not to be toyed with, not something the reality of which or the practical attainability of which are apt topics for serious debate. To deny the reality of truth, to deny the capacity of the mind to arrive at truth, is not simply to undermine philosophy, it is to subvert the very purpose of human reason. Truth can at times be tryingly difficult to attain, but the prize goes to the persevering. If the very possibility of truth is denied, words lose their proper purposefulness, which is to convey meaning, to connect mind with mind, and thus provide foundation for community. Skepticism, the sickly attitude that habitually entertains doubts about the reality and attainability of truth, is the bane of philosophy. To subscribe to it would be like a runner who voluntarily submits to being hamstrung.

Philosophy, if we are to consider it rightly, should not be regarded as the narrow and exclusive province of only a few properly credentialed individuals, as if it were a profession the professing of which depended upon the approving say-so of established professionals. Philosophy does not have to be legitimized by academic degrees. If the habit does not necessarily make the monk, neither does the degree necessarily make the philosopher. There are but two rudimentary qualifications, the meeting of which can put one on the path to being a genuine philosopher: (1) a creative impatience with ignorance; (2) an unswerving commitment to truth.

This is a book on philosophy. That apparently self-explanatory statement requires explanation. "Philosophy" can be taken in several ways, but only two of which are pertinent here. The term can refer to one thing or to many. Philosophy as one thing is what was described in the first sentence of this Introduction: it is the discipline, the practice itself—the systematic study of whatever the human mind is capable of knowing. That is what we can call the inclusive or comprehensive understanding of philosophy; it covers, umbrella-like, all the many particular philosophies, the individual systems, that have been developed over the centuries, East and West, most of which are the brain children of individual thinkers. Not all philosophical systems are equal, in terms of the quality of the philosophy they embody, the specific ideas they propose and develop; some philosophies are brilliant, some are so-so, yet others are, it has to be said, decidedly unimpressive. As to the last, the world would not be the worse had they never gone public.

Many of the books on philosophy written for a general audience, as is this one, tend to be historical surveys of philosophy, describing and explaining a number of different philosophical systems. Books of this kind are valuable, for they give the reader an idea of the range and variety of philosophical thought, especially if, as some of these books do, they start with the very origins of philosophy and end with the contemporary philosophical scene. It is good to know a number of philosophical systems, it is better to know what to make of them, to be able to distinguish the brilliant, from the so-so, from the decidedly unimpressive. In order to be able to do that you need your own philosophical frame of reference, in the form of a particular philosophy of which you have a good knowledge and to which you are intellectually committed. The difference between being an historian of philosophy and a philosopher is that the latter is dedicated to a particular philosophical system, from the perspective of which the quality of other philosophical systems can be responsibly adjudicated. Sound philosophical judgments are grounded on a sound philosophy. If you do not have specific, concrete standards on the basis of which you make judgments, your judgments can be little more than whimsical.

This book is about a particular philosophy, which can be identified as Aristotelian-Thomism, or simply Thomism, or, less often now, Neo-Scholasticism. I favor the first, because it is the most fully descriptive of the philosophy itself, although I often use "Thomism" simply for the sake of brevity. This is the philosophy to which I am intellectually committed, for the simple reason that I am convinced that, taking it all in all, it is the soundest, most fertile philosophy that is available to us.

There are three general reasons for singling out Aristotelian-Thomism for special philosophical regard. The particular reasons for doing so are many and are to be found in the substance of the philosophy itself, which will be spelled out in the chapters which follow. The first reason has to do with the roots of the philosophy, the fact that it has its origins in, and is the richly developed expression of, the thought of four of the most impressive minds Western culture has given us: Socrates, Plato, and Aristotle, of ancient Greece, and Thomas Aquinas, of the thirteenth century.

Second, Aristotelian-Thomism fosters a generously receptive attitude toward the truth, wherever it might be found, by whomever it might have been expressed. Apropos of the inequality of philosophical systems referred to above, there are some systems of philosophy which, because of the quality of the ideas they foster and promulgate, are not to be recommended, *as systems*. You would not want to accept the philosophy as a whole, but neither would you want peremptorily to reject everything that the philosophy has to say. If the philosophy contains some truth, that truth should be freely acknowledged and gratefully accepted. A philosopher should approach any philosophy that is new to him with unprejudiced openness of mind, with a wide-open eye to whatever is true in that philosophy. Aristotelian-Thomism can oppose a particular philosophical system, taken as a whole, while at the same time gleaning whatever truths might spring from the system's soil. Truth transcends all systems.

Third, Aristotelian-Thomism is closely allied with, deeply embedded within, what is known as the perennial philosophy. The perennial philosophy is not itself a specific philosophical system; it is rather the sum total, the capacious depository, of those fundamental truths that have been expressed, East and West, down through the ages of human history, such as those, for example, found in this or that particular philosophical system. The perennial philosophy has the name it has because the truths it embraces are like perennial flowers: they bloom fresh and lovely year after year. Aristotelian-Thomism, because of its openness to the truth wherever it is to be found, can be regarded as the heart of the perennial philosophy.

Should you take my word for it that Aristotelian-Thomism is the best philosophy? I very much hope not. Should you, in a moment of weakness, do so, you would be getting off on the wrong foot toward becoming a philosopher. In philosophy, the weakest form of argument is the argument from authority. We would be swayed by such an argument were we to take X to be true simply because Professor Sage says that it is true; our only evidence for X's truth would be the professor's say-so. With respect to the worth of Aristotelian-Thomistic philosophy, the burden of proof rests very much on my shoulders. I cannot simply claim that it is the finest of philosophies; I have to show cause, to make a reputable case in support of that claim. And that is the reason for this book. My aim in writing it was to present as clear and complete an account of the basic tenets of the philosophy as I could, so that it then might, as it were, speak for itself. The book relies heavily on argument; I do not simply assert that a certain proposition is true, but give reasons to support the assertion. I must *show* that Proposition X is true, give evidence that supports its truth.

By following that procedure I will be meeting my basic obligations in writing a book on philosophy. But reading a book on philosophy comes with its own obligations. A book must be read, Henry David Thoreau argued, as "deliberately" as it was written. The practical application of that lofty ideal, as far as your relation to this book is concerned, is that you must be prepared to read it actively—think about it, question it, talk back to it. If you are bothered by a certain line of argument I develop, you should stop and explain to yourself why you find it bothersome. If you decide that the argument is faulty, then propose a counter-argument that you think corrects the matter. In that way you will be responding in a genuinely philosophical way to what you are reading. In philosophy, argument is not quarreling; it is the civil exchange of ideas by two parties, both of whom are concerned with getting at the truth.

The eight chapters of this book present the essentials of a full course in Aristotelian-Thomistic philosophy, covering all its basic ideas and principles, which are expanded upon as thoroughly as space limitations allow. The book begins with a chapter on logic, which is followed sequentially by chapters on the philosophy of nature, philosophical psychology, epistemology, ethics, political philosophy, and metaphysics; the book ends with a lengthy chapter devoted to natural theology.

Logic is the prerequisite for the study of philosophy, as it should be for the serious study of any science. That stands to reason, for logic is the science of clear and correct thinking, without which no serious study of anything at all can hope to be fruitful. The philosophy of nature studies the material world, the world which is most familiar to us. In philosophical psychology we look at a specific and altogether singular aspect of material being, when it is informed by the presence of life. Epistemology explores the realm of human knowledge. Ethics is the concentrated study of human behavior from the point of view of its moral quality. Political philosophy is ethics as applied collectively, studying the behavior of man as a member of a political community. Metaphysics is the most comprehensive of the philosophical sciences, for its subject is simply being, whatever exists in whatever way it is possible to exist. In natural theology, which is an extension and the culmination of metaphysics, we engage with what has often been described in philosophy, in an overly precautionary way, as "the problem of God." This is the science of ultimate questions.

Chapter One
Clear and Correct Thinking: Logic

Begin with Thought

We human beings have been defined as rational animals. It is a flattering way to be identified, but we should not allow ourselves to be carried away by it. The definition requires proper construing. Its basic message is that we have the natural capacities to think and act rationally, but it offers no guarantees that we will do either. A natural capacity has to be developed, and then continuously exercised so as to keep it in a healthy condition. The sure sign that we have properly developed our natural rational capacities is that we actually do, on a continuous basis, think and act rationally.

The thinking of course comes before the acting, for actions follow thought, and the quality of the latter is prefigured by the quality of the former. The place to begin, then, is with thought. What is rational thought? We will get into the particulars soon enough, but for now it can be described in general as thought which is under control and heading in a definite direction so as to arrive at a precise destination. Rational thought is clear. Rational thought is correct, which means that it has what it takes to be able to arrive at the precise destinations toward which it is directed.

Logic is the science of clear and correct thinking. The knowledge which it provides is the means by which we can develop our natural capacity for rational thought. By learning logic and applying what we learn we become logical, and by becoming logical we measure up to the definition of ourselves as rational animals.

Logical Thinking as Directed Thinking

Think about day-dreaming. We have all done it, so it is an experience with which we are all familiar, although not one, I would hope, that we have become accustomed to. When we day-dream we are not asleep, and our mind is not a blank; we are thinking, but in a rather peculiar way. The thoughts that flow through our mind when we day-dream are not controlled, there is no obvious pattern to them, and they are not headed in any discernible direction. Often there is no clear connection between one thought and another, and it almost seems as if we are mere spectators to what is going on in our own minds, captivated onlookers caught up in a semi-hypnotic state.

Now, the principal feature of logical thinking is that it stands in marked contrast to the kind of thinking that is characteristic of day-dreaming. Day-dreaming is an excellent example of uncontrolled thinking, whereas logical thinking, by contrast, is the quintessential example of controlled or directed thinking. In the memorable phrase used by the logician Susan Stebbing, logical thinking is "thinking to some purpose." When we think logically we are the conscious originators of our thoughts, and we are directing them toward a specific end where we intend that they find satisfactory resolution.

The specific ends toward which logical thinking is directed can be as numerous and diverse as the stars in the night sky, specific examples of which would be the solution to a mathematical problem, the successfully working out of a crossword puzzle, figuring out the quickest way to get from Morton, Minnesota to Musselshell, Montana. But there is a single, overriding purpose to which all logical thinking is directed, and that is truth. That is a point about which there must be no ambiguity. Logic is not a self-enclosed system, hermetically sealed off from the practical realities of the often confusing, sometimes messy everyday world in which we live. Logical thinking is not a matter of playing clever word games or manipulating bloodless symbols to arrive at sterile conclusions. Logic is about the real world, about your life and mine, and it is meant to arrive at real solutions to real problems.

The Science of Logic

Logic is a science, meaning that it is an organized body of knowledge, based upon first principles, and is dedicated to the discovery of causes. The first principles of any science are simply the foundational truths on which the science is built. An important feature of a first principle is that it is self-evident. It has to be, because a first principle is a truth with which any science begins, and so there can be no truths antecedent to it and having a more basic nature than its own. First principles can be regarded as the absolute starting points of a science. If we didn't have them, as Aristotle once remarked, no science could ever take its first step. All we have to do in order to grasp a first principle is understand the words in which it is expressed. A first principle of Euclidean geometry is, "A whole is greater than any of its parts." To understand those words is to grasp the meaning behind them. The statement requires no proof, for the self-evident speaks for itself. Every science begins with truths of this kind, and they provide the foundation for everything that follows in the science.

Logic is a unique science because it is the prerequisite for all the other sciences, and its first principles are applicable to all of them. In that sense we can say that the first principles of logic are universal; they govern human reasoning as such, to whatever it might be applied. When we are thinking straight, and thereby achieving the ends toward which our thought is directed, it is because we are guided by the first principles of logic.

First Principles

The first principles of logic, and of all human reasoning, are four in number. They are: (1) the principle of identity; (2) the principle of contradiction; (3) the principle of excluded middle; (4) the principle of sufficient reason.

The principle of identity tells us that a thing is what it is; it is identical with itself, and is thus distinguishable from what is other than itself. A tulip is a tulip, and not a turtle; and this tulip here is not to be confused with that tulip over there. The principle of identity underscores the separateness of being, the stark and inviolable individuality of each and every actually existing entity. The principle of identity calls attention to the uniqueness and independence of each individual being, and introduces us to the notion of substance: that which exists in and of itself. Identical twins are amazingly similar, but Susan is not Sarah, and Sarah is not Susan.

The principle of contradiction (also called the principle of non-contradiction), succinctly put, says that being is not not-being. A common, and more developed, way of stating the principle is as follows: it is impossible for any one thing to be and not be at the same time and in the same respect. Susan cannot be, as the undeniably existing Susan, physically in

St. Paul and in San Bernardino at one and the same time. (She may have left her heart in St. Paul while a resident of San Bernardino, but in that case she would have been in two places in different respects, physically in San Bernardino, sentimentally in St. Paul.) The principle of contradiction is the reverse side of the principle of identity, for if every thing is what it is, it is impossible for it not to be what it is. This particular turtle, Tucker, cannot both be and not be Tucker at one and the same time. It would be contradictory to suppose otherwise.

The principle of excluded middle declares that either something exists or it does not exist. There is no middle ground between existing and non-existing, between being and non-being; here it is very much the case of all or nothing. Let's go back to Tucker the turtle. Tucker cannot almost exist, or half-way exist, or just about exist. He is really there, or he is not really there; no third possibility is available for our consideration. But doesn't the fact that Tucker undergoes change alter the picture somewhat? No. In order for change to take place there has to be a subject of change, an actually existing entity that does the changing. For Tucker to change he has to really be there in order to undergo the change.

The message conveyed by the principle of sufficient reason is this: absolutely everything that exists must have an explanation for its existence, as well as for the manner in which it happens to be existing at any given time. This is so even though we may not be able to come up with those explanations right on the spot which, in fact, is often the case. The idea here is that things do not just happen; they are made to happen. Nothing in the created world is the explanation for itself. A specific expression of the principle of sufficient reason, call it a sub-principle, is the principle of causality, which tells us that if the existence of a thing is not self-explanatory, there must be something other than that thing which explains its existence; that would be its cause. Beyond the explanation for the very existence of a thing, which is basic, there are innumerable causes that explain the *way* it exists, for example, as being in motion or at rest, or in this or that place, or having this or that color. In the following chapter we will have more to say about the important subject of causality.

It would be very surprising if anyone reading those descriptions of the four first principles of all human reasoning had the sense of being informed of something entirely new. These truths about reality are so basic that we all have a semi-instinctive knowledge of them; we take them as obvious, and rightly so. But we should also appreciate how foundational they are. It is with these truths as background that we begin all our thinking about the world in which we live, and about ourselves as well. Our thinking is sound if it is consonant with these principles; it is unsound to the degree that it strays from them.

The Word

Ideas can be considered as the basic building blocks of our thought. We are able to grasp the essence or nature of anything, know what any particular thing basically is, only through the medium of an idea. And the only way the human mind can communicate an idea to another human mind is through the medium of words. Think of a thing we see and recognize, let's say a table, as enclosed within an idea, and the idea as enclosed within a word, "table." In logic "word" and "term" are commonly used interchangeably. We distinguish between the *comprehension* and the *extension* of a word. The comprehension of a word is simply its meaning, the specific idea or ideas it embodies; the extension of a word is the breadth of its applicability, all of the things to which it refers. The comprehension of "tree" is clear enough, there is no need to consult a dictionary; the extension of "tree" is every species of tree to be found on the face of the earth. We can limit the extension of a word by the qualifying language we use, as when we say, "Some trees are deciduous." We can also explicitly state the full extension of a word by saying, "All trees are categorized as flora."

We need to make another important distinction regarding words or terms: that between *univocal, equivocal,* and *analogous.* A univocal term is one which has a single, unvarying meaning; "animal," "stone," "bread" would be examples of univocal terms. An equivocal term is one which has more than a single meaning, and those meanings can be quite at odds with one another. Every language has its store of equivocal or ambiguous terms, and the English language is no exception in this regard. The word "bark" has at least two different meanings; it can refer to the covering of the trunk and branches of a tree, or to a sailing vessel having at least three masts. Usually the context within which equivocal terms are used makes it quite clear what is the referent of the term. "The bark *Jessica Sandy* was tossing about in very rough seas, and Captain Watkins was reluctant to leave the bridge." If we were to read that sentence in a novel we would readily know what "bark" in the sentence is referring to. A term is used analogously when, in comparing two things, A and B, one intends to call attention to (1) how those two things are the same, and (2) how they differ. "Being" is very much an analogous term. Consider these two statements. "John Smith is a being." "A porcupine is a being." In comparing the subjects of those two statements what could we say they have in common? On the most basic of levels we could say that they both actually exist; they are both real entities. And how do they differ? Obviously, they differ in very many and radically significant ways. Whenever we think analogously, we are endeavoring, in making comparisons, to recognize both the likenesses and un-likenesses of what we are comparing.

Definition

Logic is the science, the art, of clear and correct thinking. Ideas are the building blocks of thought. The only way the human mind can come to know anything, to grasp the essence or nature of a particular thing, is through the medium of an idea. And the only way the human mind can communicate an idea to another human mind is through the medium of a word. The relation between idea and word is of the most intimate kind. Again, consider a thing we are thinking of as enclosed within an idea, and the idea in turn as enclosed within a word. The clarity of our ideas, and the reliability of the words by which we communicate our ideas, is best assured by relying on the important tool of definition. Described generally, definition is the means we use to identify and clarify the meanings of words. More particularly, there are three kinds of definition: nominal, descriptive, and logical or essential.

Nominal definition is what we commonly find in dictionaries. There a word is defined by providing verbal accounts, one or several, that serve to explain its meaning. Very often synonyms or near synonyms of the word to be defined are made use of. For example, if you look up the word "ire" in a standard dictionary you will read that it means the same thing as anger, or wrath. A descriptive definition can take three basic forms. (1) It identifies and discusses the key characteristics and features of the thing to be defined. For example, in defining man it will focus on rationality, or risibility (the capacity to laugh, as a property of rationality), and devote developed attention to them. (2) Descriptive definition defines something by identifying and discussing the causes of a thing. (3) A third way to define descriptively is though narration, by telling a story. Christ provided a powerful definition of "neighbor" by telling the deathless story of the Good Samaritan.

Logic, understandably, is most concerned with logical, or essential, definition. To define a term logically involves a simple two-step process. The first step is to put the definitum (the thing to be defined) in its proximate genus; the second step is to identify the specific difference of the definitum. In explaining those two steps we will use as a model Aristotle's famous definition of man as "rational animal." In the first step we put man in his proximate genus. A genus is simply a large group, class, or category of things. In this case we place man in the genus "animal." That is the proximate genus of man because man is essentially the same as all the other members of the genus in the sense that he has the same basic, animal-identifying powers that they have: man is self-nourishing, he grows, and he reproduces; he has sensitive powers, as well as appetitive powers (he is naturally drawn towards what he perceives as positive and naturally shuns what he perceives as negative); he has the power of locomotion. Even so, man is obviously radically different from all other animals. How is he different from them? What is the specific difference that sets man apart from all the other members of the genus animal? Aristotle discovered that it is rationality. We have completed the process and we have our definition: "Man is a rational animal."

The fact that Aristotle was able to cite only a single specific difference to arrive at a successful definite was unusual. In more cases than not it is necessary to discover several specific differences in order to be sure that you are clearly setting the definitum off from all other members of the genus. Often it is relatively easy to make the first step in defining something logically. For example, let us say we want to define "empathy." We can be fairly confident that we are making a sound first step by saying, "Empathy is a human emotion." Then what? How are we to clearly differentiate empathy from all the other emotions? It will require some hard thinking to come up with an adequate answer to the question. Perhaps in defining a term you make what you think is a solid first step but then are stalled, and you begin to doubt that you can come up with a logical definition of the term you are working with. And you might be quite right. Nonetheless, the fact that you were able to take the first step, putting the definitum into its proper category, has just in itself provided you with an important bit of knowledge. We call a logical definition an essential definition because, if successful, it reveals the essence of the definitum, the heart of its reality, the core of its basic what-ness. Powerful a tool though it be, logical definition has its limitations. There are many ideas, often the richest and most important we deal with in life, that do not lend themselves to the rigid demands of logical definition. How would one define love, or freedom, or beauty? In cases such as that, however, there is no need to give up. We can avail ourselves of the greater scope allowed us by descriptive definition.

The Statement

A statement is made up of two basic parts, a subject and a predicate. Statements can at times be very complex, but the basic structure remains the same in all cases; the complexity of a particular statement is to be found in either the subject or predicate, or in both. In logical terminology, a statement is commonly called a proposition. It is also referred to as categorical, which means that it states what is actually the case, and not just what is possibly the case. In grammatical terms, a statement is known as a declarative sentence. The subject of a statement is that about which something is said, or predicated, and the predicate does the saying or predicating, as in these two statements: "The dog is in the bog," and "The cat is not in the bag." Unlike other linguistic expressions, such as questions ("Where is the library?"), imperatives ("Shut the door."), wishes ("Oh, if only I were in Honolulu."), and exclamations ("Holy smoke!"), a statement takes a definite stand with respect to a given situation in the real world; it asserts, unequivocally, that something is actually the case or something is not actually the case, and that is why it must be either true or false. If the dog is in fact in the bog, then the statement making that claim is true; if the cat is in fact in the bag, then the statement that declares the feline is not there is false, and should be rejected without demur.

Inference

The heart of logical thinking is the mental activity we call reasoning, and the heart of reasoning is inference. Inference is the mental move by which, beginning with a true statement, we proceed either directly or indirectly to another statement which we accept as true because it follows from the truth of the initial and any intervening statement. When we move directly from one statement to another we are engaging in immediate inference; when we move from one statement to another indirectly, through one or more intervening statements, we engage in mediate inference. We will first consider immediate inference.

We have in mind two statements that we will label respectively A and B. I know statement A to be unquestionably true. As I reflect on it, I see that there is another statement that can be made, B, which is also true, and necessarily so, given how it relates to A. Because A is true it cannot be otherwise than that B is also true. That is an immediate inference. Using logical terminology, we say that the truth of A entails or implies the truth of B, and that the truth of B is inferred from the truth of A.

Now let us consider some real-life examples of immediate inference, stated in plain English. The statement that "all dogs are vertebrates" is true. From that we can make the obvious inference that "some dogs are vertebrates" is also true. We readily see the logic behind that move. If something is true of the entire membership of a class, it is necessarily true of a portion of that membership. "No males are mothers" is patently true, and allows us to make the immediate inference, also patently true, that "some males are not mothers." If something is true of an entire class it is true of a part of that class, but no certain inference can be made about an entire class in terms of what we know about part of that class. "Some women are college professors" is true, but from that I cannot infer that all women are college professors. Consider the two following statements and how they relate to one another. "Every man is mortal." "No man is mortal." It is evident that they both cannot be true, but clearly the first statement is true; this permits us easily to infer that the second statement is false. Finally, we consider these two statements: "All dogs are vertebrates." "Some dogs are not vertebrates." This is a particularly interesting pair because together they illustrate the principle of contradiction, which we introduced above; also, they allow us to make sound immediate inferences in two different directions. "All dogs are vertebrates" is true, and from that we can infer that "some dogs are not vertebrates" is false. And, starting from the fact that "some dogs are not vertebrates" is false we can validly infer that "all dogs are vertebrates" is true. In dealing with two statements that contradict one another, if one is manifestly true, the other must be false; and if one is manifestly false, the other must be true.

Argument

Every instance of inference represents an argument, however modest it may be, for an argument is nothing else but the linguistic expression, simple or complex, of the inferential move. Argument is the core of logic, its paramount concern, that around which all of its lore has been developed. If you can argue well, you are being logical in a preeminent way.

But before we proceed further in our discussion of the nature of argument, a few linguistic clarifications are in order. We use the term argument in ordinary language in ways that are entirely foreign to the way it is used in logic. Argument, in logic, is not to be confused with a quarrel, the usual object of which is to get the better of the person with whom one is quarreling, to come out as the winner in a heated verbal exchange. Quarrels are very personal and highly emotional. The object of argument is to arrive at the truth, and therefore the only winner in this case should be the truth.

There are two major categories of argument, deductive and inductive. The usual way to distinguish the two is to say that in deductive argument we move from the more general to the less general, and in inductive argument we move from the singular or the particular to the general. Another important distinction between them has to do with their conclusions. The conclusions of deductive arguments, assuming that they have been properly constructed, follow necessarily; they must be true. The conclusions of inductive arguments are probable; they may be true. In inductive reasoning there is always the possibility that new facts might be discovered that could undermine a conclusion which before that discovery seemed quite sound.

We will consider some examples of both types of argument. "All men are mortal" is a statement the truth of which we can be reliably confident. The statement is called a universal affirmative; it deals with an entire class, human beings, and it tells us that each and every member of that class is subject to death. Now, as we have noted, it can safely be inferred that if something is true of an entire class, it must be true of each member of that class. So, if "all men are mortal" is true, and it is, then it is true that Socrates, who is a human being, is mortal.

In inductive argument we do not start with generalizations, but we gather together specific facts which will serve as evidence on the basis of which we formulate what we take to be reliable generalizations. Let us consider the case of a dedicated ornithologist, Professor Bertram Byrd, who specializes in swans. He embarks upon a major research project the purpose of which is to test the hypothesis that all swans are white. After many months of assiduous efforts expended by him and his assistants, observing and recording hundreds upon hundreds of swans, all of which turn out to be white, the professor is prepared to publish his findings and the conclusion he drew from them. Now, the professor knew that they had not observed each and every swan on the face of the earth, and that it would be practically impossible to do so. However, because he and his team had sampled a significantly large portion of the world's swan population, and found nothing but white swans within their sample, the conclusion of the article written by Professor Byrd that appeared in *Ornithology Today* was succinct and to the point: "All swans are white." Unfortunately, a few weeks before he was to be elected president of the Oregon Ornithological Organization, word came from Australia, a country his team did not visit, informing them that there were black swans residing in the Land Down Under. With that disconcerting information, "All swans are white" immediately became a false statement. If it is proven to be the case that "some swans are not white (the black ones)," then there is no way in the world we can infer that "all swans are white."

Because logic is principally concerned with deductive reasoning, that will be our focus as we now push on with our discussion of argument.

The Structure of Argument

The basic composition of an argument, like that of the statement, is quite simple; while the two basic parts of the statement are the subject and predicate, the two basic parts that make up every argument are premises and conclusion. (This is as true of inductive arguments as it is of deductive arguments.) Also like any statement, an argument can be very complex, but in the case of an argument, the complexity is almost always to be found within the premises. The simplest form an argument can take is where there is but a single premise and the conclusion. The example we used above in our discussion of immediate inference could be spelled out in formal terms this way:

Because all dogs are vertebrates.
It necessarily follows that some dogs are vertebrates.

The premise part of an argument, be it simple or complex, is the supporting or proof part; it is the data which is provided, as evidence, to justify the acceptableness of the conclusion. The conclusion is the supported part of the argument; it is the statement which is to be taken as true if the premise part of the argument convinces us with the evidence it has to offer, i.e., it states something that is manifestly true. We "jump to a conclusion" in our reasoning when we accept the conclusion of an argument in a situation where there is insufficient evidence for doing so. To engage in that kind of mental gymnastics is illogical.

Mediate Inference, the Syllogism

Again, the argument just above, having to do with the character of dogs as vertebrates, is an instance of immediate inference, where we moved directly from one statement, the premise, to the statement which serves as the conclusion, with no other statement intervening between these two. This is a logically legitimate move because all the information we need to confirm the truth of the conclusion is contained in the single premise. The knowledge we have that all the members of a class have a certain trait, is all the information we need to conclude with full confidence that a proportion of the membership of the class has the same trait.

Immediate inference will often work quite well for us when we need to arrive at firm conclusions about how things actually are in the real world, but not always. Sometimes we need more information than can be provided by a single statement, and that is supplied by mediate inference, which is what takes place in a more complex form of argument, one requiring more than two statements. In mediate inference we have an argument which begins with a statement, a premise, and ends with a statement, the conclusion, but because the information in that initial statement is not sufficient to justify the conclusion, more information is required, and that information is provided by at least one additional statement, or premise, which stands between the first statement and the conclusion.

The kind of argumentation representing mediate inference has its most potent expression in what is called the categorical syllogism. "Syllogism" is the common name given to any arrangement of statements in which something is proposed, through one or more statements, and something necessarily follows from what has been proposed. Aristotle, the father of the science of logic, laid down the basic principles pertaining to syllogistic reasoning. It is called a categorical syllogism because it is made up of categorical statements. A categorical statement, recall, is one that makes a definite, unequivocal assertion about something. "There is a cardinal in the ash tree" is a categorical statement. "There may be a cardinal in the ash tree" is not a categorical statement. Here is an example of mediate inference in the form of a categorical syllogism.

> All human beings are mortal.
> All Greeks are human beings.
> Therefore, all Greeks are mortal.

Note the key features of the make-up of a syllogistic argument of this type. It is composed of three statements, two serving as premises (the first called the Major Premise, the second, the Minor Premise), and a conclusion, which is clearly identified as such because it begins with "therefore." Note also that the syllogism has three terms (words or phrases) conveying specific ideas: "human beings," "mortal" (short for "mortal beings"), and "Greeks." Notice further that one of those terms, "human beings," appears only in the premises, not in the conclusion; as such, it performs the important logical function of forging a connection between the other two terms (both of which show up in the conclusion), in such a way that what is stated by the conclusion is not simply true, but necessarily true; the situation could not be otherwise than what is there stated. Such is the beauty and logical force of the syllogism as a form of deductive reasoning. Here is the standard way in which the three terms of the syllogism are arranged.

> Middle Term — Major Term
> Minor Term — Middle Term
> Minor Term — Major Term

Now we need to look more closely at the argument, so that we can see just how the Middle Term (the term that appears in the premises but not in the conclusion) makes a connection between the Minor Term (the subject of the conclusion) and the Major Term (the predicate of the conclusion), a connection that is so tight that the conclusion is inescapably true. Let's walk our way through the argument together. The Major Premise introduces us to two large classes, human beings and mortal beings, and it tells us that the first class is entirely included within the second, larger class, It is clearly evident that mortal beings is a larger class than human beings, because the latter are not the only beings marked by mortality—birds and bees are mortal, and so are buffalo.

The Minor Premise of the argument introduces some new information, telling us that the class called Greeks is entirely enclosed within the previously introduced class of "human beings." Now, consider what that leaves us with. We have a class, "human beings," (label it M) entirely enclosed within the larger class, "mortal beings" (label it P)—such is the information provided by the Major Premise. The Minor Premise informs us that the class of "Greeks" (label it S) is entirely enclosed within the class of "human beings" (M). Given those relations, the conclusion that "All Greeks are mortal" neatly follows.

Consider it this way" If M is entirely a part of P, which we diagram as [{M} P] and if S is entirely a part of M, diagrammatically expressed as [{(S)M} P], then it is obvious that S must also be entirely a part of P. There is no way around it. With those diagrams we can literally see how it is so.

Syllogistic argument, spelled out in a formal way as I just did, might strike us as strange and even somewhat artificial, but actually, the kinds of basic mental moves which the spelled-out argument makes explicit are altogether natural to us, and reflect the way the human mind normally operates in order to arrive at conclusions the truth of which we can be completely confident. We generate specific ideas and then, considering them closely, we see how they relate to one another and the logical connections that are established by those relations. The truth of certain ideas leads us to the truth of other ideas, which previously we may not have been fully aware of. We either discover entirely new truths, or what was hitherto only implicit becomes explicit. That, very generally, is the kind of thinking we do when we reason. Reasoning is a thought process that is thoroughly dependent upon inference.

Analyzing Arguments

If argument is the heart of logic, then, if we master argument, being logical is part of who we are. Now, some arguments can get quite complicated, mainly because, as mentioned, they can contain many premises which go together to support the conclusion, but this should not intimidate us. Recall that all arguments, however complex, have only two basic components— premises and conclusion. So, the first order of business is to make a clear identification of those two components. Of the two, the premises are the more important, for if we understand what the premises are saying and how they are related to one another, then we will be able to judge whether or not they adequately support the conclusion.

In formulating an argument, there are two simple but nonetheless important points to keep in mind, both of which have to do with premises. First of all, we must be sure that our premises are true; we have to take care that we have our facts straight. The premises contain the data intended to support and substantiate the conclusion, the evidence on the basis of which the conclusion will carry conviction. If the premises are not true, the argument collapses. Like the foundation of a building, they must be solidly supportive. The premises must not only be true, they must be self-evidently true, true at face value, so there can be no question of their having to be proved. Consider the two premises of the argument we discussed just above, "all human beings are mortal," and "all Greeks are human beings." Neither statement requires proof, for the truth of both of them is immediately obvious to us.

The second thing we must keep in mind regarding the premises of our arguments is that there is a clear logical relation between them and the conclusion they support, in such a way that the conclusion clearly "follows from" the premises as their obvious consequent. Such a relation is established through the referents of the subject and predicate terms of the statements that serve as the premises of the argument. Consider the following argument.

All Greeks are mortal.
Socrates is a Greek.
Therefore, Socrates is mortal.

We can readily see how the conclusion of the arguments follows from the premises. Now consider the two following statements.

All Greeks are mortal.
Socrates is a philosopher.

What follows? Nothing. Both of the statements are true, but because the terms that compose them create no logical bond between them there is no inference to be drawn. We cannot claim that any third statement is necessarily true because of the truth of those two statements. They are simply two statements juxtaposed to one another; they do not function as the premises of a syllogistic argument. The problem here is that we have four terms, but one of the rules for the syllogism is that it must have only three terms: the major, the minor, and the middle.

Validity

Statements, as we have seen, are either true or false, depending on whether what they state does or does not reflect an actual state of affairs. Arguments, on the other hand, are either valid or invalid. Validity has to do with the structure of an argument, principally with regard to how its premises are arranged in relation to one another. For a true conclusion to follow necessarily from an argument's premises, those premises must of course be true, but that is not enough. As in the case cited just above, we have two true statements, but they cannot serve as genuine premises because there is no logical connection between them, and that is because the two statements contain four terms, whereas a syllogism is valid only if it contains no more than three terms. If we were to alter the second statement to read, "Socrates is a Greek," then "Greek" would act as the Middle Term connecting the other two terms, and a true conclusion would follow—"Socrates is mortal."

There are a number of other structural problems that result in invalid arguments, and the upshot of all of them is the same—they produce a non sequitur conclusion, one that doesn't necessarily follow from the premises. We end up with an argument that fails because of its structural problems. Consider the following argument.

> All the freshmen at Utopia U. have read *Moby Dick*.
> Constance has read *Moby Dick*.
> Therefore, Constance is a freshman at Utopia U.

You can probably sense that there is something wrong with this argument. But what is it? Let us grant that both of the premises are true. Even so, the conclusion does not necessarily follow from them, and that leaves us with a situation which could not occur were the argument valid, that is, a situation where the premises are true but the conclusion does not follow. Here is the guarantee offered by validity: If an argument is structurally sound, and if its premises are true, its conclusion is necessarily true. Given those criteria, we then know for certain that we are dealing with an invalid argument if its premises are true but its conclusion is questionable. The explanation for this problematic state of affairs is that the argument is not structurally sound.

What is wrong with the structure of the above argument that makes it invalid? The technical way of identifying the problem in logical terms is to say that the argument has an "undistributed Middle Term." An undistributed Middle Term is one which is not universal—i.e., does not apply to each and every member of the class to which it refers—in neither of the premises in which it appears. Why does the Middle Term need to be universal at least once? Because if it is not, it cannot make a connection between the Minor Term and the Major Term.

Notice that both of the premises are referring to a class of people who have read *Moby Dick*, that being the predicate terms of both premises. Notice also that both of the premises are affirmative statements. The Major Premise tells us that the freshmen at Utopia U. are in that class; the Minor Premise says that Constance is in the same class. Now, one of the basic facts regarding the structure of statements is that the predicate terms of affirmative statements are always undistributed, or non-universal. This can be proved by converting any affirmative statement, assuming its predicate term to be universal, and observing the results. To convert a statement simply means to exchange its subject and predicate terms, so "the umpire is Joe" would be the conversion of "Joe is the umpire."

Converting the Major Premise of our argument, assuming its predicate to be universal, would give us, "All those who have read *Moby Dick* are freshmen at Utopia U.," which is clearly false. And if we were to convert the Minor Premise we would end up with a statement which would say in effect that Constance is the only one who has read *Moby Dick,* which is also clearly false. Because both of the converted statements are false if we assume their predicate terms to have been universal, that proves that the predicate terms of both of the premises of the argument are non-universal, or undistributed, and therefore they cannot make a firm logical bond between the Minor Term and Major Term.

On the basis of the information provided by the premises as originally stated, it *could* be the case that Constance is a freshman at Utopia U; that is not an unreasonable surmise. But the point to be stressed is that it does not necessarily follow that she in fact is a student at that renowned institution; the premises allow for, but do not demand, that such be the case. The mistake that is made in an invalid argument of this kind is to presume that simply because two things are in the same class they are *necessarily* related to one another. In deductive argument, remember, the conclusion cannot be questionably true, but it must be absolutely true. No "could be the case" allowed, only "must be the case."

Fallacious Reasoning

A fallacy is an instance of reasoning gone wrong. In logic, we distinguish between formal and informal fallacies. A formal fallacy, as the name indicates, has to do with the form, or structure, of an argument. The problematic arguments that we discussed above are examples of formal fallacies, arguments with a faulty structure. The formal fallacies are relatively few in number, but there are many informal fallacies. An informal fallacy has to do with the contents of an argument, what it explicitly says, and what is implied or suggested by what it explicitly says. There are various causes of fallacious reasoning. It can be attributable simply to honest mistakes on our part; we all unintentionally slip up from time to time, despite our best efforts to avoid doing so. More seriously, fallacious reasoning can be the result of carelessness; we are not giving to the reasoning process the kind of focused attention it demands. The most serious cause of fallacious reasoning is when we engage in it consciously and deliberately, with malice of forethought. A fair amount of fallacious reasoning has its source in ungoverned emotion. Someone who is in the grips of anger, for example, is not in the most propitious condition for reasoning well.

A common strategy of fallacious reasoning, when it is deliberately indulged in, is to get people to take their eye off the ball, to distract them by a side issue, something that is not relevant to the principal concern of the argument, so that they are no longer concentrating on the issues at hand. Almost all of the fallacies appeal to the emotions rather than to reason.

As mentioned, there are many informal fallacies. Here I will treat briefly with but five of them, chosen for the fact that they tend to be among the most commonly committed. They are: Two Rights Make a Wrong; False Dilemma; Straw Man; Ad Hominem; and Improper Appeal to Authority.

Two Wrongs Make a Right. The name of the fallacy describes the type of bad reasoning it involves. In fact, what two wrongs actually make is not a right, but two wrongs. The fallacy often takes the following form: "If George did it, it's okay for me to do it." The thinking behind that claim ignores the moral quality of "it," the particular action that George took. Was it a good act or a bad act? If what George did was donate $1,000 to charity, then following his lead in that would be meritorious. But if George's act was bad, like cheating on an exam, then obviously the mere fact that George, or anyone else, performed the act does not justify my performing it.

This is so glaringly obvious a mistake that one would think we would rarely make it, but it turns out to be one of mankind's favorites. The fallacy, by attaching absolute value to precedent, misses the very point that should be focused on, the moral quality of the precedent, while ignoring the fact that there are bad precedents.

This is essentially a childish fallacy, but adults are quite proficient in committing it. It is a standard way by which we attempt to duck any blame for our actions by pointing to somebody else's actions of the same kind. The fallacy is committed on a grand scale within international conflicts. During World War Two the time-honored distinction between combatants and non-combatants was for all practical purposes rendered null and void by both Axis and Allied powers. In the last stages of the war the carpet bombing of population centers became common. At least some Allied commanders attempted to justify the bombing of cities like Dresden with the limp excuse, "Well they did it to us first!" That was true, but irrelevant, because it did not address the morality of the action itself. If the bombing of civilian centers is wrong, it is wrong no matter who does it. If the bad guys do something that is bad, it does not suddenly become good because the good guys decide to do it.

False Dilemma. There are real dilemmas in life: certain situations where we are faced with an either/or choice between two courses of action. It's either one or the other; we cannot opt for both. A false dilemma is created when people attempt to persuade us, through argument, that we are in a situation where we have only two choices before us, when that happens not to be the case, for in fact we have more than two choices before us. We are not limited to choosing either A or B, for there is also C, D, and E to be considered. In sum, the fallacy is an attempt to falsify reality by reducing what is truly a complex situation to a fictitious simple one. It is a way someone tries to force an issue, foisting upon people a manufactured sense of urgency so as to get them to act in the way he wants them to act.

Politicians would seem to be especially adept at committing this fallacy. "Either this piece of legislation is passed, and without delay," Senator Sly solemnly assures us, "or the consequences for the country will be truly disastrous." Is it really all that simple? Calmly reflecting on the situation will show, in more cases than not, that it is not all that simple. One could reasonably consider a third possibility: the bill is not passed, and the country goes on generally as before, without experiencing any adverse consequences.

Straw Man. In the lively back and forth of a serious conversation, or in a formal debate, where substantive matters are being discussed, we can sometimes get wrong what other people are telling us, in developing an argument, or in stating their position on this or that matter. And it works the other way around: people can misconstrue what we say as well, get us wrong in one way or another. These can be called honest mistakes if the people involved in exchanges of this kind are ingenuously endeavoring to get at the truth of the matter under discussion, and not out simply to score points against one another. If that is the case, we could expect that there will be continuous exchanges taking place among participants, where they take pains to ensure they are being properly understood, and where needed corrections or clarifications will be generously accepted by all parties involved. In such a circumstance a civilized discussion would be taking place.

But discussions are not always civilized. If, in response to an argument presented to me, I deliberately misconstrue that argument in a way that weakens it, I commit the Straw Man fallacy. The image suggested by the name of the argument is instructive. A straw man is easily dealt with; we can push him over with our little finger, or touch a match to his toes and he will quickly go up in smoke. Whenever anyone, understanding full well an argument or position presented to him, deliberately and with malice of forethought distorts them so as to weaken them, thus making them easy targets for disparagement and disposal, he is guilty of committing the Straw Man fallacy. The Straw Man argument I am responding to is not my opponent's argument, but my distorted version of my opponent's argument.

Ad Hominem. Many of the fallacies retain the Latin names originally given them, and such is the case with this fallacy. "Ad hominem" means "against the person," and the fallacy consists in attacking the one who is presenting an argument, rather than responding to the argument that is being presented, when such an action is clearly uncalled for, because it introduces something that has no direct bearing on the matter under discussion. Like many of the informal fallacies, the Ad Hominem is simply a diversionary tactic.

Jerome and I are both members of the city council. He has proposed that there be a hike in property taxes to make more money available to our less than illustrious public school system, a proposal I am dead set against for seriously questionable reasons. We are invited to debate the issue before a large audience at a local high school. Jerome is a very intelligent fellow, besides being an articulate and witty speaker, and as the debate proceeds, it becomes increasingly evident to me, because of the clarity and cogency of Jerome's arguments, that I am rapidly losing ground and stand in danger of being effectively swept off that stage. Finally, out of desperation, I start calling attention to certain aspects of Jerome's personal life, which, though true, have nothing to do with the issue we are debating. My hope is that by this maneuver, given the nature of my revelations, the audience will begin to see Jerome in a new and diminished light, causing them, however illogically, to be more open to the position I am taking toward the proposal.

So, I coyly make reference in passing to the rumors going about that Jerome, a married man with a family, has been known to be consorting with the notorious Flossie La Flame, and then there is that matter of his having been expelled from his home town high school for supposedly smoking pot. And to those I add a few more juicy tidbits. I am committing the Ad Hominem fallacy. Let us assume that everything I have to say about Jerome's personal life is true. But does that render nugatory the quality of the arguments he is making in favor of the proposal in question? Strictly speaking, it does not. A man's personal life may be less than edifying, but if he says the square root of sixteen is four, it does not become false because he says it.

Does that mean that every reference in argument to someone's personal life counts as a commission of the Ad Hominem fallacy? No. The key here is relevance to the issue at hand. If a man who is applying for a job as a school bus driver has twice in recent months had his license suspended for DUI violations, and has a known drinking problem, these are aspects of his personal life which are relevant to the question of whether or not he should be hired for the job.

Improper Appeal to Authority. The key word in the name of this fallacy is the first, "improper." There is nothing fallacious in itself about appealing to authority, so long as the authority is legitimate and can give a good account of itself. We appeal to authorities of various sorts all the time, and need to. Most of what we accept as true regarding a full range of matters is because we accept what authoritative voices have to say to us about them. We are thus exercising natural faith. I believe it is true that water can be reduced to hydrogen and oxygen, but I have never performed that experiment myself. I take Galileo's word for it that Jupiter has four moons, though I have never trained a telescope at the planet to count the moons myself.

The improper appeal to authority consists in giving undue authoritative weight to something (call it X), and presenting that as a sufficient reason for taking a certain course of action. (Because of X, Y must be done.) The fallacy commonly takes the form of attaching excessive importance to past practices or traditions; that particular expression of the fallacy goes under the name of traditionalism. It can be crudely expressed in statements like, "Look, we've always done things this way, for years in fact, and we're going to continue to do them this way, and that's that." What inspires this way of thinking is the idea that just because certain practices have a considerable history behind them, that fact alone justifies, or even demands, that those practices should continue to be followed. It is simply the lengthy history behind the practices that becomes the final say, the authority. The problem with this point of view is that it fails to focus on what should be of primary concern, the practices themselves which are under discussion. It is not that the long-standing status of certain practices should not be taken into consideration; it would be careless to dismiss them out of hand simply because they are long-standing, for that might be an argument in their favor. But their long-lastingness should not be emphasized to the point where it becomes the determining factor, and the practices themselves are not thoroughly examined. If it can be shown that the practices are deficient in one way or another, their long-lastingness then becomes of peripheral interest only. The practices should be changed to remedy their deficiencies.

This fallacy has an opposite side to it, to which I give the rather awkward name of newism. In this way of thinking we reject certain long-standing practices and want to replace them *simply because* they are long-standing. Longevity itself becomes a liability. In this case too our attention is improperly focused; we are not concentrating on the nature and quality of the practices themselves. This manner of reasoning holds that if something is new, that means it is necessarily better. Non sequitur. The "latest improvement" is not always an improvement.

Yet another form taken by this fallacy is called the Appeal to Numbers, the authority in this case being mere quantitative superiority. The point of view at play here would be reflected in the attitude that the majority always has it right, an attitude that Henry David Thoreau would have taken warm exception to. If the majority of Americans believe that abortion is acceptable, then abortion must be acceptable. If 75% of the experts in a particular field say that X is Y, then, no question about it, X is Y. It is easy to see the problem with this mode of reasoning. Simply because most people, or even most experts, believe or think that something is true does not make it true. Majorities have been known to have gotten it wrong on some very important issues. The basic problem here, once again, is that the main point is being missed. If one wants to know if the statement X is Y is true, you do not look at the fact that most people take it to be true, you give a long, hard look at X.

But if majorities sometimes, perhaps even often, have it wrong, they sometimes get it right. It would therefore be fallacious to conclude that just because most people believe that X is Y it is, for that reason alone, necessarily false. Non sequitur. Once again, peripheral matters are given undue emphasis, while the essential is being ignored. Attention should be focused on X.

We obviously have no control over the fallacious reasoning of others, but we should readily recognize it for what it is and know how to defend ourselves against it. One classic way of defending us against the conclusions of faulty reason is to employ what is called the *argumentum ad absurdum* ("an argument leading to an absurd or false conclusion," to give the Latin a fully fleshed-out translation). Let us say that someone presents you with an elaborate argument which concludes with the statement: "All philosophers are untrustworthy." You are deeply troubled by that claim, and you want to prove that it is false. To do so you avail yourself of the *argumentum ad absurdum*. You begin by assuming it to be true that all philosophers are untrustworthy, and then you turn your mind to discovering all the consequences that would follow were that in fact to be a true statement. It turns out that those consequences are absurd, they make no sense whatever. You therefore conclude that the statement cannot be true. The basic pattern of the argument, expressed in skeletal form, is as follows: We assume W to be true. But if W were true, X, Y, and Z would follow. However, X, Y, and Z are false. Therefore, W must be false.

Chapter Two

The Material World: The Philosophy of Nature

Introducing the Philosophy of Nature

Philosophy is a science made up of several sub-sciences, the first of which to be seriously engaged in, after mastering the basic principles of logic, is the philosophy of nature. The study of philosophy, taken as a whole, must be gone about in a systematic manner. We do not want to barge into the field of philosophy just anywhere, but to begin at the beginning, and the proper place to begin is with the philosophy of nature. The reason for this has directly to do with our basic psychological make-up. The subject matter of the philosophy of nature is the material world, everything having to do with physical reality. Our aim, as philosophers of nature, is to come to know that world the best we can. We are material beings ourselves—not entirely, but nonetheless very importantly—and as a result what we have knowledge of first and foremost, as we grow fully conscious of our corporeal selves and the world around us, is material being, the reality of physical things.

All human thought is rooted in material being, and even though it can transcend the realm of the material, say through mathematical abstraction, it can never completely sever ties with it. All mathematical thought has its foundation in material being. When we are presented with the mathematical statement that 2 + 2 = 4, we do not ask, with a baffled look, "Two what?" Two is an abstract concept. Adding the concept two to the concept two gives us the concept four. But the origin of the concept two, that from which it is abstracted, are two physical things—two rocks, two sheep, two pennies. Given the commanding role that the material world plays in human knowledge, as its very starting point, it only makes sense that philosophy should begin its work by thoroughly investigating that world. It is, after all, what is most familiar to us.

What Is Nature?

So, the particular science which is here the focus of our attention is the philosophy of nature, or, as it is sometimes called, natural philosophy. Our special concern, then, is nature. What is nature? There are two closely related ways of identifying what we mean by the term, one particular, the other general. Nature, understood in the particular sense, refers to that which is possessed by every individual thing, of whatever kind, and whether animate or inanimate. The nature of a thing is what identifies it as a specific this or that (a rabbit, a rhododendron, a ruby); it confers upon it a precise individuality. The nature of a thing is intrinsic to it, as a dynamic principle which accounts for the various features it displays, the various ways it behaves. St. Thomas Aquinas describes nature as a principle of motion and rest which is intrinsic to a thing. It is the action of a thing that reveals to us its nature. The nature of a thing is inseparable from the thing itself, and it is fixed and invariable. If we could conceive of a thing losing its proper nature, it would simply cease to be the kind of thing it is. It would change into something else.

Note how we use the word "nature" in ordinary language. We speak commonly of human nature, for example, and by doing so, whether or not we are consciously aware of the fact, we are acknowledging that nature is something which, though concretely manifested in individuals, is shared by many. Each of us possesses human nature in a unique way, but all of us together share the same nature. We are all participants in humanity, all part of the human family. Yet the uniqueness of the individual is not in any way diminished by reason of what is common to us all. Bob is a human being uniquely so, only in the way Bob can be a human being, and the same is true of Barb, but both are fully and completely human.

As we look around us, we cannot help but marvel at the differences among material things, be they animal, or plants, or inanimate things, down to the level of the elementary particles that go together to compose the atom. The root explanation for these differences is a difference in natures. A falcon is not a pheasant, and never the twain shall mate, and that is because they have specifically different natures. And it is different natures which allow us to distinguish between a rose bush and a birch tree, between sandstone and marble, between hydrogen and neon. I said just above that the nature of a thing is fixed and invariable. If this were not the case we would be living in an utterly chaotic world, where there would be no science, indeed where there would be no stable, reliable knowledge of any kind, for the shared aspect of natures would be gone with the wind, and the transmission of a given nature from one generation to the next would be completely unpredictable. Out of a falcon's egg would pop a pigeon; plant an acorn and you might get poison ivy. But a scenario as bizarre and disconcerting as that would not even be possible, for without fixed and invariable natures, there would be no material beings that could be clearly identified as falcons or pigeons, as oak trees or poison ivy.

Nature understood in the general sense, Nature with a capital N, is aptly described as the sum total of all material things that exist, each possessing its proper nature, each expressing that nature by the stability of certain basic features, and by the predictable regularity of the activity which is peculiar to each nature. If there is a dominant feature of nature as a whole, the physical universe, it is its orderliness. The explanation for that orderliness has much to do with the fact that the myriad of material substances that go together to compose the universe are themselves ordered by reason of the specific natures that identify them. As we shall see more clearly presently, every material substance, be it minute or monumental, acts in an orderly fashion, which is shown by the fact that its actions are predictable, either precisely or statistically. The order of the universe as a whole, we may argue, is attributable to the order displayed by all the parts (the individual substances) that compose it.

The Basic Characteristics of Material Things

As philosophers of nature, our principal concern is with material things, and that immediately suggests the question, What is matter? Perhaps it would be more useful to start with a more precise question: What is a material thing? First of all, and basically, a material thing is something that is marked by extension, which is to say that it has to it a certain spread-out-ness, and that would entail its being and that would entail its being able to be located in space, in a definite place. So, a material thing occupies a definite place. Because every material thing has extension, it can be measured, with one degree of precision or another. That is obvious enough, given our familiarity with the physical objects all around us. The top of the desk on which I am now writing has a length of approximately four feet, eleven and a half inches, a width of two feet, and a depth of about an inch. No matter how tiny a material thing is, say a subatomic particle, if it is an actually existing material thing and not just a mathematical construct, it must have extension and thus be subject to measurement. And it has a more or less definite spot in the universe.

Another basic feature of a material thing, besides extension, is its impenetrability, the practical ramifications of which is that it is not possible for two material things to be in exactly the same place at exactly the same time while maintaining their proper identity. The impenetrability of material things is a declaration of their individuality (and hence of their identifiableness as a specific this or that), and the preservation of the integrity of their proper nature. The extension of a material thing answers for its having a definite place, and its impenetrability mandates single occupancy for any given place. An archer shoots an arrow into a sand bag; we say the arrow penetrates the sand bag. We submerge a natural sponge in a tub of water and a minute later draw it out. The sponge is now heavy with water; we say the water permeates, or has penetrated the sponge. Neither of these are examples of what we refer to as the impenetrability of a material thing. If a physical thing were to lose its character of impenetrability it would lose its proper identity; its matter would be transformed. An arrow stuck into a sand bag does not cease to be an arrow, nor does a sand bag become something other than a sand bag. Neither sponge nor water loses its proper identity in the situation described just above. It is the impenetrability of material things that accounts for the phenomenon of the displacement of one material thing (a billiard ball) by another. When two electrons clash, attempting to occupy the same place we might say, they destroy one another, giving birth to photons in the process.

That brings us to the subject of relation, another signal feature of a material thing. Let us imagine there were but a single material thing in existence; we will say that it is of basketball size, and it is made of pure gold. We could speak of internal relations, those that exist among all those closely compacted gold atoms that compose the ball, but there would be no external relation, no relation, that is, between the ball and anything else, for there would be nothing else to which it could be related. It takes two to make a relation. Because there are myriads of material things that constitute the physical universe, every one of them is related to any number of other material things in any number of ways. Discovering how any particular material thing is related to other material things can tell us much about the nature of that particular material thing. The science of chemistry is very much concerned with how the basic elements relate to one another.

Let us once again descend to the lowest depths of material being, to the realm of subatomic particles. We would find there a material thing, an electron for example, which is perfectly simple, meaning that it is not composed of parts; it is pure electron, through and through. Electrons are not entirely independent entities, for they are inclined to hang around nuclei and become constituent parts of atoms. The atom is the most basic of clearly individualized material things, but even in the simplest of them, the hydrogen atom, we discover complexity. As we ascend upward from the atom, to the level of molecules, then to compounds, and beyond, the picture becomes more and more complex. This leads us to observe that another key characteristic of all material things is complexity. Once we get beyond subatomic particles, all material things are compositions; they are integral wholes—that is what accounts for their individuality—which are made up of parts. Of course, some material bodies are more complex than others, and some are stunningly so. Recent research in molecular biology has shown the complexity of the cell to be such that it is almost like a mini-world unto itself.

Perhaps the most readily recognizable feature of material things is the fact that they move, incessantly. A material thing, be it highly complex or of the simplest kind (an elementary particle, say), be it animal, vegetable, or mineral, is the quintessential Nervous Nelly; it is constitutionally incapable of relaxing and settling down into a permanent state of rest. To bring up the electron again, physicists tell us it never sits still; it is always jiggling. Given this key characteristic of material being, philosophy has come generally to describe material being as mobile being (*ens mobile* in Latin). If it is material, it is in a constant agitated state. One of the basic principles of philosophy, of metaphysics specifically, is that everything that moves is moved by another. Later in the chapter we will give close consideration to that principle. At one level the application of the principle is easy enough to see: the cue ball strikes the eight ball and sends it posthaste to a corner pocket. But what about those jiggling electrons, what's moving them? In this case we could say that their movement is accounted for by gravitational or electro-magnetic forces external to them. To move is to change, so we could easily generally describe material being as changing being.

Substance and Accident

Thus far I have been using the rather bland but eminently serviceable word "thing" to designate a specific material being, of whatever specific kind. Now we need to be more precise in our language, replacing "thing" with "substance," which in philosophical language means something very precise. We will start simply by giving some examples of substance, after which we will define the term. You are a substance, and so am I. Fido the dog is a substance, as is Caspar the cat. A pine tree, a lilac bush, gold, silver, the sun, the moon, the stars—all these are substances. We have a very wide range of diversity in that list. What all these things have in common, what qualifies them as substances, on the most basic level, is what we could roughly describe as independent existence. A substance is anything that exists "through itself," which is to say, as not directly dependent on something other than itself to have the kind of existence it has. A substance is recognizably individual, and thus distinct and separate from other substances; it has an identity which is all its own, which is acknowledged by the precise name we give to it, calling it a kangaroo, krill, or krypton. The root explanation for different individual substances is their different natures.

A good way of coming to an understanding of the idea of substance is by comparing and contrasting it with the idea of accident, a term which first needs to be defined. We have defined substance as that which exists through itself, or independently. In speaking of accident, we are not referring to a mishap, an unintended happening, which occurred, for example, when Paul dropped a plate and it shattered on the kitchen floor. Accident, in philosophical parlance, designates a way of existing for material being that is opposite to the way in which substances exist. Whereas substances exist independently, in the way noted, accidents exist dependently, as always inextricably united with the being of substances. Generally described, an accident is a trait, a characteristic, a feature, an aspect of a substance. It is the "how it is," or "how it relates," or "what it does" of substance. We have already recognized the dog Fido as a substance; Fido's height, his weight,

the color of his coat, the general state of his health, would be various examples of accidents. Notice that none of those things can exist independently, apart from the substance of Fido in which they inhere. Obviously,
accidents really exist, but always and only dependently, and what they depend on, once again, is nothing else but substance. If Fido did not exist,
none of the things that could possibly be said about him would exist. If
there is no substance, there can be no accidents. There is no such thing as
blue, just in itself, other than as an idea in your mind; there are only blue
things (i.e., substances)—books, shirts, skirts, caps, cars, catamarans. And
by the way, that idea of blue you have in your mind is another example of
accidental being; it is a quality or feature of your mind.

A qualification should be made regarding what I have described as the
independent existence of a substance. The independence in question is relative, not absolute, if by the latter we mean a mode of existence which is
completely autonomous. Every material substance owes its existence to
what is other than itself. To say that a substance exists "through itself"
means that it exists as an integrated whole, and not as a part of another
being.

Whatever really is, whatever actually exists, is either a substance or an
accident; there are no other possibilities beyond these two most basic ways
of being. Either something exists through itself, as a substance, or through
another, as an accident, that is, as a feature of a substance. That is true of
material being, but it is true of immaterial being as well, which we will have
occasion to discuss in a later chapter.

Material Being as Changing Being

As noted, one of the most prominent features of material things is that they
are constantly moving or changing, so that to say "material thing" is tantamount to saying "changing thing." If we reflect seriously on the phenomenon of change, as applied to a material substance, we discover that it can
change in four distinct ways: quantitatively, qualitatively, locally, and sub-
stantially.

A material substance changes quantitatively by either increasing or de-
creasing in size. The tomato plant you carefully plant in May is some six
inches in height; in August, when it is producing tomatoes faster than you

can give them away to neighbors, it has a height of better than five feet. A block of ice at room temperature will gradually decrease in size until eventually it is reduced to a puddle of water on the floor. Diminishment in size can be consciously controlled, as when Jasper decides to go on a diet to lose what he decides is unseemly poundage.

Qualitative change can take a wide range of forms, such as the following: leaves changing their color in the fall; changing one's mind about something; altering the voice from a whisper to a shout; learning a new language; clouds changing their shapes as they drift across the summer sky. Qualitative change has to do, generally, with alterations in the disposition of a substance, the various ways it displays its basic nature. We can easily grasp what qualitative change is by citing examples of specific qualities, as I just did, but it is not so easy to describe quality in general, and that is because the category of quality is large and various. Aristotle identified quality in general as that by which things are said to be "such and such." You may or may not find that particularly helpful. But to give us a more concrete idea of what we are dealing with here, Aristotle went on to identify four specific kinds of quality. They are: disposition and habit; capacity and incapacity; sense qualities; figure and form. They pretty much speak for themselves.

One of the most readily noticeable ways a material substance changes is by locomotion, moving from place to place. Human beings and animals can effect a change of place on their own accord. I decide that it is getting too uncomfortable sitting in the sun, so I move my lawn chair into the shade of the ash tree and continue my writing there. Fido, for whatever doggy reason, follows my lead and moves into the shade as well, where he resumes his briefly interrupted afternoon nap. Plant life is very good at growing, but has to be rooted in one place; locomotion is out of the question. Inanimate things are not self-moving but, up to a certain point, they are moveable. We can fairly easily relocate a mattress, but moving a mountain would be an altogether different affair.

By all odds, the most significant kind of change is substantial change. Of the three kinds of change we have so far considered—quantitative, qualitative, local—the substance that undergoes one or another of those changes retains, throughout the course of the change, its identical substantial nature; it is precisely the same substance after the change is completed as it was before the change began. The teenager who grows three inches in seven months is, at his new heightened state, the same person he was before it was attained. Beatrice, who now speaks fluent French, something she could not do two years ago when she departed for Toulouse, is still Beatrice for all that. The mattress that was once in the delivery truck, and is now on the twin bed in the back bedroom, is the same mattress after the move that it was before the move; different location, same substance.

In the case of substantial change, it is not some aspect of a substance that changes (its weight, its color, its place), it is the substance itself that changes, and in the most radical of ways. The substance loses its very identity, as this or that kind of material thing, and is transformed into something entirely different. When a chemist combines hydrogen and oxygen according to certain proportions and under the proper conditions, a substantial change takes place. Two highly flammable gases disappear, and their place is taken by a liquid which can be used to douse unwanted flames. And if he so chooses, a chemist can reverse that particular substantial change, analyzing water to produce hydrogen and oxygen. If a log is burned completely so that nothings remains but a pile of ash, we have there an instance of substantial change. The death of a plant or an animal is an example of substantial change.

The Essence of Change

It is one thing to describe the various ways that material substances can change, it is quite another thing, and very much a philosophical thing, to try to get to the bottom of the phenomenon so as to arrive at an accurate account of change just as such, irrespective of the particular kind of change that is taking place. The question before us is this: What is the very essence of change, any and all change?

We will start by thinking of two states, a before state and an after state. In every kind of change we witness a change from one state to another state. Before the change takes place the thing is in State A; after the change takes place the thing is in State B. Consider a change of place. A book of mine was on the shelf a few minutes ago, now it is sitting right here on my desk. That would be an example of accidental change, a change of place. We say that what underlies and explains that or any other kind of change is the transition from potentiality to actuality. In order for a material thing to change in a particular way, it obviously must have the capacity, or the potentiality, to undergo change in that particular way. The green leaf of an elm tree cannot transform itself into a pickle, for it has no potentiality that can be realized in that particular and rather fantastic way. But it does have the capacity, come October, to change from being a green leaf to being a yellow leaf. Right now, in mid-July, it is actually a green leaf, but it is also, right now, potentially a yellow leaf.

The distinction between potentiality and actuality, or potential being and actual being, is one of the most important distinctions in philosophy. It was the incomparable Aristotle who was the first to give a thorough theoretical account of it. The distinction calls attention to the two basic modes of real being. The reality of actual being is immediately apparent to us; indeed, it is self-evident. This five year old girl, Danielle, actually exists, there is no doubt about that. But what particularly interests us is that here is a five-year-old girl who has an exceptionally lovely singing voice, accompanied by perfect pitch. In all, she has a natural knack for music. On the force of that state of affairs, her Uncle Herb, an opera buff, is prompted one day to proclaim, "that kid has the potential to be a veritable diva one day!" Now obviously little Danielle is not a diva right now, but we understand what Uncle Herb is saying. (The philosopher would say that he is implicitly acknowledging the reality of potential being.) Listening to the child sing, we agree that she really could be a professional singer some day; that is not a preposterous possibility. The potentiality to be a professional singer, according to the considered estimate of Uncle Herb, is an instance of real being, right now, in this five year old girl. That potentiality is not a mere fiction. Something which is not actually the case right now but could actually be the case in the future represents a genuine dimension of being, and we call it potential being. That was Aristotle's great insight.

The fact that we recognize real potentiality in something or in someone does not mean that the potentiality is necessarily some day going to be actualized. Potentiality can be thwarted for any number of reasons, and go unrealized, but that possibility does not negate the fundamental reality of potentiality, the real capacity of something or someone to be tomorrow what they are not today. Potentiality is future-oriented reality; it is the reality that explains our natural tendency to look ahead, to make plans, to hope that what is not right now can be a year from now, or maybe even tomorrow.

The essence of all change, once again, is the transition from potentiality to actuality, or, more simply, from potency to act (*de potentia ad actum*, in Latin), from what really can be to what really is. But what are we to say of the *process* of change, that which takes place between State A and State B, between the commencement and the terminus of the change? We say that it is "the actualization of potentiality in the very condition of its being actualized." It is the arrow flying through the air, midway between archer and target. It is the now no longer completely green leaf in the gradual process of turning completely yellow. It is Danielle, today studying at the Julliard School of Music, on track for making her debut at the Metropolitan Opera.

Having made the distinction between act and potency, we now need to make a distinction within potency, between active potency and passive potency. Active potency is the capacity of a body to act upon, to move, to affect another body in any number of ways; passive potency is the capacity of a body to be acted upon, to be moved, to be affected by another body in any number of ways. If something is the source of change, displaying active potency, there is an object of change, displaying passive potency. The two are inseparable. Picture a young mother pushing a tram along the sidewalk. The pushing mother displays active potency; the pushed tram displays passive potency. Together they make a single action.

Whatever Is Moved Is Moved by Another

Earlier in the chapter, after alluding to the principle which states that whatever is moved is moved by another (*quidquid movetur ab alio movetur* is the poetic way it is expressed in Latin), I said I would have more to say about it later. This would be the proper place to do so. But first, a brief word on *ens mobile,* which I also mentioned earlier. The phrase has been traditionally used to identify the principal subject matter of the philosophy of nature, which it does very precisely, for it is literally translated as "moving being," or "changing being"; either of those would nicely serve as synonyms of material being, for it is of the very essence of material being to change.

Now, as to "whatever is moved is moved by another," the general idea behind the principle, as applied specifically to the philosophy of nature, is this: every physical body is influenced, in its motion, by other physical bodies already in motion. Here we want to understand "motion" in the broadest terms, as referring to any kind of change. Every individual thing is subject to change because it has incorporated within its very nature a receptivity to change; that is, it has within itself the passive potency to be changed in this or that particular way. In other words, we must acknowledge that a good part of the explanation for why a thing changes in the ways it does is accounted for by the nature of the thing itself. A particular physical entity of a certain kind has something to say, as it were, about how it is to be changed. A particular chemical element, because of its very structure, will submit to being changed only in certain limited ways. All of these considerations pertain to what we can call the internal factors of change.

By citing the principle that whatever is moved is moved by another, we call attention to the external factors of change; it is important to be aware of this principle because those external factors are always a very important part of the phenomenon of change. In we consider a case of local motion, where a moving physical object strikes another physical objec which was at rest and thus puts it in motion, as when a golf club strikes a golf ball, it is easy to see how one thing is moved by another. The now moving golf ball obviously did not set itself in motion, but was set in motion by the action of the golf club. A father painting his child's toy box; the sun bleaching a board fence; a loud noise waking a sleeping baby with a start; harsh words bringing tears to a sensitive teenager—all of these are changes brought about by something external to the subject of change.

One might suppose that the principle under discussion does not apply to conscious agents who have the powers of self-motion, but it does. If we consider closely the movements such agents make, we will invariably find that there is something external to the agent which is a key factor in accounting for the movement. There is no question but that the human conscious agent can, by making an act of will, move himself—that is, he can bring about certain kinds of changes in hiimself—and he can therefore rightly be said to be the source of his own movements; he moves himself by an act of will. But that is not the whole story, for the will is always moved by something other than itself, and in human behavior that turns out to be what a person perceives as a desired good and then is moved to possess it. The will moves itself, yes, but always in response to a desire to achieve a specific good of one kind or another. We might say, then, that we are moved to move ourselves.

We have seen that the essence of any change is a transition from potency to act, a movement from one state to a new and different state. In
describing that transition, we speak of a "reduction" of potency to act, and
we say that no substance can reduce itself to act in any specific way, but
can only be reduced to act (e.g., made to move) by something that is already
in act in that specific way. And this is just another way of expressing the
principle that whatever is moved is moved by another. Thinking of it again
in terms of local motion, if an object, A, is at rest and then is set in motion
by another object, B, that object, B, must already have been in motion, or,
as we say, "in act" (*in actu*) with respect to motion. So, object A, which was
potentially in motion, is "reduced" to the actuality of motion by object B,
which was already in act in that respect.

When we consider the large realm of inorganic being, which represents
by far and way the greater part of the physical universe in which we live,
and when we consider the myriads upon myriads of the changes that are
constantly taking place in that realm (*ens mobile* never stops to rest), it probably would be more correct to say, with the principle under discussion in
mind, not that things change, but things *are changed*, for change is always
initiated by something that is external to the changing thing. Perhaps the
most comprehensive way to express the principle is to say that every physical
thing in the universe is influenced by, and in turn influences, proximately
or remotely, countless other physical things in the universe. In making that
sweeping claim I have in mind what physicists now seem to agree are the
four basic forces that govern all material being: the strong force (binding
together the particles that make up the nucleus of atoms); the weak force
(governing the intra-atomic particles not governed by the strong force); the
electromagnetic force; gravity. The principle that whatever is moved is
moved by another serves to bring home to us the cosmic interconnectedness
of things.

Matter and Form

Every material substance is composed, at a very elementary level, of two
basic principles, or "parts," using the term loosely—matter and form. The
matter principle is easily enough understood; it is simply the physical stuff
of which any material substance is composed. The substance of water, for

example, is made up of molecules which are composed of two hydrogen atoms and one oxygen atom. The human body is composed of any number of organic parts—heart, lungs, muscle, bones, etc.—and at the foundational level, of countless molecules and atoms.

When we think of matter in abstract terms, we think of it as pure potentiality, what we call in philosophy primary or prime matter. Now, potentiality does not exist independently; it is not a substance, but a quality of a substance. Primary matter, as pure potentiality, exists as a principle embedded within every actually existing material substance, wood, or wool, or granite, and it is that which explains the capacity of any material substance to change into another substance or substances. It is primary matter that "stays the same," as an enduring principle, undergirding as it were the transition from one substance to another.

In speaking of the form of a material substance we do not have chiefly in mind the external shape or contours of a material body. That is indeed form, but it is accidental form. Here we are concerned with substantial form, which plays a role of the utmost importance. Substantial form is a principle in a substance which, at the most basic level, accounts for its very existence, and making it be precisely the kind of substance it is. It establishes the specific identity of a particular material substance. What, at bottom, distinguishes lead from silver from platinum from molybdenum? What allows us to say this is a tulip plant and that over there is lettuce? On what basis do we differentiate between ants and antelope, between beavers and bears, between cougars and crocodiles? Earlier I made much of the point that what explains the differences among those various kinds of vegetative and animal beings is the fact that they have different natures. But what explains the different natures? It is difference in substantial forms. Those different beings are different because they have different substantial forms. It is different substantial forms which is the root explanation for different natures. The nature of a material substance can be understood as the overt or public expression of that substance's substantial form.

Material Being Is Limited Being

Material being can be regarded as limited being in two rather basic ways. The first way has to do with what we might describe as its intrinsic susceptibility to impermanence. Material substances, as we are all readily aware, are constantly changing, and sometimes the changes are so complete that a material substance that once was no longer is. Thomas Aquinas typically framed material being within two dramatic events, generation and corruption. Material substances come into being and they fall out of being. This is especially evident with respect to animate material substances, plants and animals. We could say that, all in all, material substances have a tenuous hold on existence. An individual material substance can lose its grip on being, but matter as such holds on to it tenaciously. As the result of substantial change, a particular substance takes its departure, but the matter of which it was composed does not evaporate into thin air, as if there were a transition from something to nothing. We give due recognition to the principle of the conservation of matter/energy.

In that remarkable phenomenon which is substantial change a particular substance loses its proper identity and is transformed into an entirely different substance, or substances. Consider the dramatic sequence of events that takes place at the atomic level where uranium goes through a series of transformational steps until it eventually ends up as lead; the uranium has disappeared, and now we have lead. When fall arrives and the heavy frosts set in, the marigold plant is smitten; the life principle is driven out of it and the plant dies. It ceases to be a marigold plant, and the matter that was once so nicely integrated as to constitute a single and particularly attractive living substance, disintegrates and takes the form of any number of elementary inanimate substances. There are dramatically different time frames within which the impermanence of material substances manifests itself. The mayfly lives for only a few hours; it takes a very long time for uranium to pass through the staged natural process which terminates in lead.

The second way we can regard material being as limited being relates to the fact that potency is an inextricable part of its nature, is indeed part of its definition. To say "material being" is effectively to say "potential" being. In the ordinary way we think of potentiality, we tend to regard it as very much a positive factor, suggesting progress, improvement, the promise of better days ahead. And well we might so regard it, for clearly there is a pronouncedly positive aspect of potency. But let us think about potency as the engine of change. Why do material things change? They change because they have a need to change, a need that is explained by the fact that they are imperfect beings. Material things change because they have an inherent impetus to make up for their limitations, to fill gaps in their being as it were. If a material substance were perfect it would have no inclination to change. In sum, material being is limited being because it is potential being, and thus imperfect. Echoing the words of the Thomist philosopher H. D. Gardeil, we can say that wherever there is potency there is necessarily *imperfection*. He went on to note that potency relates to act, in a given substance, as a state of imperfection to a state of perfection or completion.

The Aristotelian Categories

In delineating the basic features of material being I cited the item of relation: every material substance is related in any number of ways to any number of other material substances. In enumerating the four ways in which material substances can change, I cited quantitative and qualitative change: material substances can become larger or smaller, can become heavier or lighter; they can change with regard to any number of their characteristic features, external or internal. Now, because relation, quantity, and quality are among the categories identified by Aristotle, it is fitting, to put those three categories in their proper context, that I introduce all of the categories here and briefly describe them. There are ten categories in all. The first category is substance, which, as we know, is a material thing that exists through itself; it is, as it were, a free-standing material entity. (There are substances other than material substances, which we will deal with in a later chapter, but as philosophers of nature our principal concern is with material substances.) The remaining nine categories are accidents, which represent a type of being that can only exist in another, that "other" of course being a substance. I will first simply list the nine categories of accident, then briefly discuss each of them. We already know the first three categories, for they are quantity, quality, and relation; after them come action, passivity, time, place, position, and habit.

Before I get to that, though, I need to make some observations about the categories as a whole, and the important roll they play in our thinking, about material substances, about things in general. In a statement or proposition, its subject, for our purposes, will be a material substance, and what is said of that subject, what is predicated of it, will be one of the nine accidents listed above. The remarkable thing about that list is that it pretty much exhausts every informative thing that can be said of a material substance. Such was the genius of Aristotle in composing that list. If we can predicate of any substance that we are interested in each of those nine accidents, those nine modes of accidental being, we will have a very complete knowledge of that substance. Here is a brief description of each.

Quantity. Recall that the first thing we had to say about material being was that it is extended, which is to say that it is in the category of quantity. Material being, because extended, occupies a position in space; it can be measured, according to the language of quantity, which is mathematics.

Quality. This category, if not the largest, is certainly the most varied. As we saw, it is difficult to describe in general terms, but we can try. We could say that the category has to do with what philosophers have come to call qualia, which, broadly considered, would include all the phenomena we experience through sensation, as well as that which we experience internally, such as thought and imagination, and the various emotions. The more qualia of a substance we can identify, the better we know it.

Relation. When we focus our attention on quantity or quality we are concentrating on individual substances; when we have relation in mind we are concerned to know how substances are related to one another. To know how a particular substance relates to other substances can tell us much about that particular substance. Perhaps it is a relation of location in space: Putterville is six miles due east of Somber City. Perhaps it is a matter of blood relation: Lu Lu Mae is a cousin of Betsie Lee Dells.

Action. To know the kind of activity that is common or habitual to a particular substance is revealing of the basic nature of the substance. Actions speak louder than words, as the old saying has it, and truly enough. A person's patterned actions are revealing of the character of the person. It is active potency, identified earlier, which is behind the actions of any substance.

Passivity. The passivity of a material substance tells us what it is receptive to, and it is explained by the aforementioned passive potency. We must not think that the passivity of a substance is inconsequential information. Passivity should not be confused with weakness. A good example of it would be intellectual docility. Students who assume an open-minded and attentive attitude to the lectures they hear and the books they read put themselves in a promising learning mode.

Time. To know when something happened is to give it specific historical placement. Actions do not just happen; they happen at a particular time. On occasion they are instantaneous, like the firing of a pistol, but in most cases they are marked by temporal endurance, going on seemingly interminably, like a concert whose music is an offense to ears and mind. Temporal sequence is important: it is helpful to know that World War I came after the American Civil War.

Place. Actions do not just happen; they happen in a particular place, and where they take place can have a bearing on the quality of a particular action. It is a good thing to pray, but not viva voce in the town square at high noon, for the express purpose of calling attention to your self and demonstrating to your fellow townspeople what a pious fellow you are. Knowledge of correct geographical placement is important; if I want to get to Putterville in time for the meeting, it is important for me to know that I am heading in the right direction on the Tentative Turnpike.

Position. This accident refers to the general disposition or to the arrangement of the parts of a material substance. It is best explained by examples. The rake is leaning against the side of the garage, but the hoe is lying in the driveway. All the drawers of the bureau were half open. Various positions taken by the human body: sitting, standing, kneeling, crouching, arms akimbo, arms folded, arms raised overhead.

Habit. This category can be generally described by a situation where you have one substance contiguous with another. Clothing is the example usually given. Brother Elias is never seen not wearing his Carmelite habit. Dew on the grass, frost on the roof, rust on a knife blade, can be taken as examples of habit. The categories of position and habit are probably the least informative of the accidents, but sometimes the information they provide can be valuable. The fact that the man who robbed the filling station was wearing a bright red ski mask, a green sweat shirt, and faded blue jeans proved to be helpful to police inspector I. M. Delving.

I will now describe a particular substance, a young man named Bartholomew, by predicating of him all nine of the accidents. I will give but a few examples for each category, but for some of them, especially quality, dozens of examples could be given. Bartholomew stands six feet, two inches in height and has broad shoulders (quantity); he has pitch-black hair, brown eyes, and a ruddy complexion (quality); he has a brother who is five years older than he, and a sister who is five years younger (relation); he played three years of varsity high school basketball, besides being on the swimming team (action); he received his high school's Latin Prize two years in a row, and when the basketball team won the state tournament his senior year he was awarded the Best Player trophy (passivity); he was born on February 12, 2000 (time) in Putterville, Pennsylvania; at the moment he is sitting in the local library, his legs crossed, reading Aleksandr Solzhenitsyn's *The First Circle* (position), wearing a blue double-breasted suit, a pale blue shirt, and a red bow tie (habit).

Place and Space

As we have seen, extension is a basic property of every material substance. However great it might be, extension is necessarily limited. To be a physical body is to be limited by definite boundaries, and this makes the body measurable. To imagine that there could be a physical body of infinite size would be, as Aristotle showed centuries ago, to imagine the impossible, for we would be supposing there to be in existence something without boundaries, but something without boundaries could not be identified as a body, for a body is a specific, identifiable entity, so we would not even know what we were talking about. A body is, by definition, that which is bounded, limited in space. A physical body infinite in size is, then, a contradiction in terms. It makes no sense.

It is the boundaries, the physical limits, of any given material substance, that are the foundation for what we call place. But it is not those boundaries alone that serve that function. We need to take into account the matter—gaseous, liquid, or solid—which is other than the material substance which we say is in a particular place, and which surrounds that substance. The idea of place is based upon a relation between the object which is in place, and its physical surroundings. We are here talking about something that common sense readily recognizes. It would be unintelligible to speak of the place of a physical object without reference, albeit only implicit, to something physical other than that physical object. A material object is always somewhere, and that somewhere is constituted by material reality. The coat is in the closet; the clock is on the mantel; the diadem is on the head of the princess.

Do you remember the solid gold basketball-sized object that I brought up in our discussion of relation? I asked you to imagine that it was the only body in existence. The point of that thought experiment was to show that if the golden basketball-sized object were the only material object in existence there would be no relation. Again, it takes at least two to make a relation. Now, let's bring that solid gold globe back into play. If it is the only material thing in existence, not only would it have no relation, it would have no place as well. Where could it possibly be if it were the only thing in existence? We would have one of the elements necessary for the constitution of a place, that is, the dimensions of the golden globe itself (that would allow us to talk intelligently about the internal space of the globe), but we would lack the other necessary element in order to constitute a real place, matter of one kind or another which is other than and external to the matter of the golden globe.

Space, roughly defined, is the sum total of places. It is the existence of physical bodies, with their extension, which makes space possible, space now being more precisely defined as the interval between any two physical bodies. And that interval, like the extension of any physical body, is measurable. As I now look out my window, I estimate that the distance between the front steps of the house and the street is about thirty feet. The astronomers tell us that the distance from the earth to the sun is some 93,000,000 miles. But note this; the standards by which we measure intervals of space are provided to us by the extension of individual material objects. Consider the distance from here to the sun—93,000,000 miles. What is a mile? It is 5,280 feet. What is the standard that we refer to as a foot? It is the measured extension of a human foot, a rather large one at that. Whatever standard we might appeal to in our measurements, the metric system for example, it is ultimately traceable back to the measurement of the extension of physical objects.

All this comes down to the fact that what we call space is entirely dependent upon the existence of material bodies and their extension. We might be tempted to imagine that if there were no physical objects at all in existence (not even that lonely golden globe), then there would still be space, utterly empty space. That was the opinion of Isaac Newton, who believed that before God created the physical universe, space existed. In this case, Aristotle proved to be the better physicist. If the existence of all physical bodies was to be subtracted, the remainder would not be space. There would be literally nothing. It is material being that makes space possible. Einstein was in Aristotle's camp on this question, not Newton's.

Time

We noted earlier that one of the favorite ways philosophy has of describing material being is to call it mobile or changing being (remember *ens mobile*?). It is of the very nature of matter to be constantly in motion. The whole physical universe is on the move. What we have in the ubiquitous, incessant motion of matter is the foundation for what we know as time. Aristotle famously, and succinctly, defined time as the measure of motion. That definition needs to be carefully examined.

A general description of time, one based on our common experience of the phenomenon, would reasonably start by noting that it is a kind of duration, more exactly, successive duration, one thing after another. But what are the "things" that are succeeding one another? In order to answer that question satisfactorily, we cannot avoid referring to motion, the constant motion of matter, or, to be more precise, of physical bodies. We can confidently state that motion is the *foundation* of time, but it is not time itself.

Recall how, just above, we saw that two elements were necessary to establish the reality of place—the particular material object we say is in a place, and the material objects external to it to which it relates. We have a comparable situation here in dealing with time. There are two elements to consider: first, the aforementioned motion of physical bodies; we could call that the objective element of time. Second, there is the subjective element, which is the conscious awareness and keeping track of the motion of physical bodies by the human mind. In observing the motion of any physical body we take note of its succession. To put it in simple but very ordinary terms, we notice a before and after aspect of motion: first this happens, then, afterwards, that happens; one perception follows another. When we are conscious of the passage of time what we are really conscious of is the passage of the various phases of a particular kind of motion we are consciously aware of. There is the successive motion; there is our conscious registering of that motion.

In practical fact, any successive, regular motion can serve as the foundation for time. Galileo, who lived before watches came along, once used his pulse (tracking the regular motion of heart beat), to time the arc of a slowly swinging chandelier. But there is one kind of motion, cosmic in dimension, which, because it is so prominent and immediately obvious and accessible to everyone, has become the universally accepted standard for time, and that is of course the relative motion between the earth and the sun. We have become so used to clocks and watches that we tend to forget that what those time pieces are recording is the rotational motion of the earth with respect to the sun, which gives us days. Then there is the orbital motion of the earth around the sun, another standard for temporal measurement, which gives us seasons.

Let us begin with the year and work our way down through increasingly smaller segments of time. A year is the time it takes the earth to make one orbit around the sun. We then, with an eye to the phases of the moon, divide the year into smaller units we call months, the number of which is conventional; months we divide into weeks, the number of which is also conventional; and weeks we divide into days, once again the number of which can vary by convention, but the number of days has now been pretty much universally fixed at seven. A day is the time span created by the earth's making a complete rotation on its axis as it relates to the sun. We divide the day into twenty-four hours by convention, and convention divides the hour into sixty minutes, and the minute into sixty seconds. It does not stop there. In modern physics, it is not unusual to measure in milliseconds (one thousandth of a second) and in nanoseconds (one billionth of a second). Note that all those various units of time, from the year down to the nanosecond, are no more than different ways of regarding and dividing up the motion of the earth relative to the sun. Our time is founded on the measure of cosmic motion.

In our earlier discussion of space we claimed that if there were no physical bodies with their measurable extension, there would be no space. Something comparable to that is to be said of time: If there were no physical bodies in motion, there would be no time, for time is nothing else but the measuring of that motion. On this point too Isaac Newton thought otherwise, and argued that even if there were no physical bodies with their motion, there would still be time. Here again, Newton had it wrong, and Aristotle had it right.

We should not be too hard on Sir Isaac, however, for most of us are in-clined to think of time as something which is entirely free-standing and in-dependent, as if it were a substance of sorts, albeit perhaps an immaterial substance, and an elusive and mysterious one to boot. We suppose that it is not based on motion, as the measuring of that motion; rather, it is that by which the motion itself is measured. In other words, time does not fol-low upon motion but is antecedent to it. To support that way of regarding time we might appeal to a scenario such as the following: Coach Carlson is standing by the track, stop-watch in hand, timing one of the members of his team as he runs the 100-meter dash. Is that not a clear case of time measuring motion? One could say that, but let us consider the situation more closely. What is that thing the coach has in his hand? It is a stop watch. What is that stop watch doing but recording very small segments of the motion of the earth as it makes a single rotation on its axis? So, the watch time which is measuring the motion of the runner is completely de-pendent on the motion of the earth in relation to the sun. If that cosmic motion did not exist, there would be no watch time. We are back to the unavoidable fact that motion is the foundation of time, and because time is therefore dependent on motion, it cannot exist independently of motion. If motion stops, so does time.

The Four Causes

If we can identify the causes of material substances, or of anything in our universe, we are equipped with a most valuable kind of knowledge. De-scribed in the most general terms, a cause is simply an explanation. On the most basic level, a cause of a thing is the explanation for (a) its very existence or (b) modifications in the manner in which it exists. So, the cause of the handsome cabinets in the Smiths's kitchen is the cabinet maker who made and installed them; later, he is the cause of the changes that he thought should be made in them. Usually, when we think about the cause of some-thing, we have in mind what in philosophy is called the efficient cause. The cabinet maker just alluded to would be the efficient cause of the Smiths's cabinets. However, efficient causality does not exhaust the realm of causal-ity, for there are three other causes besides the efficient cause, three other ways of explaining a particular object we want to know about. They are:

the material cause, the formal cause, and the final cause. Those four causes—yet another product of Aristotle's inventive genius—when used as a means of analyzing a material substance, will provide us with a comprehensive account of that substance. In Chapter One we introduced the principle of sufficient reason, one of the basic principles that govern all human reason. It informs us generally that there is a reason for everything that exists; if that "reason" is other than the thing itself, then it has a cause; it is not self-explanatory. A material substance lends itself to fruitful analysis in terms of the four causes. It is a simple and illuminating process.

In describing that process I will make use of the example used by Aristotle, though altering it slightly. The object which we want to analyze in terms of the four causes is a statue of St. Joan of Arc. We begin with the material cause and the formal cause; these are called intrinsic causes, because they are internal to the object itself. The material cause of the statue is the matter, the physical stuff out of which it is made, which in this case would be marble. The formal cause of the statue is, on an obvious level, simply its form or shape. The next two causes, the efficient and the final, are called extrinsic causes because they are external to the object itself. The efficient cause of the statue would be the person who made it, who happens to be none other than the world-renowned sculptor Federico Famoso. The final cause answers the questions, Why was it made? What is the statue's purpose? The sculptor himself has answered those questions: "To give due honor to a saint, and one of the most remarkable women in Western history." (Mark Twain would thoroughly agree with that assessment of the Maid of Orleans.)

The material and formal causes are intimately related to the important distinction we introduced earlier between matter and form, the two fundamental components of every material substance. To speak of them in terms of causes is simply to draw attention to their explanatory value in understanding the basic nature of a material substance. A substance of that kind is, by definition, one that is composed of matter and form. Notice that in identifying the formal cause of the statue, just above, I said it was the statue's shape or form. Some qualifications are now in order. In the first place, to accurately describe that form we must identify it as an accidental form. Secondly, I assumed that in analyzing the statue we were dealing with a material substance; that is acceptable if we understand that the term substance is being used analogously. This is to say that I am using it in less than its strict sense. A statue, obviously, is an artifact, a man-made object. It is not a natural substance, and therefore, *as a statue,* it does not have what we earlier identified as a substantial form; it has only an accidental form, the form given to it by the sculptor. Is there anything in this circumstance that could be identified as a substantial form? Yes, there must be; if we were to focus our attention, not on the statue but on the marble of which the statue is made, it is there we would discover substantial form. Recall our identifying matter and form as the basic components of a material substance. There we saw that the form in question is not accidental form but substantial form, which plays the altogether crucial role of establishing the very existence, and the proper identity, of a material substance. So, turning our attention to the marble out of which the statue of St. Joan of Arc is made, we would, to explain the basic fact that it exists and the way it exists, call attention to the substantial form of the marble, for it is that which explains marble as marble.

Thomas Aquinas, referring to the four causes, identified the final cause as "the cause of causes," by which he meant that it is the explanation of the other three causes. In attempting to illustrate his line of reasoning here, I will return to the work of Federico Famoso in his sculpting the stature of St. Joan of Arc. Before he picks up his mallet and chisel to take the first chip out of the marble, he sits down and plans what he wants to achieve. He generates an idea of the statue he wants to sculpt, the form he intends the marble to take. That idea is called the exemplar cause. (The exemplar cause is not a fifth cause; it is simply the formal cause as it exists as an idea in the mind of the sculptor.) In artistic production, what is last in execution, the artifact (the statue) is first in cognition (the idea). Now, what prompts Famoso to take action and start chipping away at the marble is his intention to realize his idea. Thus, the efficient cause is explained by the final cause because the action of the efficient cause is ordered toward achieving the final cause; the formal cause is explained by the final cause because the content of the formal cause is the final cause (the completed statue), and the material cause is explained by the final cause because without it the final cause could not be realized. Famoso would not have been able to achieve his end or purpose without the marble; it would have remained but a beautiful idea in his mind.

Efficient Cause and Final Cause

It is customary for the philosophy of nature to concentrate its attention on the efficient cause and the final cause. Typically, the efficient cause is distinct and separate from that which it causes, the effect. It is the agent that gives existence to another, or changes its way of existing. The young mother carrying her baby across the room is the cause (along with her husband) of the existence of the baby, and right now she is the cause of the change in the way the baby is existing, as being moved from one place to another. We saw that the material cause and the formal cause are inseparable; they are two aspects of one and the same thing. We will soon see that the efficient and the final causes are also inseparable.

Cause and effect are correlatives, meaning that you cannot have one without the other; like "right" and "left," the meaning of one depends on having a direct relation to the other. It would make no sense to identify something as a cause if there were no effect, nor would it make sense to call something an effect if it did not to have a cause. Given the intimate relation between cause and effect, there is another philosophical principle that tells us that every cause communicates something of its own nature to whatever effects it brings about. It is as if the cause left its personal signature on its effects. It is particularly important to keep this principle in mind. We can know with certitude that every distinct fact of nature has a cause. Things don't just happen; they are caused to happen. But there are situations where we may have clear and indisputable facts before us, effects (they must be effects because nothing can be the cause of itself), but we are unable to pinpoint their cause or causes. In such a situation what we need to do is to subject those facts, those effects, to the closest kind of scrutiny, with the purpose of finding in them indications or hints that suggest the nature of the cause or causes that are behind them. We endeavor to read the signature of the causes in the effects. That is the common procedure of scientific investigation.

There are a number of refinements that can be made regarding the efficient cause, but here I limit myself to a discussion of two prominent sets of distinctions—between the primary cause and the secondary cause, and between the principal cause and the instrumental cause. I will begin the treatment of each with an example. Consider a 100-car freight train, now passing through the town of Putterville, PA. The last car is a caboose. What is the cause of the movement of the caboose? It is the box car right in front of it, to which it is coupled. That car is the immediate cause of the caboose's movement, and it is a secondary cause. So too are all the intervening box cars between the caboose and the engine. The engine is the primary cause; it is its movement that accounts for the movement of all the cars to which it is coupled. Notice something important about this state of affairs: without the movement of the engine, none of the box cars would move, and thus neither would the caboose. This is to say that without the active causal agency of the primary cause, none of the secondary causes would be able to exercise real causal agency. The movement of the primary cause, the engine, is simultaneous with that of all the cars in the train.

This is not always the case with respect to the relation between primary and secondary causes; sometimes, as in the case of animal generation, secondary causes can exercise their agency, act as generative causes, without the primary causes exercising their causal agency. Consider a pop and mom poodle. Mrs. Poodle has just given birth to three poodle puppies. She and her consort were the generative causes of those puppies. They were able to exercise their generative powers because they themselves were generated by their respective parents, and their parents in turn were generated by their parents. Let us designate the grandparents of pop and mom poodle as the primary generative causes. Those eight canines have long since departed this mortal coil, so it is obvious that they do not exercise generative causality, but that does not inhibit pop and mom poodle from exercising theirs.

A good example of the distinction between a principal cause and an instrumental cause is that between a musician and his instrument, let us say a between a violinist and his violin. Here, as with the distinction between primary and secondary cause we have subordination, of the instrumental cause to the principal cause, but in this case the causation of the instrument is absolutely dependent upon the causative action of the principal cause. Violins do not play themselves. Hammers are not self-hammering nor are hand saws self-sawing. There are some rather interesting relationships between a musician as principal cause and the musical instrument. One could have one of the finest violins available, a Stradivarius, and yet because the musician playing it is not all that accomplished, the instrument is not producing the quality of sound it is capable of. Or think of the opposite kind of circumstance. Let us imagine that a masterful violinist like Isaac Stern or Itzhak Perlman, because of a bizarre series of mishaps, finds himself having to perform with an instrument that is decidedly less than first-rate. Even so, it is very likely that, because of the superiority of his skills, either of these musical geniuses would be able to get more out of the instrument than could a musician of lesser talents. There is mutual dependency between principal cause and instrument: the principal cause needs a good instrument; the instrument, so to speak, needs a good principal cause.

We mistakenly tend to think of the relationship between cause and effect to be sequential: first the cause acts, then the effect follows. In fact, however, cause and effect are simultaneous. Consider again the simple example of the cue ball striking the eight ball and setting it in motion. There may be action preliminary to the actual causation, such as the cue stick striking the cue ball and setting it in motion, and action following the actual causation, such as the motion of the eight ball after it is struck, but the actual causation itself takes place precisely when the cue ball strikes the eight ball. At that instant cause and effect are simultaneous. There is no delay or gap between the two.

Another aspect of the relation between cause and effect is that the cause is greater than its effect. Obvious though that is, it is important not to take it casually, for we may make serious mistakes by doing so, assigning to objects causal capacities that are beyond them. An old saying has it that one can't get blood from turnips; if we were to think the case to be otherwise we would end up defending a situation where there is an effect, blood, which is a substance that is ontologically superior to, representing a higher order of material being than, its putative cause, the substance which is a turnip. Here we could cite the unpretentious principle which tells us that something can't give what it doesn't have. Common sense and philosophy are on friendly terms.

One of the signal features of the world of nature, Aristotle points out, is that in that world every agent acts for the sake of an end; its action is directed toward achieving a specific end. We can take that to be a general rule of nature: finality, or purpose, is ubiquitous in nature. The operative presence of finality is obvious enough in human agents. Unless we are seriously deranged, virtually every action we take is directed toward achieving a specific end. Describe any human act, and in that description you have the declaration of the end or purpose of that act: writing a letter, singing a song, giving a donation. It is equally evident that animal actions are purposeful (the nest-building of birds), and plant behavior is purposeful as well (the water-seeking action of roots), and it is even true of the actions of inanimate material substances. If a chemist mixes hydrogen and oxygen in the right relations and under the right conditions, he knows how things are going to end up. Action can be purposeful, i.e., end-oriented, without being conscious. Thomas Aquinas had this in mind when he referred to what he called "natural appetite," the tendency of even the actions of inanimate substances to act for the sake of an end. In sum, every kind of action in the universe is ordered toward a determined finality, a particular completion, a specifiable resolution. It is this ubiquitous presence of end-oriented activity in the universe that accounts for its unity and its order. And, by the way, it is what makes scientific prediction possible.

For decades now there have been philosophers and scientists who have denied the reality of final causality, but they do so in vain. Those same philosophers and scientists would without hesitation admit to the reality of efficient causality, but by doing so they are admitting to the reality of final causality as well, for the two cannot be separated. Cause cannot be separated from effect, as we have seen, but the effect which is brought about by the action of any cause is nothing else but the finality of that action; it is the purpose of the causal action. Every movement of ever-moving material being is a declaration of purpose.

Chapter Three
The Living World: Philosophical Psychology

The Great Gap

In the philosophy of nature we are engaged with material being, the world of physical things, endeavoring to come to a reliable understanding of the principles that govern that world. In the science of philosophical psychology we narrow our focus and deal with material being of a very special kind. Here we focus our attention on material being that is possessed of that wondrous something we call life. There is a huge gap, a yawning chasm in fact, that separates animate from inanimate matter. The sun that illumines and warms our earth is an awesomely impressive celestial body, and most needful to us; we literally could not live without it. The sun vivifies, yet it is itself utterly lifeless. For all its size and potency, for all its blinding brilliance, the sun cannot hold a candle to the minute, one-celled amoeba. The amoeba, just for the fact of its being alive, having life, is superior to the sun, to a million suns, to the whole inanimate physical universe put together. Inanimate material being is wondrous enough in its own right, and we can devote a dedicated lifetime attempting to penetrate and figure out its deeper secrets, and still fall short of realizing our ambitions. But when material being is animated, takes on life, matter undergoes a profound transformation; we are introduced to an altogether new dimension of reality.

Modern psychology, which saw its beginnings in Germany in the middle of the nineteenth century, has today developed into a number of different schools, all of which, however they might differ, are expressions of what is a specifically human psychology, with much attention being given to the individual person. Philosophical psychology, to be sure, is very much interested in human psychology, but our interests are more extensive. Human psychology is the culminating concern of our science, but it is something we work up to systematically. From a philosophical point of view, there are a number of very basic issues, concerning the nature of life, that need to be addressed before we enter the realm of human psychology.

The principal difference between philosophical psychology and general psychology is that the former, precisely because it is a philosophical science, is concerned with the most fundamental questions regarding the nature of life itself, in all of its forms, whereas the latter is principally concerned with human life, paying special attention to the cognitive and emotive aspects of the individual person. Given philosophical psychology's broader scope, given its interest in animate material life as such, it has as one of the first things on its agenda the need to bring some clarification to that key term, "animate." What does it mean, in specific terms, for something to be animate? What is the basic difference between animate being and inanimate being? Responding to those questions must be the first order of business.

A Clear Indication of the Presence of Life

What is it we first notice about living things? Is it not that they are self-moving? As we saw in the previous chapter, movement is a characteristic of all material being. The electron never stops jiggling. But that jiggling, and the movement of all inanimate material things, is a response to external stimuli or forces of some kind or another. The jiggling motion of the electron, as we noted, is best explained by various motivating influences coming from its environment, such as an electromagnetic field, or the attracting and repulsing forces of other inanimate bodies. The movement of the electron would thus seem to be entirely reactive; its instigating source is external to the moving body itself.

Thinking in terms of much larger material bodies than electrons, we are aware that the earth moves through the heavens in its remarkably regular way because it is urged to do so by the commanding presence of the sun. What is unique about the movement displayed by animate beings, such as a petunia plant or an elephant, is that its instigating source is within itself. When an elephant moves, in its typical lumbering way, we are inclined to say that there is something like choice behind its movements. There is an impetus within the elephant that accounts for its earth-shaking trip to the water hole.

Before we proceed we must pause here to deal with a possible problem. In the previous chapter we cited the principle which tells us that in the material realm whatever is moved is moved by another. But here we cited self-movement as one of the most obvious characteristics of animate material life. Do we have a flat contradiction on our hands, or are we simply to say that the principle which holds that whatever is moved is moved by another applies only to inanimate, and not to animate material being? There is no contradiction; the principle applies universally, to animate material being as well as to inanimate material being. To explain how that is so, we need to look more carefully at what we call the self-movement that we associate with animate creatures. Self-movement is, to be sure, a key identifying aspect of animate material substances, and the source of that movement is intrinsic to the substances. Now we want to consider that more closely. To get the complete picture of the movement of animate material substances we need to take into account more than the intrinsic source of the movement.

With regard to the internal movement, we can surmise that there is a distinction between a moving element and a moved element within the being itself. The elephant we see making its ponderous way to the watering hole is in motion not because the initiating source of that motion was seated in its legs. We would say that his legs are moving because a message was sent from the elephant's brain through his nervous system to the muscles of its legs. So, the mover here would be the brain, and the moved would be the legs, or the elephant as a whole. There, roughly sketched, we have the internal aspect of the mover/moved distinction as it manifests itself in animate beings. But there is an external aspect as well. The elephant is moving because it is thirsty and it wants to get to the water hole. Perhaps most of the movements made by animate beings are in response to something external to themselves, either something positive, which they want to move toward, or something negative, which they want to move away from. The same general idea applies to the movement that we find in plant life, the flora of the world. Consider the water-seeking movement of plants, displayed in an especially remarkable way in trees, which will send penetrating roots great distances and to great depths in search of water. The source of that movement is internal to the tree, specifically to its roots, but it is an external factor, the water, that accounts for that movement. One could also cite the heliotropic character of plants, explaining the way they move their leaves to get maximum direct exposure to the sun. Again in this case, the source of the movement is internal to the plant, but it is something external, the sun, that instigates the movement.

The Essence of Life

We saw, in our excursion into the philosophy of nature, that the root identifying principle of any material substance, that which makes it precisely the kind of thing it is—silver, gold, platinum—is substantial form. This is true of all material substances, be they inanimate or animate, but there is a decisive difference between the substantial forms of inanimate substances and those of animate substances, which reflects and explains the huge difference between non-living things and living things. The substantial form or identifying principle of an animate substance determines it to be, not only a particular kind of substance, but a *living* substance. We can conveniently refer to the substantial form of a living substance as its soul, by which we simply mean its life principle; it is that within the substance that explains the fact that it is alive. The word soul is traceable back to the Greek *psyche,* the original meaning of which is "breath of life," or "spirit." The Romans translated the Greek word into Latin as *anima*, from which we get our English word animate, along with its negation, inanimate. An inanimate substance is soulless. We speak of an especially lively person as animated. An animal is a creature that has an *anima*, soul, a life principle which, again, explains the fact that it is alive.

In his book *On the* Soul, Aristotle identifies the soul as the "actuality of a living body," meaning, as he explains, that it is the cause or source of a living body , the very essence of that body precisely as living. Aristotle's book, by the way, which is now often identified by its Latin title, *De Anima* (On the Soul), can be regarded as the work that inaugurated what was to develop into the science of philosophical psychology. The soul, as the "form" part of the matter/form combination that constitutes a material substance, is contrary to the "matter" part, and therefore is itself immaterial. That is a very important point, and we will have more to say about its implications later in the chapter when we consider more closely the human soul. We cannot see a life principle or soul, any more than we can see gravity, but we conclude the existence of both by their demonstrable effects. We know gravity is real by observing the way the earth and the moon behave in relation to one another. We know the reality of the principle of life, or soul, because it is the only reasonable explanation for the radical differences we observe between organic and inorganic matter. Live material substances—plants, animals, and human beings—can do things of which inanimate substances are completely incapable; they are possessed of powers that are nowhere to be found in the world of inanimate substances, wide and richly varied though that world might be. The most fundamental of those powers, upon which all other powers depend, are nutrition, growth, and reproduction.

Life's Three Basic Powers

Every living substance dramatically demonstrates its vitality by its capacity to nourish itself, to grow, and to reproduce its kind. The capacity to nourish itself is basic to the two other capacities, for without food there would be no growth, and without growth leading to a mature state there would be no reproduction. In the philosophy of nature we learned of substantial change, the most radical kind of change, whereby a particular substance loses its proper identity, ceases to be what it once was, and is replaced by an entirely different substance, or substances. The process of nutrition, by which, through ingestion and digestion, a living substance keeps itself alive, is a process which involves substantial change. Living substances incorporate into themselves substances other than themselves, and transform those substances into their own substances. They thus, in a real physical sense, internalize what is external to themselves. The root systems of plants and trees, which Aristotle, in an uncharacteristic display of poetry, compared to the mouths of animals, take in minerals found in the soil and effectively animates them by assimilating them into their living vegetal being. The grass consumed by the cow, at least some of it, becomes part of the cow, and so it is with the hapless earthworm serving as breakfast for Robin Redbreast. The grass as grass is gone, and the earthworm is no more. The self-nourishing capacity of a living body is an instance of immanent action, meaning that it is action which has its source within the body, remains within the body, and is for the benefit of the body. This is in contrast to transitive action, exemplified by one physical body moving another physical body.

Food is the fuel that prompts growth, a process which continues to the point where an organism reaches a mature state. The quantitative augmentation of living substances is the most obvious manifestation of growth. Most organisms start very small, but then can demonstrate an amazing increase in size in a relatively short time. We human beings begin our life on the planet as a single-cell organism, so tiny that it would require a microscope to be clearly seen. Compare that single-cell creature, as it was twenty-six years ago, to the six foot six, two hundred- and eighty-five-pound professional football player, whose body contains trillions of cells, which it has become today. Of course, those impressive athletic dimensions would never have been arrived at had not the football player continuously received requisite nourishment over the course of his twenty-six years, beginning with the nine months he spent in his mother's womb.

But there is qualitative growth as well as quantitative growth, the importance of which cannot be minimized, especially as it applies to human beings. When we refer to a mature man or woman, we do not only have in mind the fact that they have reached their maximum physical height, but also to the fact that they have grown up mentally and emotionally. In many respects healthy qualitative growth is dependent on healthy quantitative growth, if we recognize the latter as entailing everything that accompanies physical health. The ancient Romans promoted the condition of what they called *mens sana in corpora sano,* "a healthy mind in a healthy body." It is a commendable combination.

One of the more sobering facts of life is that it inevitably comes to an end. Living material substances do not live forever, however impressively lengthy some animal lives are. There are certain species of terrapins and parrots that seem bent on challenging the record for longevity set by Methuselah. And then there is the amazing longevity of the sequoia trees of California. But even very long lives come to an end. However, though the individual organism eventually dies, it can be said to enjoy a kind of immortality in its progeny, a progeny that is made possible by reproduction. There are two kinds of reproduction, sexual and asexual, the latter being subdivided into fission and budding. What the two asexual kinds have in common is that in both kinds an individual organism can take care of reproduction on its own, without any help from another organism of the same species. Single-cell organisms typically reproduce by fission, a process by which they simply split apart (meiosis is the technical name for it), and from the original or mother cell there result two daughter cells. In budding, commonly occurring in plants, the organism forms protuberances, or buds, which ripen to the point where they drop off from the organism and grow into a new organism, carrying on the living tradition of the organism from which they budded. Hydras and yeast reproduce by budding.

With regard to sexual reproduction in plants, it is typically the case that both sexual elements are found within a single plant, but often there is need for help from outside to bring them together, a service that is provided by pollinating insects. In sexual reproduction in animals there is established the foundational distinction between male and female, the physiological basis for the distinction being that they bear different reproductive cells, the male bearing the sperm, the female bearing the ovum. When male and female unite on the macrocosmic level, in coitus, there can be a microcosmic replica of that union on the microcosmic level when sperm and ovum unite. As soon as the sperm penetrates the ovum a substantial change takes place, and the single cell which then comes into being, the zygote, is different in genetic make-up from either of the two cells from which it came.

The Three Great Realms of Life

The lilac bush out in the back yard is alive; the dog lying under the lawn chair taking an afternoon snooze is alive; the young lady sitting on the lawn chair reading Nathaniel Hawthorne's *The Blithedale Romance* is alive. And there we have in close proximity to one another representatives of the three great realms of life, the vegetative, the sensitive, and the rational—in other words, the realms respectively of plants, animals, and humans. These three distinct ways in which life manifests itself are of course markedly different from one another, but for all their differences they have in common the three powers of nutrition, growth, and reproduction. The lilac bush, as well as all other plants, or flora, to be found around the globe are limited to those three powers. There is a distinct hierarchy to be recognized among the three forms of life, beginning with plants, ascending to animals, and culminating in human beings, a hierarchy which has an objective foundation in terms of the number of powers possessed by each particular form.

Plants, by reason of their having the powers of nutrition, growth, and reproduction, fully qualify as animate substances. But when we move from the level of plant life to that of animal life, we encounter a whole array of new powers, no less than twenty-one of them. Nine of these powers can be grouped together and labeled the sense powers; eleven of them are categorized as emotive powers, otherwise known as the appetitive powers or the passions; and then, standing alone, there is locomotion, the power to move from place to place, something which the lilac bush in the back yard, fortunately, is not able to do.

The Sense Powers

The sense powers are divided into the five external senses, with which we are all quite familiar—sight, hearing, smell, taste, touch—and four internal senses. Of the four internal senses, two of them, imagination and memory, are powers that we readily recognize in ourselves. But dogs can form images from what they learn from their external senses, and those images, stored away, provide material that memory draws upon. Colleen's pet collie fairly wags his tail off in greeting her when she comes back home from school, and that is because he remembers what she looks like, the sound of her voice, and her signature scents. The two other internal senses are the common sense (not to be confused with what we ordinarily mean by that term) and the estimative sense, which in human beings is called the cogitative sense. Let's consider the estimative sense first. This is an animal's initial, instinctive response to something external to itself, another animal, say, which alerts the sensing animal as to whether that other animal is a friend or a foe, either harmless or dangerous. The chicken that espies a chicken hawk circling languidly above the barnyard immediately flees to the protection of the coop. This is the chicken's estimative sense in action.

We infer the presence of a power called the common sense to explain an animal's ability to integrate and coordinate the data that is provided to it by its five external senses, which are called the proper sensibles. A sensible is simply that which is sensed. Each of the five external senses has a power which is proper to itself: sight—the visual; hearing—the audible; smell—

the odiferous; taste—the savory; touch—the tangible. The five external senses do not communicate with one another; the eye knows nothing about hearing, for example, and the ear cannot discriminate among smells. The task of the common sense is to inform the animal that the various specific sensations it is experiencing at a given moment, supplied by different external senses, have their source in a single object. So, the dog knows, instantaneously, that what he sees, hears, and smells have their origin in the quail pecking about in an open field some twenty yards ahead of him.

There is another way in which we can understand the function of the common sense. As noted, each external sense organ has its proper sensible in which it specializes, but there are certain sensibles that can be detected by more than one sense, and for that reason they are called the common sensibles. They are motion, rest, number, shape, and size. Let us consider motion. We can detect motion by sight and by the tactile sense. We see that the train is moving out of the station. If we are sitting with our eyes closed in a plane right before takeoff, we can feel when the plane begins to move down the runway because our body is suddenly pressed back against the seat. But hearing can also detect movement, as when we judge that a truck is moving toward us because the noise of its motor becomes steadily louder. And perhaps in some cases the sense of smell can register motion, as when the especially pungent smell of an object becomes increasingly less strong as the source of the smell, Skippy the Skunk, moves farther and farther away from us. (Unless Skippy had left a squirt of skunk perfume on one's clothes as a memento of his visit.) The common sense would be behind all these experiences.

The Basic Emotive Powers

The English word emotion has its roots in the Latin *motus*, which means movement. The emotions are motion-inciting responses to sense information; they move animals, and us, toward or away from certain objects or situations we are made aware of by the information provided us by the external senses. The external senses inform us as to what is going on in the external world, and we react to what they tell us with one or another of our basic emotions.

The emotions can be arranged in two groups, six in the first group, five in the second. The six emotions in the first group are called the concupiscible emotions. That formidable word "concupiscible" comes from the Latin verb *concupiscere*, which means to desire, to covet, to long for. These emotions are love, desire, pleasure, and their opposites, hate, aversion, pain. They are, as you will recognize, very basic emotions. The term "love" is of course freighted with all sorts of meanings, so we must be very clear about how the term is being used here. What we mean by love, as referring to the principal concupiscible emotion, is simply a positive emotive response on the part of an animal (including the human animal) to what is being sensed. A dog can be said to love a bone because he is strongly attracted to it. Love is the initiating emotion, activating the emotions of desire and pleasure. If we love something we desire to possess it, and if we succeed in possessing it, then we take pleasure in the possession.

The three emotions opposite to them, once again, are hate, aversion, and pain. Sometimes an animal's response to sense information can be quite negative, and we give the name hate to that response. The hatred here obviously has no moral connotation attached to it; it is simply a negative emotional response. The animal senses something which in no way meets with his approval, and therefore, rather than get close to it and possibly possessing it, he wants to get as far away from it as he can; that movement is prompted by the emotion of aversion, which is the natural follow-up of hatred. But what if the animal does not succeed in safely distancing himself from the hated object? In that case he experiences pain in one form or another.

The Emotive Powers for Difficult Cases

We introduced above eleven basic emotions, six of which we have already examined. The name traditionally assigned to the five basic emotions yet to be discussed is the irascible emotions. As "irascible" is to be found in a standard English dictionary (meaning "easily angered"), it does some service as a description of the five basic motions to be treated here. The word irascible comes from the Latin verb *irasci*, meaning "to be angry." Before describing each of the irascible emotions individually, we need first to make some general comments pertaining to all of them, which will establish a context within which these particular emotions can be better understood. There is a very basic fact about human psychology, and for that matter about animal psychology as well, and it is this: We naturally respond in an emotionally positive way to what we perceive to be good, and we endeavor, in some manner or another, to possess it; we just as naturally respond in an emotionally negative way to what we perceive as bad, and we endeavor to flee from it or perhaps, in one way or another, to overcome it. "Good" here means what we perceive as potentially beneficial for us; "bad" means what we perceive as potentially harmful for us. However, some perceived goods are difficult to achieve, and some perceived evils are difficult to escape from. It is the task of the irascible emotions to enable us to deal with situations such as those, specifically, by providing us with effective emotional responses to difficult goods and difficult evils. No problem arises if, in a particular situation, an animal sees something that is estimated as good, accordingly loves it, desires it, and, everything proceeding smoothly, succeeds in possessing it and thereby experiences pleasure as a result. Nor would there be any problem if, conversely, an animal sees something which is judged to be evil, hates it, and succeeds in escaping from it. But because there are some goods that are difficult to attain, and some evils that are difficult to avoid, we need special emotions to handle those circumstances, and that is where the irascible emotions come in. These are the emotions that are designed to deal with the problematic.

Sometimes an animal perceives something as good, and thus loves and desires to possess it, but to gain possession of it will be no easy task. In such a circumstance the animal needs the aid of the emotion of hope, which keeps alive in him the sense that the achievement of the desired good, though difficult, is a real possibility. Accompanying that optimistic impetus is the emotion of audacity, or courage, a persistent pertinacity, a determined stick-to-itiveness in dealing with the difficulties encountered in order to attain the perceived good. Audacity could be regarded as the emotion that props up hope, keeps it alive.

The two emotions opposite to hope and audacity are fear and despair. An animal experiences the emotion of fear when it senses that it does not have what it takes to achieve a difficult good or escape from a difficult evil; its strength and cunning may not be up to the task. Fear can be beneficial to an animal in that it apprises him of his limitations. An animal that was absolutely fearless would not be around for long. The emotion of despair (which has nothing to do with theological despair; we are talking here about an elementary emotion) takes over when an animal finally gives up the battle and admits defeat. The emotion of despair may in some cases be the key to his survival, for it could be telling him that he has taken on more than he can handle in pursuing a particular difficult good, and it would be to the benefit of his overall welfare to cease and desist in his efforts. There would seem to be a kind of instinctive smarts in animals that tells them when to quit.

The fifth irascible emotion is anger, which stands alone, having no opposite. It is an interestingly complex emotion in that it has two stages to it, a passive stage and an active stage: first, there is an offending stimulus of some sort; this is then followed by an avenging or rectifying response to that stimulus. A dog, given its territorial nature, will commonly raise a barking ruckus in response to a stranger coming into the yard, regarding that as an offensive intrusion which he has to do something to rectify, if only by putting on a noisy show. Let us consider this emotion as it applies to the human animal. What typically happens when we become angry? Someone says or does something at which we take offense, and if the emotion is allowed to play out as it typically does, we respond in a retaliatory manner, meeting what we see as a need to even the score as it were, by our words or action. Perhaps we regard our response as an attempt at somehow re-balancing the scales of justice. In the heat of anger we often end up saying or doing things which, later, in calmer moments, we come to regret. But that is a matter for ethics rather than for psychology. What I described above is simply the basic structure of anger, the pattern according to which the emotion is typically expressed, setting aside the questions of whether the anger expressed is justified or unjustified, rational or irrational. Those would be questions for ethics to settle.

Locomotion

There is not much that needs to be said about an animal's power of locomotion, other than to draw attention to how closely it is related to the sensational and emotional powers we have just reviewed. In more cases than not there is a set sequence to be observed: first there is sensation, to which there is an emotive response, which in turn triggers an external action of some kind or another. When Roger sets down Rover's bowl of dog food,

Rover, lounging on the far side of the kitchen, perks up, identifies a good, desires it, scrambles to his feet, and makes a bee-line for the bowl, to gain full possession of the bowl's contents.

The goods and evils that animals, and ourselves, encounter in life very often have more or less definite physical locations; they are to be found in specific places. What locomotion allows us to do—no small benefit this—is to get to places where good is typically to be found, and to get away from places where evil tends to prevail.

Some Summarizing Observations on Sensation and Emotion

Besides the power of locomotion which we share with animals, we also have in common with some but not all of them the above described nine sense powers and eleven emotive powers. Comparable to the hierarchy that characterizes the three great realms of life, beginning with plants, ascending to animals, and culminating in human beings, there is a hierarchy of sorts to be recognized within the animal realm. There is an empirical basis for distinguishing between higher and lower animals, according to the number of sense and emotive powers possessed by each species. The highest-ranking animals would have all nine sense powers and all eleven emotive powers, as would be the case, for example, with dogs and cats and horses. Animals such as bats and moles, who lack the sense of sight, could be regarded, simply for that reason, as ranking lower in the animal hierarchy. No living organism would qualify for admission to the animal kingdom if it were totally lacking in sense powers, but at the very bottom of the hierarchy, where we find single-cell creatures like amoeba and paramecia, it would appear that they possess only one sense power, the sense of touch, which can be regarded as the most basic of the senses. It is the sense by which these tiny animals maintain physical contact with the world about them.

In comparing powers shared by animals and human beings, we must be careful not to think in narrowly quantitative terms; there are qualitative differences to be considered. While the higher animals and human beings have in common the nine sense powers and the eleven emotive powers, they experience and express those powers in radically different ways, the higher animals as higher animals, human beings as human beings. Rover sees, hears, smells, tastes, and feels, as does Roger, his owner, but Rover does those things as a dog, Roger, as a human being. With Roger the rational element in him pervades and colors all sense and emotional experiences. We humans do not simply feel, we think about our feelings, talk about them with others, write books about them. We noted above that what we call the estimative sense in animals is called the cogitative sense in humans; the purpose of the change in terminology is to indicate that there is something special about this sense when it is operative in rational creatures. St. Thomas maintains that at times the cogitative sense can operate like a rudimentary form of reasoning. For example, we may not simply feel that we are in a dangerous situation, but have thoughts as to how to deal with it.

The strength or force of any sense or emotive power can vary among the members of any specific animal species, and of course that is true of human beings as well. Some people have better eyesight than others, some people have more vivid imaginations or better memories than others; some people are naturally timorous, others are reckless daredevils. The sense powers of some animals far surpass what is to be found in human beings. The olfactory and hearing powers of dogs put ours in the shade, and we are all positively myopic in comparison to hawks and eagles. The particular sense organs for four of the senses are readily identifiable—the eyes for seeing, the ears for hearing, special cells within the nose for smelling, taste buds on the back of the tongue and palate for taste. As for the tactile sense, the entire body could be designated as its organ, although some parts of the body are more sensitive to touch than others. Aristotle regarded touch as not so much a single sense as a group of senses, given the variety of sensibles it can register.

The Great Leap into the Realm of the Human

Human beings eat, grow, and reproduce, which are capacities they share with plants and animals. Like all animals, they have the power of locomotion. And, as we have seen, they share with the higher animals the nine sense powers and the eleven emotive powers. But to that total of twenty-four physical and psychic powers, the human animal can lay claim to two more powers which are of momentous significance: intellect and will. To call attention to the fact that human beings have intellects, that we come equipped with minds, is not merely to note that we are conscious creatures who are aware of the world around us, as something distinct from ourselves; that much could be said of many animals. More tellingly, we are aware of others precisely as others, and ourselves precisely as ourselves. In other words, the distinction between the subjective order and the objective order is a fundamental fact of our consciousness.

Even the lowest animals, those that can boast of nothing beyond the tactile sense and the power of locomotion, can be imagined as having something comparable to consciousness, in however crude and primitive a form it may take; this would be displayed, for example, in tactile irritability and aversive movement. As to the higher animals, such as dogs, cats, and horses, there is no doubt at all that they are possessed of consciousness, and in a manner that we can readily relate to. But what is unique about human consciousness is that we are conscious of ourselves precisely as conscious; we are aware that we are aware. We have a deep-set, ineradicable sense of self. We can think, and, moreover, we can think about thinking, which is to say that our minds are reflexive; they can turn back on themselves, as it were, and examine their own cognitive operations. We were doing a considerable amount of thinking about thinking when, in Chapter One, we were dealing with the principles of logic. Rover, for all the canine smarts he is sometimes capable of displaying, is blissfully unaware of the fact that he is a dog, much less an English Setter. All this comes down to saying that animals are completely bereft of ideas. The higher animals can create sense images, and this enables them to remember things, but they cannot conceptualize. They entertain no ideas, good, bad, or indifferent, about the world around them.

What radically separates human beings from all other animals and makes them sublimely special has everything to do with the nature of the human soul. It would be a good idea if we were at this point to review some basic facts about ourselves as rational creatures. Recall that we established that a human being is a substance, a material substance, which means that a human being is a composite of matter and form. The matter part of man is of course the body; the form part is the soul. Body and soul are not equal to one another, existentially, in the manner in which they exist, as if they were on the same level of being, for the body is completely dependent upon soul for the fact that it exists as a living body; the soul is the substantial form of the body, its animating principle. Soul, as form, is the direct opposite of body, as matter, which then means of course that the human soul is entirely immaterial. Today there are not a few philosophers and scientists who, because of their commitment to a materialistic philosophy (a philosophy which maintains that all reality is material), reject the immateriality of the soul; indeed, they would reject the very concept of soul. They do not deny the existence of the human mind, but to them the mind is no more than the brain, a physical organ. To think in those terms is to indulge in materialistic reductionism. As a matter of fact, however, the human mind, rightly understood, is to be recognized as the principal power of the immaterial soul. If it were true that the mind, the human intellect, were material, we would not be capable of the kind of knowledge, specifically intellectual knowledge, that is proper to us as human beings, as rational creatures. That is a point that demands closer examination, which we will be doing presently.

There are two distinct, but never entirely separate, forms of human knowledge: sense knowledge, and intellectual knowledge. The basis for the distinction between the two are the objects of knowledge which are peculiar to each. The proper object of sense knowledge is the concrete particular, individual things in the external (i.e., extra-mental) world, this particular umbrella, that particular lawnmower. The object of intellectual knowledge is the abstracted essence or nature of individual material things, or the universal concept. It is intellectual knowledge that allows us to identify this thing here as an umbrella, and that thing over there as a lawnmower. We are aware of the particular as an instance of the universal, that is, we recognize an individual thing as not being absolutely unique but as one of a kind. That thing over there next to the garage is a member of the class of things called lawnmowers. It is only our knowledge of universal concepts that allows us correctly to identify individual things. It is only because I know of umbrellas and lawnmowers in general that I can easily identify this thing as an umbrella and that thing as a lawnmower.

All of our knowledge begins with sense experience, but if it were to end there our ability to know the world would not be appreciably different from that of animals. If we were limited to sense knowledge we would be fully aware of the material world all around us, but our knowledge of that world would be markedly superficial; we would be aware of physical objects in all their concrete particularity, but they would be impenetrable to us with regard to their natures. We would know *that* they are there, but we would not know *what* they are. If the only knowledge of which I was capable were sense knowledge, and I beheld an elephant before me, I would register its impressive size, note its shape and color, be aware of its tusks, trunk, ears, see the ponderous way it moves about, and various other of its features, but I would have, literally, no idea of what it was. To see how our sense knowledge rises to the level of intellectual knowledge, which is to say, becomes fully human knowledge, we need to consider the remarkable process by which we give birth to ideas. By doing so we will see that it cannot be otherwise than that the human mind is immaterial, which necessarily implies that the human soul is immaterial.

The Birth of Ideas

The process by which ideas are born in our minds, very roughly sketched, is as follows: In response to what is registered by our external senses, and the integrating work done by the internal senses (the common sense, imagination, memory, and especially the cogitative sense), a sense image is formed, an image or mental representation of a concrete, particular thing out there in the world, say an elephant. This image is presented to the intellect which focuses its illuminating attention on it and, through its penetrating power of abstraction, effectively ignores its material aspects, and reveals its immaterial form, or nature, which provides the intellect with what it needs to conceive an idea, the idea of elephant. What is presented to the mind is the substantial form of the elephant, not of course the substantial form itself, that stays with the elephant, but the substantial form as abstracted, which is an intellectual image, a replica of sorts, entirely immaterial, of the elephant's substantial form. As the result of these mental operations something like a marriage takes place, an intimate conjoining of the abstracted form of an object external to the mind and the form which is the mind, or, more precisely, simply the human soul. What we know thus becomes part of the very essence of what we are. In a sense, we become what we know.

The power of abstraction is the key to our capacity for intellectual knowledge, the knowledge which is composed of ideas, the ideas which inform us of the real natures of things external to the mind. Abstraction, when it reveals to us the nature of material things in the world, functions as a de-materializing power. The specific immaterial object, resulting from abstraction, is the intellectual image of the substantial form, revealing its nature, of the material object we come to know. If I know, through the medium of an idea, that the material object I am now looking at is a chair, it is not because something material has been transferred from the chair to my mind, such as molecules of wood, for example. (There were some philosophers in ancient times who believed that this was what actually took place.) A transfer did indeed take place, but it involved an immaterial sense image which was then upgraded to the status of an intellectual image, or idea. If we try to imagine the process of human knowledge as something which is entirely material, as the philosophic materialist is forced to do, we end up with nothing but a tangle of absurdities. What abstraction does, by its de-materializing power, is to raise things to the immaterial level of the mind, for things are only intelligible to us, we are able to grasp their nature or essences, only to the extent that they are immaterial, that is, only to the extent we have immaterial ideas of them. So, the marriage I alluded to above, which is productive of intellectual knowledge, is not between the material, and the material—that would be impossible—but between the immaterial and the immaterial. Because human intellectual knowledge begins with sense knowledge it is rooted in the material realm, but once intellectual knowledge has been gained through the operation of abstraction, the workings of the human mind can carry on quite happily without any further dependence at all on matter. The first definition my dictionary gives of "spiritual" is "having the nature of spirit, not tangible or material." On that account it could be said without undue distortion that we human beings are essentially, given the nature and workings of the intellect, spiritual creatures.

The human soul as the immaterial life-giving substantial form of the body, is the source of all of the body's actions, from the beating of the heart to the growth of the toenails. We have identified the principal power of the soul, its glory one might say, as the human intellect, and this explains why Thomas Aquinas commonly refers to the soul as an intellectual substance. As such it is essentially a knowing substance. The human soul as immaterial is, in contrast to the body, simple, meaning that it is not composed of parts, of extended things juxtaposed to extended things, such as are the various organs of the body. This fact has very significant implications, for it provides an argument for the immortality of the soul. Anything that is composed of parts can fall apart. Put differently, anything that is an integrated whole can disintegrate. What that means for living material substances is that they can die. The existence of a living material substance is framed between two poles, generation and corruption; it comes into being, and it exists from being. The essence of death, for a human being, is the falling apart, as it were, of its two basic components, matter and form, body and soul. Once the body is bereft of its animating principle, the soul, it loses its integrity as a physical whole; it disintegrates, the many parts of which it is composed lose their composition. But nothing comparable happens to the soul, and that is because, as simple, it is not composed of parts, and because it is not composed of parts there can be no decomposition, in a word, no death of the soul. The body dies, but the soul lives on serenely, its integrity as an immaterial substance immune to any disintegrating influences.

The Proper Object of an Idea

We have duly noted that the object of sense knowledge, its intention or that toward which it is directed, is a physical object found in the external world—a table, a chair, an elephant. Sense knowledge, just as such, would be ignorant of the natures of those objects. The object of intellectual knowledge, represented by an idea, could very well be in any given instance the same as the object of sense knowledge—a chair, a table, an elephant (we can simultaneously be looking at an elephant and entertaining the idea of elephant)—with this grand difference, that with the idea we would have full knowledge of the physical object, the satisfying awareness *that* the object is, it actually exists, but also, and most importantly, *what* it is. Our ideas are the means, the absolutely essential means, by which we gain knowledge of things in the external world. But a cautionary note must be sounded here. Ideas are the necessary means by which we connect with objects in the world, but they must not be confused with the things to which they refer, nor, worse, to be thought of as superior to the things to which they refer. We must not allow ourselves to become so enamored of the ideas which are the means, that we allow ourselves to forget that of which they are the means—that chair, that table, that elephant. The proper object of an idea is not the idea itself but its referent, that to which it refers.

Philosophical idealism is a manner of mis-thinking that attaches more significance to ideas than to what ideas are about, the objects which were the initiating causes of the generation of the ideas. We must keep our eyes on the elephant, constantly monitoring that idea, checking its soundness, to ensure that our idea of the elephant is an accurate representation of the real elephant out there in the world. The danger of supposing that human knowledge is principally about ideas is that our thinking can then tend to become too much an in-house affair, with the result that the subjective world of the mind becomes increasingly cut off from the objective world outside the mind. The mind of the philosophical idealist becomes stocked with ideas which do not have their initiating causes in the objective realm but are generated internally, by his imagination. The extreme philosophical idealist eventually comes to believe that it is his mind, the contents of his mind, and not the world external to the mind, which is the center and the source of reality.

Ideas and Language

We embody our ideas in words which, besides being a quite natural move, is an altogether necessary one, for without it we would not be able to communicate with one another. Using the term "idea" in a somewhat loose but not entirely inaccurate way, we can say that one kind of idea refers to individual things, and another kind to collections or classes of things. In grammatical terms, this distinction would be represented respectively by proper nouns and common nouns. The Eiffel Tower, the Roman Colosseum, and the Washington Monument are examples of proper nouns; tower, stadium, monument, table, chair, dog, cat, and elephant are common nouns. The difference between the ideas that these two types of nouns signify is that proper nouns signify an idea that applies to one thing, whereas common nouns signify an idea that applies to many things; the latter kind of idea is known as a universal. A universal, Aristotle plainly put it, is that which refers to many.

The special importance of universals, ideas that refer to entire classes of things and not just to individuals, is that they convey to us the nature or the essence which is common to all the members of the class to which they refer. "Elephant" is a universal because it refers to all animals of a particular kind, all those that share the same nature. There have been some philosophers who have denied that universals perform that important task for us. They argue that common nouns are just names, labels of convenience, and they are not to be taken as evidence for the fact that the many individuals to which they are applied share a common nature. This erroneous point of view, which is called nominalism, has very serious ramifications. We use the term human being, or person, to refer to all individuals who, despite their many and varied differences, are essentially the same. They are all members of the same family, which we identify abstractly as humanity. To deny that all those individuals have the same nature, human nature, and that they are therefore essentially the same, leaves the door wide open to all sorts of abuses such as bigotry and racism, providing fuel for the despots of the world who want to claim that all men are not equal as to their nature, but that some are intrinsically superior to others, and these have a right, if not a duty, to exercise mastery over the supposed inferior types. History teaches us that this sorry scenario is not an imaginary one.

The Speculative Intellect and the Practical Intellect

In making the distinction between the speculative intellect (sometimes called the theoretical intellect) and the practical intellect, we are not suggesting that human beings have two intellects, two minds, but simply that we use our one mind in two distinctly different ways. That this distinction is a real one, and not something dreamed up by philosophers just to make things more complicated than they need be, can be readily verified by appealing to your own personal experiences. There are times when we seek to know things for the simple sake of knowing them. We just want to assuage our curiosity, to find out something, ascertain the facts, discover the truth. That is the speculative intellect at work. There are other times when we seek knowledge, not for its own sake, but for the sake of the uses to which that knowledge can be put. We want, for example, knowledge that will guide us in our behavior; that is the kind of knowledge moral philosophy or ethics is able to provide. Or we want knowledge that will direct our actions in making things; that is the kind of knowledge which is the concern of art, understanding art in the broadest terms as referring to any kind of human making, from baking a cake to building a bridge to composing a symphony.

When we think along those lines, wanting to know how best to act or how best to create, we are exercising our practical intellect.

In a later chapter, when we discuss moral philosophy or ethics, we will give a good deal of attention to the workings of the practical intellect as it is applied to human behavior, and there we will also have some general observations to make about art. But for now we want to focus our attention on the speculative intellect, the principal aim or purpose of which is simply to arrive at truth, be it pertaining to things great or things small. There is a set of virtues which pertain specifically to the speculative intellect and, appropriately enough, they are called the intellectual virtues.

The Intellectual Virtues

They are three in number, but before naming and describing them a few preliminary remarks must be made. The term "virtue" (it comes from the Latin *virtus*, which means strength or vigor) is to be understood as referring to a specific power or capacity of the intellect. Second point: a virtue, be it an intellectual virtue or a moral virtue (the latter we will treat in a later chapter), is classified as a habit. A habit is a fixed disposition, meaning that it is a certain capacity which we are not born with, but which we come to acquire as a practically permanent part of our psychological make-up, and which is put in place by repeated acts that pertain to a particular virtue. Habits, as we all know, can be either good or bad.

The three habits which are the intellectual virtues are all definitely good, for when we put them to work they contribute directly toward realizing the purpose of the speculative intellect—attaining the truth. The three intellectual virtues are: understanding, reason, and wisdom.

It is through understanding that we are able immediately to grasp those elementary, self-evident truths which are the foundation for all human reason, such as, for example, the principle of identity, the principle of contradiction, the principle of the excluded middle, and the principle of sufficient reason, which we became acquainted with in Chapter One. Consider the principle of contradiction. It is through the virtue of understanding that without straining our mental capacities we see that it is patently obvious that something cannot both be and not be at the same time and in the same respect. It is impossible to say in the same breath, and be making sense, that Napoleon died on the Island of St. Helena and he did not die on the Island of St. Helena. The principle of sufficient reason tells us that every fact must have an explanation. We may not know, right at the moment, what is the explanation for Fact X, but we know for sure that it has to have an explanation.

Reason is that intellectual virtue to which we gave a good deal of attention in the chapter on logic. The reasoning process, we saw there, has many ramifications to it, but inference lies at the heart of it: inference, that mental move by which, from an already firmly established truth, we derive a new truth, one that follows necessarily from the truth with which we started. Knowing that helium is lighter than air, I can confidently conclude that if I let go of the string attached to this helium-filled balloon, it will soar into the wide blue yonder. I can count on that outcome.

Wisdom is the crowning intellectual virtue. It is the mental capacity which enables us to order all things rightly, meaning that we direct all our actions toward their proper ends. Wisdom is the "big picture" virtue, in that it takes account of the whole, and sees to it that the parts (i.e., specific acts) fit the whole. We speak of people who have their priorities straight; that is an accurate enough way of describing what wisdom is all about. Wisdom sorts things out judiciously, identifying all those things that are really important, in that they contribute toward a life that is truly and fully human, and then consistently guides us to act accordingly. Only an ordered mind can order all things rightly, and it is the virtue of wisdom that makes for the ordered mind.

We identified the intellectual virtues as habits, that is, capacities that do not come naturally to us but which we must acquire through our own efforts. This is manifestly the case with reason and wisdom, but it is somewhat different with respect to understanding, for that comes close to being a mental capacity which, among adults of sound mind, would seem to be innate. We seem to be endowed with an intuitive sense that allows us to recognize the self-evident precisely as self-evident. It does not have to be proven to us; it speaks for itself, as it were. All that does not mean that we cannot strengthen the virtue of understanding, work on becoming more keenly aware of those elementary truths that undergird the whole of human reason.

Mind and Emotions

The basic emotions, identified above, are an integral part of what we are as human beings. We can acknowledge our spiritual part, the soul, but we cannot forget that soul is warmly embraced by body, and on that account we are inescapably emotional creatures. But we are also rational creatures, and those two basic facts about our nature are inseparable. Even our most abstract cogitations are not devoid of emotion, although they might be of a highly refined kind. One thinks of the mathematician, dwelling in the upper stories of the ivory tower, who is fairly transported, emotionally, by a new insight he has had regarding number theory. But emotion, in human beings, is never pure emotion; it is never entirely separated from ideas, the general workings of reason. Emotion need not necessarily hamper reason, but it can; the important thing is to maintain the right relation between the two. Reason performs a vitally important guiding and controlling function with respect to emotion, for without that guidance and control, maintaining a balanced emotional life would be impossible.

Our emotional life becomes unbalanced when the emotions gain ascendency over the intellect and dominate it. There is a rigid law of human psychology of which we are all quite familiar through personal experience, telling us that there is a direct relation between the intensity of an emotion, on the one hand, and the ability to think straight, on the other. We all know how difficult it is to keep our wits about us and cogitate coherently when we are in the grips of a strong emotion, such as fear or sorrow or elation. It is precisely because the emotions, taken in themselves, are non-rational that they must be subject to the beneficent governance of reason. To say that the emotions are non-rational is not to denigrate them, but simply to point out that they operate on a different track than does reason.

There are two extreme attitudes that can be taken toward the emotions, both of which have unfortunate consequences. One can take a decidedly negative attitude toward the emotions, regarding their influence to be so detrimental that it is necessary to subjugate them totally, even to the point of trying to root them out of one's psyche. This would be to play a most dangerous game with what are integral to our human nature, and intrinsically good. In the first place, it would be simply impossible to extricate completely any given emotion, that is, to try to permanently cancel out its

influence. Secondly, even persistently to make such an attempt would ensure for the person who engages in such a futile effort general psychological
disorder of a very serious kind.

The emotions are a permanent and positive part of our human make-
up; we have a fundamental need for each and every one of them, as identified and discussed above. Take the example of fear; it is a legitimate and
altogether natural emotional response to what are objectively fearful things.
Regulated fear, fear under the control of intellect, is a preservative of a person's equanimity and general well-being. The key to the whole matter is the
need for the rational control and guidance of the emotions. If the emotion
of fear were to break free of that control and guidance, and become itself
the dominant controlling factor in a person's life, the person (assuming an
extreme case) could become petrified, incapable of taking any effective action at all in trying situations. And what would we say of a person who
knew nothing of the emotion of love? Might we not say that such a one
would be scarcely human?

The second extreme attitude that can be taken toward the emotions,
just as potentially damaging as the one just described, and which has been
given much play in recent decades, even by certain philosophers, is to grant
to the emotions ungoverned governing powers. The general attitude towards the emotions taken by the advocates of this position cannot be contested, for they rightly recognize that the emotions are intrinsically good.
It is where they go from there that trips them up and leads to a fall, for the
argument is made that the emotions are so good that they are in effect superior to reason, and that therefore they, not reason, should be in charge of
our lives. To adopt this attitude would represent an elevated instance of the
tail wagging the dog. The glib directive, "follow your gut feelings," if it is
taken as a mandate for allowing emotion to be the court of first and last resort in determining the life-shaping decisions we make, is extending a cor-
dial invitation to disaster. To make a systematic practice of being led by
one's emotions is to give oneself over to what will inevitably become mindless behavior, which is to say, sub-human behavior.

Emotions under the governance of reason are altogether on our side,
working for what is truly beneficial for us. What would we do without that
militant audacity which enables us to plow on ahead when the snow is deep
and the biting north winds howl? But audacity that breaks free of reason

and goes it alone becomes recklessness, and when recklessness dominates we have the kind of situation described by Alexander Pope, and we see "fools rush in where angels fear to tread."

Will

The two formidable powers that are distinctive of the human animal, that set us apart conspicuously from all the other species in the genus, are intellect and will. The will, like the emotions, is a moving power, but of a distinctly different kind than the emotions, for the will moves us as enlightened by intellect, and that is why it is called by philosophers the intellectual appetite. ("Appetite" derives from the Latin *appetere*, which means to reach to, wish for, hunger after, desire.) The movement of the emotions typically takes the form of the elementary stimulus-response pattern. They are immediately activated by sense data of one kind or another. As non-rational, the emotions do not ponder and decide; they just act, but again, always in response to sensations. The will, for its part, responds to information supplied to it by the intellect; in other words, the movement of the will is a rationally informed movement, based on knowledge. Most of the will acts we make over the course of a day do not concern monumental matters, and therefore are made more or less spontaneously, and are preceded by little or no reflection on our part. When the girl at the checkout counter asks if I want the groceries placed in a paper or plastic bag, I usually do not spend a great deal of time mulling over the question. But when we must make important decisions, those that may entail serious consequences, then the act of will behind the decision can take on an interesting complexity.

It all begins when the will focuses on something the intellect has presented to it as good, something seen as beneficial to possess or to do. By that move the will sets for itself a specific end to be achieved. Because of the seriousness of the matter at hand, we do not press ourselves to make a quick decision. We stop and deliberate, and if we think it needful, we seek the advice of others, people whose judgment we trust, asking them how we could best go about things in order to achieve the identified end. We might, for example, realize that the end we aim at admits of a number of means by which it could be achieved, and that therefore we will need to narrow the field and choose what looks to us to be the best means possible. Once we have done that, we are ready to take action. Having carefully considered the matter we then simply say to ourselves, all right, now do it! And the contract is signed, or the job offer is accepted, or the house is bought, or the girl is proposed to, or you finally decide to accept the Nobel Prize after all.

Since time immemorial there have been people who have called into question the freedom of the will. In more cases than not, those people have been philosophers, those who, so it seems, have a weakness for finding problems where there are no obvious problems to be found. The average Joe and Jane on the street (what would we do without them?) do not fret over free will; they just go about exercising it. And the same must be said, by the way, of those philosophers who deny it. One of the most popular words used by the philosophers who deny free will is "illusion," as in "the illusion of free will." If free will is an illusion, it surely has to rate as one of the most potent and spectacular illusions of all time. Here is a supposed illusion which has been steadily entertained by the overwhelming majority of human beings throughout the entire course of the history of the race, and it is as tenacious today as it has ever been. How is one to explain so remark-able and persistent a phenomenon, if it is no more than an illusion? It is highly unlikely that a genuine illusion could be so durable and long-lasting, and so emphatically universal. We humans can be gullible, but not bound-lessly so; there are limits to our limitations.

It would be worth our while to reflect for a moment on the position taken by those who deny freedom of the will. Let us assume that the position is a sound one, and that freedom of the will is in fact a fiction; human beings are without it. There is, then, only one other alternative, and that is philosophical determinism, the position which maintains, to state it in its strictest version, that human beings, no more than animals or plants, are not the originating source of their actions but are, in whatever they do, merely following a program of cosmic proportions which was set in place at the very beginning of time. We are much like computers that have been programmed to function only in certain set ways: what we think, feel, and do has all been determined beforehand by the program. Or, to use a differ-ent image, it is as if our lives have been scripted down to the very last detail by a cosmic playwright of sorts, and everything we do—we cannot do oth-erwise—is a matter of following the script. I may think, when I decided to raise my right arm to take a book off the top shelf of a bookcase, that I was performing a free act in doing so, but the philosopher who denies free will would typically tell me that I am only deluding myself by thinking along those lines. That supposedly free act did not have its originating source in myself, but in a source external to myself.

When we reflect on the matter, we recognize that virtually all of our conscious acts are preceded by thought. Before I raised my right arm to take down that book I first thought about it, in however cursory a way. A more complicated bit of behavior is enacted when, sitting at my desk, I have the thought that it's about time for a break, so I decide I will go to the kitchen and get a cup of coffee. Here too, thought precedes act, the thought in this case being a bit more elaborate. Given the close bond between thought and act, it would seem that both would have to be determined, and presumably the determinist would agree with that. So, we are determined in every respect, in what we think as well in what we do.

Now, if our thoughts are not the freely born brain-children of our minds, but are, like our actions, entirely determined, that means that the philosopher who thinks that free will is a fiction is determined to think along those lines; he has no choice in the matter. And we who believe that free will is a fact are determined to believe that way; we have no choice in the matter. The philosopher who takes the position that free will is a fiction of course wants us to accept that position as sound; he wants us to take what he says about the nature of the human will to be true. But if both of these mutually contradictory positions are determined, the philosopher who denies free will has no basis for claiming that his position should take precedence over ours. Could he reasonably argue that what he is determined to think is superior to what we are determined to think? Would he not be determined to argue that way, just as we would be determined to argue against his argument? But if everything is determined, there would be no possibility of stepping outside the realm of the determined and, from a standpoint taken there, form a disinterested, non-determined judgment as to which argument is true. Given that state of affairs, (1) the issue can never be decided one way or the other, and (2) the philosopher who denies free will has no grounds for doing so. The conclusion of these reflections is that if determinism is true, then not only the question of free will, but any question whatever, could never be satisfactorily resolved. But that is manifestly not what happens in the world in which we live, where we commonly and confidently satisfactorily resolve countless questions; we make firm judgments over what is true or false, good or evil, beautiful or ugly, on the basis of the quality of the ideas intrinsic to the arguments put forward in defense of one or the other. Determinism, therefore, is false.

That argument is essentially negative in the approach it takes, and follows the pattern of the *argumentum ad absurdum* that I introduced at the very end of Chapter One. But a more positive approach can be taken, which I will now pursue. One of the key acts of the will is choice, the act by which we determine which means are to be taken to attain a specific end, an end to which the will is already committed. In the particular situation in which I now find myself, a choice is necessary because I have discovered, after deliberating over the situation, that there is more than a single means that could be taken in order to achieve the desired end. If there were only a single means which would be adequate to achieve the end, no choice would be necessary. What I in fact discover, though, is that there are two possible means, both of them equally adequate, as far as I can see, to achieve the end—A and B. After carefully considering both, I eventually decide to choose A. I follow A, and the end is successfully achieved and I am quite satisfied. Now, some time after making that choice, and as the result of reading a book by a philosopher who denies freedom of the will, I ask myself: Was my choosing A a free act, or was I determined to make that choice? In resolving that question I ask myself another one: Could it really have been otherwise, that is, could it have been possible that, instead of choosing A, I would have chosen B? Reflecting seriously on that question, I reached the point where it became abundantly clear to me—it was something I was firmly convinced of—that there was nothing at all that would have prevented the possibility of my choosing B; it was a real possibility, a genuine option, and that is precisely how I regarded it at the time. If in fact I were determined to choose A, I could not have given serious thought to the possibility of choosing B, but as a matter of fact for some time I gave quite serious thought to that possibility; for a while I was actually leaning toward choosing B. In light of all these considerations, I conclude that the act I made to choose A was a free act, of which I was the originating source; I know that to be true because I know for certain that I really could have freely chosen B. If I were determined to choose A, there would be no basis for that knowledge.

Some Closing Comments on Personhood

A "human being" and "person" are synonyms. The sixth-century Roman philosopher, Boethius, classically defined person as "an individual substance of a rational nature." As a formal definition, that provides us with a sound philosophical understanding of what we are as persons: (a) we have real independence of being, in that we exist through an act of existence which is proper to each of us; (b) the individuality of our personhood is complete, manifesting itself in a unique way in each of us; (c) as rational, we are creatures possessed of irrepressibly inquisitive minds, marked by a driving passion for truth. Richly informative though it is, the definition has its limitations, but so would every attempt to provide a formal definition of person. The most salient fact about any person is that he or she, just as person, cannot be defined. A person cannot, in the poignant imagery of T. S. Eliot, "be set sprawling on a pin," as would be the fate of a netted butterfly, neatly categorized and precisely labeled. What the Boethian definition does for us, though, and does well, is give us a general description of the nature of personhood, what is common to all persons. But the individual person cannot be defined precisely because of the emphatic singularity, the uniqueness, of each person. While we are repeatable as human beings, we are not repeatable as persons. Each person is simply his own self, her own self. That is a truism which is rife with a multitude of individually specific truths, truths that pertain to one and to one alone.

In this chapter, following the standard procedure of philosophical psychology, we began with the basics, considering questions having to do with life in general, whatever particular form it may take. We saw that the three great realms of life—plant life, animal life, and human life—have in common the three rudimentary powers of nutrition, growth, and reproduction. Focusing on animal life, we then took careful note of how amazingly complex life becomes in that realm, with the presence of the sense powers, the emotive powers, and locomotion. Finally, we turned to the culminating concern of our science, human life, and there we found a form of life which is not simply different in degree from plant and animal life, but different in kind, for here we encounter the preeminent powers of intellect and will. Those two powers have a transformative effect on all the lesser powers, for with intellect and will, the sense powers, emotive powers, and locomotion take on a decisively human stamp. We exercise our sense powers, we show emotion, we move from place to place, all in inimitably human ways.

The guiding concern of the later sections of the chapter was to keep in mind the individual human being as a whole, in the individual's culminating completeness, and that is to recognize the foundational reality of personhood. If we were studying human anatomy, we could claim that the "wholeness" of a human individual, looked at from a purely physical point of view, is the sum total of the individual's composing parts, but that kind of synthesis will not work for psychology, and much less for philosophical psychology. The person is obviously not reducible to the purely physical. We are all unquestionably material beings, but there is a significant "more" that must be taken into account if we are to do full justice to our subject. And that "more" can prove to be well-nigh inexhaustible. To the extent that philosophical psychology chooses to make the human person, or more broadly the nature of personhood, the focus of its investigations, it is most unlikely that the book that results from those investigations will have a definitive final chapter.

Chapter Four
How Do We Know? Epistemology

What Is Knowledge?

Epistemology is the philosophical science that is devoted to the study of human knowledge. What are the basic types of human knowledge? How do we come to know what we know? What is true knowledge? What is certain knowledge? These are the kinds of questions we pursue in this particular branch of philosophy. The name of the science, epistemology, is derived from the Greek *epistemē*, which means knowledge or skill. Many of the terms we use in philosophy have their origin in the Greek language, which should not surprise us, for the Greeks, after all, were the first systematic philosophers. It can be said without too much exaggeration that the Greeks invented philosophy.

What is knowledge? To begin at the beginning, bearing in mind that philosophy is always looking to discover the causes of things, we need to ask another question: Where does knowledge come from, what is its source, its genesis? The answer is obvious: we are the source of knowledge. Knowledge is the inevitable outcome of the irrepressible natural impetus on the part of rational human agents to know, to assimilate, to make part of themselves, what is initially other than themselves. To put it more directly: we are creatures who, by nature, crave to know, to incorporate within ourselves the world around us and the people who inhabit it. This craving is proof positive of our essentially spiritual natures. As our bodies need food to live, so too do our souls, our minds, need knowledge to remain intellectually vital.

There are three basic elements that go together to compose what we may call the knowledge-engendering experience: there is the knower, the one who knows; there is the known, what the knower knows; and there is the knowing, the act itself, the process by which the knower comes to know what is known.

The source and storehouse of knowledge is the conscious human agent, the person. In the strictest sense, knowledge exists only in the human mind. A chemistry textbook contains a lot of information about chemistry, but the book does not know chemistry. Knowledge involves an inseparable aspect of self-knowledge. Jack, besides obviously knowing what he knows, also knows himself precisely as a knower, and is therefore aware of what he had to do to gain the kinds of knowledge he has. That reveals the reflexive power of the human mind, meaning that the mind is able to make itself the object of its considerations. In the previous chapter emphasis was given to the important fact that we are not only conscious (the higher animals are that) but self-conscious as well (which the higher animals are not). The human animal is aware of himself as a conscious being, and that opens up a distinct and endlessly stimulating dimension of the knowledge that is available to us. We think a great deal about ourselves.

Knowledge always has an object, that which is known. We are never simply conscious; we are always conscious *of* something. There is no such thing as pure consciousness, if by that is meant that it is possible to have consciousness without content. It would make no sense to say that someone simply knows; to know is always to know *something*, to have an object of knowledge. Knowledge necessarily involves content, that which is known. The content of our knowledge can be divided in the broadest of terms into two categories which together are exhaustive: knowledge of ourselves, and knowledge of everything that is separate from ourselves (the me and the not-me). There is of course much correspondence between these two realms, but they are nonetheless quite distinct, something which a dedicated philosophical idealist is apt sometimes to get confused about.

Knowledge and Truth

From the very beginning of our reflections on philosophy we have stressed the centrality of truth, making any number of references to it along the way. Now is the proper occasion, as we engage in the discussion of the science of epistemology, to solidify our understanding of this most important subject. What is truth?

At bottom, truth is a relation, a relation of congruency between thought and the object of thought, what the thinker is thinking about. If there is a correspondence between thought and object, the condition for truth is thereby established. I have an idea in mind to which I attach the word "cardinal." I have that idea because I am looking out the window and see a bird that I take to be a cardinal perched on a branch of the ash tree in the backyard. Now, let us say that I have correctly identified the bird. There is, as a matter of fact, a cardinal in the ash tree; in that case, my idea would be a sound idea, and if I were to incorporate it into a statement and say, "There's a cardinal in the ash tree," that statement would be true. There is a correspondence between what the statement is affirming and what is actually the case in the objective order of things.

Truth is founded upon and expressed through thought that reflects a factual state of affairs, the way things really are. Truth binds us to the real, makes us justifiably comfortable in the world in which we live because our thought is conformable to that world. If I am thinking that Napoleon was born in Corsica in 1769, that he crowned himself emperor in 1804, and that he died on the isle of St. Helena in 1821, I would be thinking correctly, because my thoughts square with the facts. Broadly described, truth is a relation of consonance between the subjective realm, our minds, and the objective realm, the world—a happy marriage between the mental and the extra-mental.

If I say "cardinal" and ask you whether that is true or false, you would justifiably be puzzled, and would probably ask me in return, "What about the cardinal?" The word cardinal, and the idea behind it, are neither true nor false. And that recalls something we encountered in logic. For "cardinal" to be either true or false, something has to be said about it, predicated of it, and that gives rise to the statement, or the proposition. Ideas and the words which express them are either sound or unsound, depending on how they relate to their objects. "Cardinal" is sound if it refers to the bird that answers to that name. Only statements or propositions are either true or false, because they make assertions about the objective order of things which are based on what is either factual or non-factual. "The cardinal is a nonmigratory bird" is a true statement. "The cardinal is deep blue-black in color, a scavenger in its feeding habits, and prominently present in the Pacific Northwest" is a false statement. I will have more to say about the correspondence criterion of truth further on.

Knowledge in Relation to Philosophy in General

The philosophy that is being presented in this book is a realist philosophy, a philosophy which, as the name indicates, takes the real at face value. "Real" can mean many things, so we must be clear how the term is being used here. What is real is taken, in the first instance, to refer to anything that exists apart from and independent of our minds; the reference, in other words, is to extra-mental reality. (The ideas and imaginings in our minds are certainly real, but they represent intra-mental reality.) Extra-mental reality is objective; everyone has potential access to it. Intra-mental reality is subjective; only the subject has direct access to it. A real thing is actually "out there"; it is not a feature of my mind, such as an idea would be, nor is it something I am imagining, nor is it what I am feeling at the moment. A real thing is not only distinct and separate from my mind, its existence in no way relies on my mind. The point here is that I do not have to be thinking about a thing, or registering it by one or another of my five senses, for it to be precisely what it is, where it is, and doing whatever it happens to be doing. We obviously have knowledge of our own thoughts and imaginings, and of the firmest kind, and we can cleanly identify that as subjective knowledge.

There have been philosophers who have taken the position that our knowledge of the external world is to one degree or another dependent upon the thoughts we have of it. There have been other philosophers who have taught that it was philosophically beneficial to entertain doubts about the existence of the external world, even of one's own body. The most extreme position imaginable has been taken by some few thinkers—one hesitates to call them philosophers—who were prepared to entertain serious doubts about the existence of anything apart from their own minds. This position is called solipsism, and one would have to be an eccentric of the first class to adopt it. The neighbors right next door and their constantly barking dog should provide a continuing challenge to the solipsist's ego-centric mental meanderings.

Philosophical Realism Versus Philosophical Idealism

How could anyone, but especially someone who identifies himself as a philosopher, take seriously as a real possibility that the external world, the world just outside his window, might not really be there at all, that it's all in his head? It could only be someone who, in such a case, has not only been influenced, but fairly swept off his feet, by the seductive charms of philosophical idealism. For almost four hundred years now philosophical idealism, to one degree or another, has been a pervasive feature of Western philosophy. What is philosophical idealism? It cannot be neatly described in twenty-five words or less, for it is a philosophical position which sports several variations, but what is common to them all is a set tendency to give more weight to ideas (the subjective realm) than to the extra-mental referents of those ideas (the objective realm). The idealist philosopher is inclined to attach more value to what's going on in his mind than to what's going on in the world around him. Not that he completely ignores the external world, for he believes that his ideas can have a shaping effect on the constitution of that world, which would then make the objective realm in a sense subservient to the subjective realm. A philosophical idealist might rightly be called a devoted subjectivist.

A clarifying distinction is called for here. We are talking about a *philosophical* idealist, someone who adopts a particular philosophical world view. He is not to be confused with those people whom we identify in ordinary language as idealists. To be a philosophical idealist is highly problematic, which is usually not the case with the ordinary idealist. Calling someone an idealist is more often a compliment than a censure. Such people are not to be recklessly disparaged. It is a good thing to have a number of healthy idealists in a population; they can act as spirit-raising leaven. There is no necessary incompatibility between ordinary idealism and philosophical realism.

Knowledge of the External World

The knowledge which we gain of ourselves is of a very private kind, and unique, for we are both the subject and the object of that knowledge. We reflect upon ourselves. But we do not do so—we could not do so—in complete isolation from the world all around us. We learn significant things about ourselves by the various ways we interact with that world. A deepening of genuine self-knowledge commonly comes accompanied by a deepening of our knowledge of the external world. Paradoxically, we can only come to really know ourselves by making a periodic practice of getting out of ourselves. Looking outward sharpens the mind's eye for insight.

We have immediate access to ourselves; but access to the external world, the world of the non-self, is mediate, and it is gained, first of all, through the medium of sense knowledge. All of our knowledge begins with sense knowledge, but it culminates in intellectual knowledge, the knowledge of ideas. It is knowledge of ideas which qualifies as specifically human knowledge, for it is through the medium of ideas that the mind merges with things external to the mind. That merging of the mental and the extramental, the conjoining of the subjective and the objective, is one of the most intriguing aspects of human knowledge. The ancient claim that "we become what we know" is not mere idle poetizing or careless philosophizing. When we have the experience of coming to know something new, a process of assimilation takes place within the mind of no small consequence; the knowledge becomes an integral part of who we are and, depending on the kind and quality of that knowledge, it can have a life-altering effect on us. Ideas have consequences, as Richard Weaver reminded us; this is true for us personally, and for the world at large. Consider the disastrous consequences for twentieth-century history of the ideas of Karl Marx, as interpreted by his more passionate disciples. It cannot be brushed off as insignificant that both Benito Mussolini and Adolf Hitler were admirers of the ideas promulgated by the philosopher Friedrich Nietzsche, another thinker whose thought has had wide and mainly deleterious influence.

The Three Acts of the Intellect: Simple Apprehension, Judgment, Reason

Simple apprehension is the mental act by which we conceive ideas. This is where it all begins, for ideas are the basic building blocks of human knowledge. What is so singularly important about an idea is that it embodies within itself the essence, the proper nature, of its object, that in the external world to which it refers. When I have a clear idea of "rabbit," I know exactly what I am thinking about. Ideas represent intellectual knowledge, which is quite different from sense knowledge, the knowledge that derives from the five external and the four internal senses. I can see and hear the high-pitched sounds of that flying nocturnal rodent we call a bat, but I know it is precisely a bat I am seeing and hearing because of the idea I have of bat. Sense knowledge puts us in immediate contact with material being; intellectual knowledge tells us what kind of material being we are dealing with.

Judgment is that act of the intellect by which we put ideas together in such a way that we establish the truth of factual circumstances regarding the extra-mental world. I can have an idea of a bat, and thus have a perfectly reliable understanding of what a bat is (its essence, nature), but that idea alone provides no basis for my supposing that there are real bats actually existing in the external world. But if I say, and speak truly in saying it, "there's a bat flying around in the attic," I have moved out of the realm of ideas alone, and have made an existential statement, that is, a statement that makes a claim about an extra-mental state of affairs. We know for certain that there is at least one really existing bat in the world, and it happens to be up in the attic. The dodo bird and the passenger pigeon are both extinct species. Professional ornithologists might have very elaborate and detailed ideas of these two avian creatures, but they could make no existential judgments about either; the hard facts of the external world will not allow it for, sadly, there are no longer any dodo birds and carrier pigeons to be found. Ideas alone do not ensure real existence. Think of all the fantastic ideas you may have entertained, for which there was not nor will there ever be, any referents in the world outside your mind.

We are already familiar with reason, having dealt with it at some length in Chapter 1, so here we need only to make a few reminders regarding its basic features. Considered as the third act of the intellect, reason, which depends upon simple apprehension and judgment, is that rudimentary mental operation by which we put judgments together (a judgment is expressed by a statement) to form arguments, by which we expand and deepen our knowledge of the external world. To the true judgment that "All mammals are warm-blooded" we conjoin the equally true judgment that "Bats are mammals," and from those two judgments we confidently conclude that "Bats are warm-blooded." Reason can be generally described as that mental process by which we discover new knowledge.

In discussing the three intellectual virtues in the previous chapter, we learned that one of them is reason. What is the difference between reason as an intellectual virtue and reason as one of the three acts of the intellect?

The difference comes from regarding the same thing from different per-
spectives. Reason regarded as an act of the intellect focuses on its practical
operations, as the means by which the mind makes the inferential move
from premises to conclusion in an argument. Reason regarded as an intellectual virtue focuses on its status precisely as a habit, as that which enables
us to exercise our innate rational capacities efficaciously, not simply to reach
conclusions through the reasoning process, but to reach conclusions that
are true. That is reason acting virtuously. The efficacious exercise of our rational capacities results in the attainment of truth, or in action that is good.
Someone can exercise his reason not to attain the truth, but to wallow in
falsehood, not to do good, but to do evil. Such a person would be exercising
ratio, reason, but not what St. Thomas calls *recta ratio,* right reason; he
would lack the intellectual virtue of reason.

Further Thoughts on Truth

Knowledge is simply what we know, the furniture of our minds. We recognized that it is not a single homogeneous quality. We make any number of
distinctions regarding it: we speak of good and bad knowledge, significant
knowledge and trivial knowledge, "need to know" knowledge and "nice to
know" knowledge. What would measure up to being good knowledge? That
would be knowledge which is beneficial to the knower, beneficial in the
deepest and most significant way, whereas bad knowledge would be knowledge that is positively detrimental to the knower. It would be naïve to suppose that all knowledge is somehow neutral, in terms of the effects it can
have on the person that harbors it. Knowledge is food for the mind, but
the consumption of that food must be guided by prudence. There are certain kinds of knowledge which can corrupt the mind, dehumanize the person. The distinction between good and bad knowledge comes down to, is
rooted in, the foundational distinction between truth and falsity.

   In reflecting on the nature of truth it can be helpful to think about
it in common, unsophisticated terms, as related to our ordinary, everyday
experiences. Is it not often the case that what alerts us in the first instance
to the foundational reality of truth, sensitizes us to its commanding importance, are those situations in which we are confronted by its exact opposite—falsity? We may initially feel confused and disoriented by this

confrontation, then perhaps angry, because we sense that something is basically wrong, out of kilter. We read something or hear something said, and what we read or hear does not square with what we know for a fact to be the case, or perhaps it is at odds with what we are convinced *should* be the case. We react indignantly to these incongruities, not as if we were responding to a purely personal affront, but because we think much larger issues are at stake. We have the disconcerting sense that reality itself is being tampered with. A head-on encounter with negation—and falsity and evil are examples of pure negation—can be a way of making us sharply conscious of the foundational affirmation which is truth. The shock of the No re-sensitizes us to the primacy and absolute importance of Yes.

The Correspondence Criterion of Truth

Epistemology lays down two basic criteria for ascertaining whether any given statement is true; they are the correspondence criterion, which we have already become acquainted with, and the coherence criterion. We have noted that knowledge is at bottom a relation, a relation between the subjective and the objective, between the mental and the extra-mental. A relation of any kind is stable and sound to the degree that there is established a firm bond between the two terms of the relation, and that would mean, in this case, a firm bond between subjective and objective realms, specifically, between the knower and the known. Such a bond is firmly established, the correspondence criterion of truth tells us, if any statement made by a knowing subject ("The main library is on Main Street") is true if there is a correspondence between that statement and the objective state of affairs, what actually obtains in the real world. The statement happens to be true because, in fact, the main library is on Main Street.

In many cases it is relatively easy to ascertain the truth or falsity of a statement, and it can be done rather quickly. Sometimes, though, we have to work at it. There are circumstances where we hear or read something and we are not immediately sure whether or not it is true. There are any number of reasons why this might be so. It could be simply a matter of ignorance on our part: we just don't know enough about the subject to which a statement is referring to be able to say one way or another if it is true.

But if the subject does not particularly concern us, or interest us, it is not likely that we will pursue the matter.

However, if we should hear or read something touching upon a subject that directly concerns us, and if we have doubts about the truth of a particular statement, then we are prompted to do some digging to find out the truth of the matter. This may take some concentrated effort. The truth can sometimes be exasperating in its elusiveness, difficult to nail down in a definite way. Even so, we have to keep up our confidence that the truth is really available, waiting to be discovered by the persistent pursuer.

The Coherence Criterion of Truth

The basic idea behind the coherence criterion of truth is this: A given statement can be accepted as true if it fits into, coheres with, a well established system or theory that is itself considered to be sound. Albert Einstein's general theory of relativity, although not empirically demonstrated to be true in every particular, has, in the minds of the majority of physicists, been sufficiently verified so that they regard it, taken as a whole, to be a sound and reliable theory. Let us say that a research scientist at Prestigious University formulates, as a result of prolonged research, a new theory about the physical universe. He reveals his theory in a talk he gives at a national conference of theoretical physicists; subsequently his paper is turned over to a special committee of physicists, which is assigned the task of determining whether or not the theory has real merit to it, whether it can be taken to be true in the broad sense. After giving the theory close study, the committee decides in its favor, and they do so for the specific reason that it is coherent with Einstein's general theory of relativity, which they all regard as essentially true. In sum, it is in accord with, coherent with, a theory which is regarded to be generally sound.

Judging any particular statement, or set of statements, as true by relying on the coherence criterion of truth is reliable only if an important condition is met: the theory or system to which the statement or set of statements is being compared must itself be sound. If I decide that X is true because it agrees with Y, the question which then naturally arises is: What is the status of Y with regard to soundness or truth? If Y is questionable in that regard, then X would also be questionable. There should always be a prudent tentativeness in applying the coherence criterion of truth. It can be seen that of the two criteria for establishing the truth, the correspondence criterion is the more basic; it provides us with the most reliable standard by which we determine the truth of any statement or set of statements, or of any theory or system. Apropos of the example we used just above, if an established theory to which a new theory is being compared itself meets the correspondence criterion, we can then be fairly confident that the new theory is true.

Certitude

Larry is an ardent baseball fan; he prides himself on the width and depth of his knowledge of the great American pastime. One evening he is at a social gathering with friends and during the course of an animated conversation on the subject of baseball history he notes in passing that the Chicago Cubs won the 1945 World Series. A neighbor, who himself had more than a superficial acquaintance with baseball lore, says to Larry, "Are you sure about that?" "Sure?" Larry promptly responds, "I'm positive."

We want to know the truth of the matter, especially if it relates to something in which we take more than a casual interest. We seek the confidence that comes with the assurance that we are right, that we have gotten things straight. In sum, we do not simply want to grasp the truth, we want that grasp to be as firm as possible. We want to be certain of what we know. Certitude, like truth itself, can be elusive at times. We can be fooled; we can fool ourselves. We all have perhaps had the experience of being "positively sure" about something, only subsequently to discover, perhaps much to our embarrassment, that we were positively wrong about being positively right. It has not been reported whether Larry suffered any embarrassment when he learned that it was the Detroit Tigers, not the Chicago Cubs, who won the 1945 World Series.

What is this certitude which, ideally, we should always want to be a feature of our knowledge? In pursuing that question, we first make a distinction between subjective certitude and objective certitude. Subjective certitude is a state of mind. It is the firm confidence I have that what I know is exactly as I believe it to be. I harbor no doubts about the matter. Objective certitude refers to the actual state of affairs in the extra-mental world. Between the two, subjective certitude and objective certain, the latter is foundational with respect to the former: if X is not objectively certain, then that renders null and void any subjective certitude that would regard X as certain. Larry had subjective certitude that the Chicago Cubs won the 1945 World Series; however, his subjective certitude lacked a firm basis, and that is because, in the final analysis, objective certainty has the final say. The reason for this is clear, for objective certainty simply refers to what is actually the case, the plain facts of the matter. We should see that in the relation between subjective and objective certitude we simply have a specific application of the correspondence criterion of truth. I am justified in being certain about my knowledge of X, if my knowledge corresponds with what is actually the case with regard to X. My subjective certitude must coincide with objective certitude.

As we shall see presently, subjective certitude is not always a matter of pure black or pure white; there are gray areas, which is to say that there can be degrees of subjective certitude. There can be no degrees of objective certitude; something either is or is not the case. What are we to say of people who persist in being "absolutely sure" about something which the facts contradict? What if Larry continues to insist that the Chicago Cubs won the 1945 World Series? That is a problem I would prefer to pass on to the psychologists.

The Criteria of Certitude

There are three basic criteria which, if met, allow us to confirm a state of justifiable subjective certitude. First of all, the knowing subject is able to give firm assent to a particular statement or proposition. When we are certain about something, there is no wavering on our part, no vacillation; we entertain no doubts about the possibility of our being wrong regarding the assent we have given to a particular statement, such as, "Napoleon was born on the island of Corsica."

Secondly, there is an absence on the part of the subject of any rational fear that he might be wrong in giving his assent. The key word here is "rational." We are speaking of a situation in which we cannot provide ourselves with any good *reasons* for doubting the rightness of our assent. But human emotion, or a lively imagination, can enter the picture and make life difficult for us at times, by stirring up any number of irrational fears, that is, fears for which, by definition, there is no real basis in fact. Such fears might be called abnormal, or illogical; the psychologist might call them phobias. The pestering presence of irrational fears can usually be easily enough dismissed, by a moment or two of cool, calm reflection, re-rooting oneself in the real. Damian is at times bothered by fears that Dorothy does not really love him, even though: (a) she has told him she loves him time and time again; (b) she has *demonstrated* her love in any number of ways; (c) she has never done anything that even suggests she doesn't love him. Damian is being bothered by irrational fears. In this case there was objective certitude, but Damian had problems giving it due regard.

Thirdly, we must have an objective basis for our certainty, which supports the firm assent we have given, and this must be accompanied by the absence of any rational fear that we are wrong in giving that assent. I am certain that Napoleon was born on the island of Corsica because I have consulted several authoritative and impeccable sources regarding the matter, and all of them, without exception, agree that Corsica is precisely the place where he was born. When this third criterion is met subjective certitude and objective certitude merge and become virtually one and the same. Subjective certitude alone, as we have seen, without a foundation in objective fact to support and authenticate it, is, as the philosopher Frederick Wilhelmsen poignantly put it, "intellectually irrelevant." To be certain of something which is not true is simply to be divorced from reality.

The Degrees of Certitude

Certitude and doubt are incompatible; certitude drives out doubt, and doubt drives out certitude. But certitude is not without its variations. There are three degrees of certitude, the highest being metaphysical or absolute certitude; next comes physical certitude, and then there is moral certitude. The rationale behind this hierarchical arrangement of certitude has to do with the firmness of subjective certitude in each case, and this in turn, quite logically, has directly to do with the objective certitude in each case. As we descend from absolute certitude, through physical certitude, to moral certitude, the quality of the subjective certitude alters, from the most firm with absolute certainty, to less firm with physical certainty, and to the less firm still with moral certitude. But it is important to note that in each case we have real certitude, a subjective state that is not haunted by doubt. The degrees of certitude apply only to subjective certitude, to the level of confidence that we have in our knowledge, and not to objective certitude. It is clear why this is so, for objective certitude, recall, is simply the certitude of objective reality itself, having to do with the way things actually are. Something is either objectively true or it is not; here there can be no question of degrees. We recall the principle of excluded middle from our logic: there is no middle ground between being and non-being. But the firmness with which we assent to objective truth can vary, and this admits of degrees.

Absolute Certitude

Absolute certitude, which is also known as metaphysical or perfect certitude, describes a state of mind in which we assent to a particular truth (expressed in the form of a statement) with complete and impregnable confidence. Our confidence is based on the fact that the nature of the truth to which we give our assent is such that it would be impossible for it not to be true, for that would involve a contradiction; therefore, were we to refrain from assenting to the truth we would simply be slipping into the slough or irrationality. The truths to which absolute certainty is the only appropriate response admit of no exceptions. The arithmetical statement, $3 + 3 = 6$ is a truth about which we can be absolutely certain, for we cannot conceive, or imagine, how it could be otherwise.

The third criterion for certitude, recall, is that it has an objective basis. The objective basis for absolute certitude is as sound as it could possibly be, for it is nothing less than actuality, the way things simply and unalterably *are*. As the most elevated form of certitude, it is something to which, in our pursuit of knowledge, we should ardently aspire. There could be no more secure and reassuring a position, from the point of view of knowledge, than being sure of something beyond the slightest shadow of a doubt. And it is not so distant and difficult to achieve as perhaps we might suppose. Consider, in terms of your own experience, the number of things the truth of which you would have no hesitancy in saying you are absolutely sure, and—this is the crucial test—you could easily justify, give sound and convincing reasons for. Or they are of the kind that any reasoning on their behalf would be unnecessary, as if they needed to be proved. Many of the things we are absolutely certain about we take to be self-evidently true, with good reason. Can there be any serious doubt about the truth of the four first principles of human reasoning, which we have articulated and discussed in previous pages? We can be absolutely certain of firmly established historical facts. I have more than once referred to the island of Corsica as being Napoleon's birthplace. That is something about which we can be absolutely certain, for it is not subject to change. We can be absolutely certain that John Adams was the second president of the United States, that Albert Einstein formulated the Special and General theories of Relativity, that Babe Ruth hit 60 homeruns in 1927. The sequential nature of time is fixed and irreversible: we can be absolutely certain that the American Civil War came before the Second World War, and that came before the coronation of Queen Elizabeth II. The past can be reinterpreted, but it cannot be rewritten. There are any number of subjective states about which, though of no great consequence for the world at large, we can nonetheless be absolutely certain. Joshua, who is in fact very much alive, can be absolutely certain that such is really the case, that he has a mother and a father, that he is married to Genevieve, and that, right now, he is taking a stroll in Kimberly Park.

The foundation for subjective absolute certainty is objective certainty, or what is the actual state of affairs. The test of absolute certainty is to measure it against the principle of contradiction. I am absolutely certain of the truth of X. I ask myself, Could it be otherwise? Can I reasonably entertain the possibility that X is false? If I can emphatically answer those questions in the negative, then I can be absolutely certain that X is true. Joshua knows who he is, where he is right now, and what he is doing right now. For him to suppose for a second he does not have that knowledge would be simply silly.

Physical Certitude

If the actual state of affairs is the objective basis for absolute certainty, the objective basis for what we call physical certitude is what actually obtains in the physical world as we know it. The knowledge could be conveniently summed up in what we identify as the laws of nature, or the physical laws, which are simply descriptions of the observed regularities, the established patterns of the manner in which material substances consistently behave. We could call it, comprehensively, the cosmic order that constitutes the physical universe as an intelligible whole. Physical certainty consists in this, that we can be confident that the consistently regular ways inanimate material things behave will not be interrupted; they will continue to behave in the future as they have invariably behaved in the past. Because to date the sun has never failed to rise, we can be certain that it will rise tomorrow morning. We can be confident that what we may generally describe as the established pattern of the regularities of nature is entirely trustworthy and will hold firm, that the regularities it embraces will not cease to be regular in their operations. It is the regularities of physical nature that makes empirical science possible, and justifies the confidence it has in its predictions. You do not have to be a physicist to know that if you let go of a hammer you are holding it will promptly drop to the ground, so you had better not be barefoot when you try that scientific experiment. Physical bodies obey the law of gravity with punctilious predictability, which is simply to say that there are regular ways that physical bodies relate to one another, at least on the macro level, which are not known to vary.

Our knowledge of the regularities of nature, though impressive, is far from exhaustive. Moreover, we can have a sound theoretical knowledge of the physical laws, but on the practical level at times fail to take into account how those laws could be operatively present because of conditions that we ourselves have brought about, and this could result in seriously negative consequences that we did not foresee. Those who, in the summer of 2007, were driving across the I-35W bridge spanning the Mississippi River as it flows through Minneapolis, surely had no idea in mind, as they approached the bridge, that it would collapse beneath them as they were in the process of crossing it.

The basic idea behind physical certitude is that we can be confident that the basic regularities of physical nature, which explain its orderliness and predictability, will not vary, that buildings and bridges will hold up, that ceilings won't cave in on our heads or floors give way beneath our feet, that the plane we are flying in will make it safely to the airport. Those various expressions of our confidence are the basis for physical certitude. But if we can trust the consistency of the regularities themselves, either our imperfect knowledge of them, or our ignorance of how they could operate in particular circumstances, can result in unfortunate outcomes. The regularities of nature, the physical laws, were not departed from when the bridge collapsed in Minneapolis, but the man-created circumstances which provided the occasion for the laws operating just as they did and just at the time they did proved disastrous. It was a series of human faults that set the stage for the disaster. The actual physical condition a bridge may be in, coupled with accompanying circumstances at a given time, can make its collapse if not inevitable, at least a dangerous probability. Unfortunately, this is the kind of knowledge we come to learn almost always only after the fact.

Moral Certitude

The basis for moral certitude is the confidence we have that the people we regularly encounter in our quotidian comings and goings are going to behave humanly, that is, as rational creatures who are guided in their actions by an elementary respect for their fellow human beings, and will not do harm to them on account of their incompetence, or carelessness, or outright maliciousness of purpose. Generally, we can rely on the fact that, by and large and for the most part, human beings will behave as rational creatures and responsible moral agents. So, for example, I need not entertain any doubts that the strangers I encounter on a day-to-day basis will not lie, cheat, or steal in their dealings with me. If, whenever I meet someone new, I were constantly to torture myself with questions like, "How do I know this guy is not lying to me?" I would be entertaining irrational fears. We have to trust that people are trustworthy, and we commonly do. If we made a practice of not doing so we would in short order drive ourselves batty.

With regard to the basis for moral certitude, prominence of place should be given to the natural law, the universal moral law that governs the behavior of the entire human race. The reality of this law could be said to have been given significant expression by the Universal Declaration of Human Rights, which was promulgated in 1948. The document was drawn up by a commission made up of people from around the world, representing, for its diversity, something like a cross-section of the entire human race. Despite this diversity in cultures, in religious affiliation, in philosophy, in economic status, in country of origin, etc., there was common agreement among the members that there are certain fundamental moral principles to which all human beings subscribe, allowing the commission to specify a set of basic rights that can be commonly acknowledged. Such a document was possible because it reflected something essential about us as human beings, that we have a deeply ingrained shared moral sensibility. By our very nature we have an ineradicable tendency to behave benevolently toward one another. We do so because we have an inherent awareness of the elementary distinction between good and evil, with the natural inclination to do good and avoid evil. When we do not act benevolently toward one another we are acting contrary to our nature.

It must be acknowledged, however, that though the objective basis for moral certitude is firm, it lacks the kind of firmness to be found in the objective basis for physical certitude, or in the objective basis for absolute certitude. Human behavior is in the main stable and dependable because people live according to the natural law, and that is why, with full assurance—we seldom think twice about it—we expect that people will behave justly and charitably and not do any harm to one another. However, we can and do at times, for a variety of reasons, act contrary to that law. The behavior of human beings can sometimes be rather quirky, if not, on occasions, radically aberrant. There are two important factors to consider here: (1) our human nature is wounded, and that affects the quality of our compliance to the natural law; (2) we are creatures possessed of free will, and we can exercise that will in ways that are contrary to the natural law. We also have to take into account the sad fact of psychopathology, as well as the fact that people can be caught up and captivated by nihilistic ideologies that impel them to do willful harm to their fellow human beings. We can be generally confident, be morally certain, that parents will not sell their children into slavery, much less kill them. But it happens. We can be morally certain, should we decide to step out on a pleasant spring evening to see a play or hear a concert, that no one is going to suddenly appear in the theater or hall with an automatic rifle and indiscriminately open fire on the audience. But it happens. We can be morally certain, if we board a plane for Los Angeles, that the pilot will not deliberately fly it into a building. But it happens. But inhuman behaviors such as those are rare; they represent departures from the norm. The happy fact is that human beings, dominantly, behave toward one another in a benevolent fashion, which serves to demonstrate that, in doing so, they are acting out of something which is fundamental to their nature.

Summing up the three degrees of certitude: absolute certitude is the full assurance with which we assent to a truth because we know it would be impossible for it to be false (e.g., I am absolutely certain that the whole is greater than any one of its parts, and that Duluth is north of Corpus Christi). Physical certitude endows us with the confidence that the regularities of nature will continue in their regularity (e.g., I am physically certain that fire burns, and that water freezes), and that all will be well if the regularities of nature are intelligently taken into account when we work with the various material substances provided to us by nature. With moral certitude I can reasonably rely on the fact that people will, by and large, act in accordance with the universal moral law (e.g., I am morally certain that the twenty-dollar bills the bank teller counted out for me this morning are not counterfeit, and that when Jack told Jill he loved her she can be certain that he meant it).

Ignorance

Ignorance is simply the absence of knowledge. It is a subjective state which may be good or bad, depending on the real-life circumstances in which ignorant subjects find themselves. But a distinction is immediately called for here, between negative ignorance and privative ignorance. (I might note parenthetically that philosophy is all about making distinctions, and we should be grateful for that fact. Good distinctions make for clearer thinking.) Negative ignorance is the lack of unnecessary knowledge, knowledge for which a particular person at a particular time has no pressing need. At the moment I am totally ignorant of Swahili. I might say to myself on dreamy afternoons in late fall that it would be nice to know that language; if I did know it perhaps I could be of some use to people in certain situations. But given my situation here and now, and the peculiar tasks and obligations I have, there is no pressing need for my being conversant in Swahili. My ignorance of the language is negative.

Privative ignorance is of an entirely different sort, for this is a lack of a specific kind of knowledge on the part of a person who should have that knowledge. This would be "need to know" knowledge for that person.

Norbert learns that there is a call for umpires to officiate at games for a local amateur baseball league that will be playing numerous games over the course of the summer. Norbert always wanted to be an umpire, is avid to act in that capacity, volunteers his services, and is accepted by the league officials. He shows up dutifully for the first game to which he is assigned, and he is designated as the home plate umpire. Things do not go well at all, for Norbert, despite his love for baseball and earnest good intentions, has but scant and confused knowledge of the rules of the game. The calls he makes are so egregiously questionable, if not flatly wrong, that he does not make it through the entire game. After five innings the managers of both teams (Norbert was not biased in the bad calls he made, distributing them fairly evenly between the two teams) ask him, politely but firmly, to leave the field and retire to the bleachers, convinced as they were, and rightly, that Norbert was doing excessive damage to the venerable game of baseball. Here was a clear case of privative ignorance. It is imperative that a baseball umpire be thoroughly familiar with the rules of the game if he is competently to meet the various tasks he has to fulfill.

We can all attest to the fact that overcoming ignorance of whatever sort is sometimes no easy accomplishment, requiring a considerable amount of time and much concentrated effort. In learning something which is entirely new to us, usually the job is made easier if we start with a completely blank slate, where we are more or less completely ignorant of the subject that we wish to master. Why is that? Imagine this situation, having to do with Penelope Price, who has an abiding love of history, in which she took several courses while she was in college. She initially grows suspicious and eventually becomes convinced that her knowledge of modern history, roughly from mid-seventeenth century to the present, is rather shaky, and that is because the college courses she took in modern history—she has come to learn this from her continuing post-college reading—were all rather poorly taught. As a result, Penelope finds herself in a state of affairs where she is burdened with any number of questionable theories, unsupported opinions, strained interpretations, and, coming from a couple of the courses she took, some downright erroneous factual information regarding modern history.

Being the enterprising young lady she is, she decides to do something about the current state of affairs. She learns that the university in the city in which she is now living has a first-rate history department which regularly offers a number of night courses in modern history. Over a two-year period she takes all of the available courses, in all of which she acquitted herself very well. But in many ways it turned out to be an especially challenging experience, for she discovered that she had to unburden her mind of much of which she had previously been taught on the subject of modern history. It was a matter of first clearing the decks, so to speak, to make room for a whole new set of deck chairs, sturdy pieces of furniture that were well designed.

In the dialogue entitled *Sophist*, Plato identified what he called a "large and grievous kind of ignorance," which would be exemplified, he explains, "when a person who supposes that he knows, and does not know." What makes this form of ignorance "large and grievous" for Plato is that it is "the great source of all the errors of the intellect." He has another name for it—stupidity. With that alternative way of describing the kind of ignorance Plato has in mind we might conclude he believed that anyone who was beset by it was beyond remedy, but this is not the case. Someone who supposes he knows but really doesn't is stupid, but Plato is convinced that stupidity can be overcome. What is the situation of someone whom Plato calls stupid? It is by no means the case that his mind is a complete blank; far from it; in more cases than not he has all sorts of opinions which he tenaciously clings to because he is convinced they are all true. The problem, and it is a "grievous" one, is that they are not true. In other words, the stupid person may be possessed of all sorts of knowledge, but it is erroneous knowledge, so he is in a state where he thinks he knows (that is, he has the truth) but he does not know (he does not have the truth). To have one's head packed with erroneous knowledge is to be ignorant, not to be knowledgeable in the true sense of the world. But his case is by no means desperate, for if stupidity may be called a mental illness (which I think Plato would be inclined to do), then it is curable. The cure for that type of ignorance, for Plato, was education, a special kind of education that he calls purgation, or purification of soul. The stupid person must be willing to submit himself to a point-by-point critique of everything he supposes to be true but which is in fact is false. His educator must prove to him, with solid, irrefutable evidence, that the positions he holds have no basis for them. He is thus "purged of his prejudices," and he is thus brought to the point where he realizes "that he knows only what he knows, and no more."

The kind of ignorance Plato describes in the *Sophist* calls attention to the kind of problem we may have to contend with at one time or another in our lives, even though the problem might not be serious as the one Plato had in mind, where a person is deserving of being called stupid because he is overburdened by erroneous knowledge. Just above we considered the situation Penelope Price found herself in. Penelope was in no way stupid; in fact it was her own perspicacity that made her realize that she had in store much information about modern history that was highly problematic, and she therefore saw the need of purifying her soul of it, so to speak, so she could build up a solid and reliable body of knowledge on that important subject. There are any number of factors that can be the cause of being in a situation where our mind is burdened with erroneous knowledge, the most basic and immediate effect of which is that it prevents us from having the kind of grasp on reality which is essential for us to have if we are to think and act as rational creatures. The first order of business, then, facing a debilitating situation of that sort, is to pursue the special type of education recommended by Plato, an education which will purge us of our prejudices (i.e., erroneous knowledge), thus providing ample space for truth.

"It is never too late," Henry David Thoreau wrote, "to give up our prejudices." This is a heartening thought, but the older we grow and the more set in our ways we become, the more difficult it is to rid ourselves of questionable or positively erroneous knowledge, especially if we have been nurturing it for the better part of our adult lives. It requires courage, and the kind of unflinching self-knowledge that is not easy to come by. It also requires, importantly, intellectual humility, the willingness to admit that on this subject or that, we have not been fully and unambiguously on the side of truth, that we have been harboring enfeebled ideas, and perhaps even foisting them upon others. And then we must be willing to take radical corrective action, in order to, as Plato put it, purify the soul.

Doubt

What does it mean to be in a state of doubt, to be doubtful about something? It is most clearly exemplified in a situation where we are faced with two alternatives and cannot make up our minds between them, cannot bring ourselves to choose one or the other, and be confident that we would

be right in doing so. We are stymied, at an impasse, and this has directly to
do with the state of our knowledge regarding the two alternatives with
which we are faced. One possibility is that we are lacking adequate knowledge of one or the other or both of these alternatives. Another possibility
is that we may have plenty of knowledge of both, but it is inconclusive.
The situation just described points to the distinction between negative
doubt and positive doubt.

Negative doubt is a product of ignorance. I am faced with a decision:
I must choose between A and B. As it happens, however, I am almost totally
ignorant of both A and B. Now, if the whole matter were trivial, it really
would not make much difference how I choose; there is nothing of consequence riding on my choice. I could with a clear conscience point arbitrarily
to either A or B, or I could simply walk away from the situation, choosing
neither, deciding that the whole business is not worth bothering about. But
let us say that it is not at all a trivial matter; much is a stake here, and
weighty consequences follow upon whatever choice I make. In that case
my ignorance is seriously incapacitating and calls for immediate remedy. I
have my work cut out for me, and have to scramble to educate myself regarding both A and B so that I will be able to make an informed decision.
I do so, but even with that I discover that my troubles are not yet over, for
now I may find myself in a state of positive doubt.

To be in a state of positive doubt is not to be in a state of ignorance.
Here knowledge is ready to hand, perhaps there is even an abundance of
knowledge, but the knowledge with which I am now endowed is such that
I am still hampered by doubt. I did my homework conscientiously with regard to both A and B, researched both options with commendable thor-
oughness, but here is the situation in which I now find myself: all the
positive data I was able to gather about A is nicely balanced by all the positive data I gathered about B. At this stage, for all the relevant information
I have available to me, I still cannot make up my mind between A and B.
I look at A; that seems to be a reasonable choice. I look at B; that too seems
to be a reasonable choice. How am I to get past this log-jam? There is no
magic solution to the problem. The only thing I can do is roll up my sleeves
and go back to work, keep digging until I find enough additional information to tip the scales one way or another, however slightly, in favor of either
A or B. (In light of what I have learned of the two thus far, the tipping of

the scales would expectedly be slight.) Then I do the rational thing: choose the option that has more evidence in its favor, however small the difference between the two might be. Remember, this is a situation where I must choose one way or the other; I cannot opt for both. And I cannot wash my hands of the whole business by simply refusing to make a choice.

Once upon a time there was a pulchritudinous young damsel named Samantha who received, within the span of a mere three days, marriage proposals from two young gentlemen, both of whom were quite remarkable, each in his special way. Their names were Jeremiah and Joachim. Now Samantha knew both young gentlemen very well; as it happens, the three of them had grown up together, and she had the highest regard for both of them; more, she loved both of them. Samantha was in a quandary, or to be more precise for our philosophic purposes, she was in a state of positive doubt. She loved Jeremiah; she loved Joachim equally well. On Monday, it was Jeremiah she was going to say "yes" to; on Tuesday it was Joachim who would get the nod; on Wednesday she was back to Jeremiah. She went back and forth like this in her mind for days, for weeks, then for months. Finally, both Jeremiah and Joachim got tired of waiting, went off, eventually met other pulchritudinous young damsels whom they married, settled down with, and lived happily ever after. Samantha thus found herself deprived of both Jeremiah and Joachim. To dawdle excessively over a decision is to run the risk of sooner or later finding yourself in a situation where the decision has been taken away from you.

The French philosopher René Descartes (1596–1650), commonly acknowledged as the father of modern philosophy, had so low a regard for what he perceived to be the general state of philosophy in his day that he decided it was necessary in effect to start all over again, developing an entirely new philosophy, one superior to all its predecessors. He laid it down as a general rule that all philosophy should begin by engaging in a process of systematic doubt: everything that one had previously learned should be called into question, and if it could be doubted then it should be scrubbed out of the mind. He proposed this extraordinary program, it is important to note, not because he was advocating doubt as such—he knew doubt was the bane of philosophy—but because he thought that this was the only way eventually to overcome doubt and arrive at certain knowledge, clear and distinct ideas that were indubitable. Descartes' program of methodical doubt came to a screeching but reassuring halt when he realized that there was something which he couldn't doubt, and that was there was someone in the vicinity who was doing the doubting, and that turned out to be René Descartes. All his doubting thoughts were proof positive that he existed for, after all, if there is thought, there is a thinker. That was something he could be absolutely certain about. Given these illuminating revelations he triumphantly proclaimed: *Cogito, ergo sum,* "I think, therefore I am."

The Scottish philosopher David Hume (1711–1776) took warm exception to Descartes' plan of action. He curtly pointed out that it is simply impossible to doubt everything. Furthermore, to suppose that attempting to do it was the right way to begin philosophizing seriously was foolhardy, for the results could be disastrous. The dedicated systematic doubter, wading into a veritable sea of doubt, put himself in danger of eventually drowning in it. The first step in philosophy, for someone like Hume, would be simply to open your eyes and take careful note of what they and your other senses tell you about the world in which you live. In choosing between M. Descartes and Mr. Hume I will, on this particular matter at any rate, gladly agree with Mr. Hume.

Truth's Ugly Opposite

We have given much stress to the notion that truth is the result of the fruitful merging of the subjective realm and the objective realm. It is, specifically, the state of mental affairs where the ideas in my mind correspond with, faithfully reflect, real facts in the external world. Falsity, of course, would be just the opposite of a relation of that kind; here there would be a breakdown, a serious disconnection, between the mental and the extra-mental. Let us assume that I say or write something which is clearly false. My doing so in a given instance may be the result of what we politely designate as an honest mistake, which could be defined as a mistake that is not accompanied by culpability. If I make such a mistake I cannot simply brush it off as just "one of those things," especially if I am dealing with serious matters. I should feel obligated, as soon as I am made aware of the gaffe, to take immediate action for the purpose of setting the record straight. Not all mistakes can be said to be honest, however, as would be the case, for example, if they are traceable to carelessness on my part. If a shortstop makes an error because he's playing his position in a sloppy manner, he should be prepared to be bawled out by the manager when he gets back to the dugout.

A word needs to be said about sincerity as it relates to truth and falsity. It goes without saying that we must be sincere in believing that the ideas we hold are true, that the positions we maintain and defend are defensible, but sincerity in itself is not enough. We say that sincerity is a necessary but not a sufficient condition as a crucial support for a person's intellectual integrity. However, it would be naïve in the extreme for me to think that, because I sincerely believe X to be true, that is adequate to ensure the truth of X. One of the most problematic ways of being wrong is to be sincerely so, for in such a circumstance sincerity has a peculiar way of obscuring our awareness of our alienation from the truth. We attach more weight to how we feel about a matter than how we think about it. "How can I be wrong when I'm so sincere?" The answer to the question is simple: "You can be sincerely wrong."

To promulgate falsehoods knowingly and with malice of forethought is to lie, which is an attempt directly to undermine the truth. A lie reflects a situation where there is a radical discrepancy between what a person publicly claims to be the case and what the person knows to be the case. He says, "X is true," when he knows full well that X is not true. I know full well that Napoleon was born in Corsica, but for some devious reason I say that he was born in Naples. Because a lie reflects an absence of consonance between thought and linguistic expression it always begins as an intra-personal affair. Others may not know that the liar is lying, but the liar always knows. If he did not know that there was a discrepancy between what he says and what is factually the case, he would not be lying. This leads to the conclusion that before we can lie to others we must first lie to ourselves. We make mistakes about the facts, in many instances, simply because we are not paying enough attention to matters at hand. However, we cannot be mistaken in telling lies, for lying is a conscious, deliberate effort to deceive, intentionally to provide our audience with—to put it in general terms—a distorted picture of reality.

Language is meant to be a means for the communication of truth. Surely the single most serious abuse of language is to use it as a vehicle for the undermining of truth, for the trafficking in falsity. The words communication and community have the same Latin root. If communication is corrupted, which happens when it is laced with lies, then the coherence of community is threatened, and those who populate it face being dehumanized. When community breaks down, "the people" is replaced by "the masses." It has become a truism to say that if a lie is proclaimed boldly and loudly enough, and repeatedly, it can be eventually accepted by many as if it were true. The truth of that truism has been borne out by several examples in recent history. It is as if the programmed and noisy promulgation of a lie has the psychological effect on people of wearing down their common-sense defenses against the phony and nonsensical, to the point where, mentally disoriented, they finally acquiesce to a completely fake version of reality in order to fit into a disoriented society. The holdouts, those who do not buy into the lie, are either marginalized or eliminated by the promulgators of the lie.

Truth, it is said, will in the end prevail. That may be so, but what often happens is that in certain situations a long prohibited truth has to reassert itself in a landscape, physical and social, that has been devastated by the prolonged dominance of lies and their damaging consequences. "The end" at which truth will eventually prevail can be long delayed in coming, and that is what typically happens with solidly entrenched totalitarian regimes. Truth may in due course win out, but before that much desired victory occurs, a great deal of permanent damage can have been done. Important truths, such as those that are integral to the natural law, which have been badly battered by incessant and prolonged lies, often need time to fully recover their vitality and resume their proper place of prominence in a society that for too long has been composed of the masses rather than the people.

Opinion

Everyone is entitled to one's own opinion, as the old saw has it, to which everyone would supposedly agree, maybe because we all have an intuitive sense of what opinion is really worth. To have an opinion about something is not to be in the strongest possible position as far as knowledge is concerned. At least not according to Plato, and Plato is worth paying attention to on this subject. In his *Republic* he is quite definite in maintaining that knowledge, true or certain knowledge, is one thing, and opinion quite

another. To have an opinion about something is not to be in a state of ignorance, nor is it to be in a state of doubt. It is to give your assent to something you take to be true, but there is a tentative quality to your assent.
You leave open as a real possibility that what you take to be true may turn
out to be false.

To illustrate Plato's point, let us return to the situation we discussed
above, one in which we are faced with two alternatives, say, two scientific
theories. I will put myself in that situation. I give both theories long and
concentrated study, as the result of which I decide that Theory A is the
sounder one; I accept it as true. I am not in a state of doubt about the matter, and the proof of that is my having made a definite decision in favor of
Theory A. Furthermore, I am confident in the conclusion I arrived at regarding Theory A. But I would describe the attitude I have toward the theory as an opinion, and not certain knowledge, and that is because I
acknowledge the possibility that my attitude could one day be shown to be
untenable. In other words, I realize that it is possible that new evidence
might materialize which would show that Theory A has serious flaws and
therefore has to be abandoned. If that should in fact happen, I would not
find the circumstance to be, in itself, all that unusual. Such is the history
of science. But the point to stress is this: according to the best evidence
now available, Theory A has all the earmarks of a sound theory.

To sum up: to have an opinion about something is to hold, with good
reason, that it is true, but at the same time be willing to acknowledge the
fact that there would be no contradiction involved if what is held to be true
today is proven to be false tomorrow. I am putting the matter in rather extreme terms for the sake of clarity, but things are seldom so starkly simple.
Apropos of Theory A, new evidence regarding it may in fact come down
the pike someday, but the nature of that evidence would lead us, not to
abandon the theory altogether, but rather to make some critical adjustments
to it. It turns out not to be a question of all or nothing.

Error

To be in error is to be in a situation where you think something is true whereas
in fact it is false; you are on the wrong side of reality regarding a given matter,
commonly something of significant import. It is to mis-take something, that

is, take it in the wrong way, as true when in fact it is false, and then to stick with it, perhaps even tenaciously. Error can be differentiated from simply getting something wrong in a particular instance—we are all apt to do that—in that it tends to be a state, if not a permanent one, at least a prolonged one.

There are many ways we can fall into error regarding the truth, but generally what happens is that our mind is not properly oriented toward the objective order of things. And that usually comes about because we are not keeping careful enough watch over our ideas, allowing them to wander away from the measures established by the way things actually are in the external world. Self-delusion is a fairly common cause of error; we have a persistent penchant for preferring how we want things to be rather than acknowledging the way they actually are. Unreality, especially if it is of our own manufacture, has its seductive charms.

There are several specific causes of error, the most prominent being inadvertence and carelessness. The pursuit of truth demands our full and undivided attention, and if we fail to give it that pursuit can turn out to be a wild goose chase.

Imagination is one of our most powerful possessions; it can be immensely valuable to us in the pursuit of truth. Some of the greatest discoveries in the history of philosophy and science have started with a hypothesis, not a clear idea of what is so, but a conjecture, a guess, as to what might be so. It is imagination that makes the first daring moves toward significant discovery, but those initial imaginative moves eventually prove fruitful because they commonly take place within the ambit of an appreciable store of knowledge. A viable hypothesis is not a reckless stab in the dark; it is a guess, yes, but an educated guess, a reasonable supposition. Under ordinary circumstances imagination needs constantly to be reined in, kept under the benign governance of reason. If imagination breaks free of reason and charges off on its own, it can be a cause of error.

As with imagination, so too with our emotions: if they are the principal impetus in the pursuit of truth, we are heading for a dead end. Attention has already been called to the basic psychological fact which tells us that it is difficult, if not impossible, to think clearly when we are in the grip of a strong emotion of one kind or another. The successful pursuit of truth depends on our ability to think clearly, to be led by logic. Someone who is blinded by anger cannot see where he is supposed to be going.

Some truths can be gained after a relatively short pursuit. To gain others, and these invariably are the more important ones, we have to realize that we are in it for the long haul. And this points to the need for patience and perseverance. Another cause, almost a guarantee, of error is impatience and impetuosity. Both go hand in hand with carelessness. If we are impatient "just to get something done" it will in more cases than not lead to the undoing of any successful pursuit of truth. Impetuosity makes us jump the gun, rushing pell-mell toward too easy conclusions, conclusions that often will eventually be shown to be insufficiently warranted. The special value, and beauty, of patience is that it brings about self-possession. Patient people have it admirably "all together."

Ideological obsession can be another cause of error. To be ideologically obsessed means to be so completely and uncritically caught up in and committed to a theory, a set of beliefs, a world view, which themselves have not been subjected to close critical examination. As a result, you live, in terms of how you typically think and act, almost entirely within the narrow confines of the theory to which you are passionately but uncritically committed, and this necessarily distorts your perspective on reality. Everything you encounter is measured against, and must be rigidly judged according to, what you regard as the unquestionable truths of your theory, belief system, or world view. And if something you encounter doesn't measure up to, doesn't fit, the theory, then it is summarily rejected. Ideological obsession is a rich breeding ground for error, for it amounts to solidifying oneself in what has all the earmarks of a delusory state of mind.

Finally, we must mention the critical importance of will. To be successful in the pursuit of truth the very first requirement is a rightly ordered will. We must will, and with all our might, to gain the truth with regard to whatever particular subject we are dealing with. But as is the case with imagination, and with emotion in general, will must be guided by reason. To suppose that we can achieve truth without prudent reasoning, but simply by allowing ourselves to be driven by raw acts of will, unenlightened by mind, as if the pursuit of truth were no more than a prolonged power play, and as if the truth itself were something which is to be subdued by us, to be made a submissive vassal to our imperious blind desires, this would be to undermine the whole enterprise. We may yank our bootstraps as vigorously as we like, but our feet remain planted on the cold concrete. The

Oxford English Dictionary provides a very precise definition of "willful": "governed by will without regard to reason."

Evidence

Recall the third criterion we cited as a test of certitude: we are able to base our certainty on objective facts, on what is actually the case in the external world. Now, let us say that I have arrived at a state of certainty regarding a particular matter. That would mean that I have satisfied myself that there is an objective basis for my certainty. If people should ask me to give a reason for my certainty I should not, in response to that request, be tongue-tied. I should be able to present them with evidence, by spelling out for them the particulars of the objective basis for my certainty.

Evidence, generally described, is simply the information we present to make evident what is not self-evident. One does not have to speak of the estimated time of arrival of a train that is already in the station. But what should we do if people are unwilling to accept the self-evident as self-evident, if they have a blind eye for the obvious? Throwing up our hands in frustration might be the proper gesture here. But this is not a problem for logic or philosophy, but for psychology. And, once again, I will gladly turn it over to the experts in that field.

There are two large categories of evidence, one of which I will call material evidence, the other the evidence of reasoning. With regard to material evidence I am using "material" in the literal sense, as that which is composed of physical stuff, and therefore can be directly confirmed, at least in most cases, by our senses. If my neighbor does not believe that I have a dog, all I have to do in his presence is give a tuneful whistle, and Bosco the Boxer will promptly show up at my side, wagging what he has of a tail in neighborly fashion. If my neighbor happens to be the kind of latter-day disciple of René Descartes who is reluctant to accept the data provided by his senses, then Bosco and I will politely excuse ourselves and retire to the den, I to read, Bosco to nap. There is not much else you can do if people will not accept evidence as evidence.

You will be acquainted with the evidence of reasoning by having read Chapter One of this book. It is possible to present compelling evidence for something which is not manifestly self-evident, by providing a sound argument to support your case, an argument, that is, whose structure is valid and whose premises are manifestly true. In some instances, the evidence of reasoning can be just as strong, if not stronger, than material evidence, for what is presented as material evidence may not be conclusive. However, even given an argument that meets the above conditions (it is valid and its premises are true), in order for evidence from reasoning to be successful, that is, for an argument to be compelling, it must be met by an audience which is properly receptive to it. A properly receptive audience is one which has the willingness and the wherewithal to follow an argument. The audience must be capable of giving a reasonable response to the reasonable. This is something which we always hope for but which is not always the case; in any event, it is quite beyond our control. Whatever the situation in that respect, we must do our part as competently as we can, formulating arguments that we hope will fulfill the task for which they were intended.

An important form of evidence is that which rests upon personal testimony. American historians who today write about the Battle of Vicksburg were obviously not eyewitnesses to any aspect of that corner-turning event, so in order to give as accurate an account of it as they can, they must rely on the written testimony of those who were on the scene at the time, such as is to be found in the *Memoirs* of Ulysses S. Grant. The reliability of testimonial evidence rests squarely on trust. We must be willing to trust the person who is giving the testimony, but our trust cannot be blind; it must have a foundation to it, and that means that we must have substantial evidence, of whatever sort, that justifies our trust. Given the abundance of the material regarding him we have available to us, we can reasonably accept General Grant as being thoroughly trustworthy. By way of dramatic contrast to that personage, someone who has, in this day and age, gained the reputation of being a proficient prevaricator, can scarcely be worthy of our trust.

Skepticism

Skepticism has its source in a basically disordered epistemological state of affairs. The particular feature of its disorder is that, with regard to the process by which we come to have true knowledge, it reverses the right relation between mind and world, between the subjective realm and the objective realm. We are all now quite familiar with what that right relation is, but it wouldn't hurt to do a little quick recall to freshen up our memories. In reflecting on the correspondence criterion of truth, we saw that the foundations of truth are always to be found in the objective order of things, the way things actually stand in the external world. When it comes to establishing the truth, then, we are, as it were, measuring the mind against the standards of ontological truth, the truth of being, the way the world in fact is. The mind is not the measure, but that which is being measured.

Now, the skeptic has it wrong because he is basically disoriented; he begins, not by looking outward but by looking inward. He looks first to mind, next to world, then mentally adjusts the world so that it conforms to the ideas he has about it. He puts the subjective order before the objective order; for that reason skepticism can be recognized as a form of subjectivism, and subjectivism is rooted in philosophical idealism, that way of mis-reasoning, recall, that places more stock in ideas in the mind than in the things in the extra-mental world to which sound ideas faithfully refer. As a result, what skepticism pleases to call truth is without objective stability and permanence, and it is therefore the expression of a philosophical view which is contrary to the view held by philosophical realism. I will briefly note some of the key attitudes assumed by a person who may be described as a typical, run-of-the-mill skeptic. He may also be designated as a moderate skeptic, because he judiciously avoids extreme skepticism, the position that denies outright the very existence of truth, and which I will discuss later on. In accordance with the generalizations made above, our skeptic regards truth as essentially a subjective, mind-based phenomenon; it has no stable, objective status. For him, the truth is something fluid and fluctuating, continuously being adjusted and changed to accommodate changing times, changing conditions, and especially changing attitudes pertaining to morality. Truth can be adjusted so as comfortably to fit different personalities; in especially magnanimous moments, he is even prepared to recognize "private truth," that is, truth that is accepted by only one person. Although he believes truth to be essentially a subjective phenomenon, the skeptic is willing to concede that the truths of science and mathematics may be recognized as having something like objective standing. However, even here he is prepared to be doubtful. Doubt is the court of last resort for the skeptic, for he is willing to take it almost as axiomatic that we can never be certain of anything. But that position poses a knotty logical prob-lem for him. If, as he claims, we can never be certain of anything, that im-plies we cannot be certain of our uncertainty. The skeptic would paint himself into a corner by consistently abiding by that principle.

The skeptic has no tolerance for the notion of absolute truth, and this clearly reveals the serious limitations of his thinking, for he does not realize, or does not want to realize, that any statement that is in fact true cannot be anything else but absolutely true, which simply means, (1) it cannot be anything other than what it states (e.g., $7 + 3 = 10$) and (2) it is permanent and unchangeable (e.g., it will always be true that $7 + 3 = 10$). It is not only in mathematics that we find absolute truths. All firmly established historical facts are absolute truths; it will forever be true that Napoleon was born on the island of Corsica; that is an immutable truth. Furthermore, things about which we can have absolute certitude can also be said to be absolutely true, because of the fact that they cannot be thought or imagined to be other than they are. There are any number of personal experiences which the per-son experiencing them can with complete confidence acknowledge to be absolutely true. Not to do that would be to succumb to contradiction. A reader now reading this book is fully conscious of that fact, and knows he cannot be now reading the book and now not reading the book. There is nothing relative about that knowledge.

Philosophical skepticism has a long history behind it, dating back to ancient Greece, to the time when the great schools of Athens, the Academy and the Lyceum, founded respectively by Plato and Aristotle, lost their bear-ings and chose to develop systems out of disjointed ideas. A particular form of skepticism to come out of these ancient schools, described as epistemo-logical agnosticism, espoused a position that did not deny truth outright, but despaired of the possibility that the human mind would ever be able to attain it. Accepting that as incontrovertible fact, these skeptics then ad-vocated suspending one's judgment regarding the whole question of truth. They were so closed-minded and despairing in adopting that crippling point of view that they were unwilling to allow for the possibility that they were up against what might prove to be only a temporary impasse, one which could be overcome by a dedicated and persevering pursuit of truth. These philosophers perversely maintained that man's incapacity to attain the truth was permanent; moreover, they maintained that their attitude was the only proper one for philosophy to assume. To make it a policy to permanently suspend one's judgment regarding something as vitally important as truth is an act of intellectual suicide. To claim that you are incapable of making a positive decision with regard to truth (that it can be attained) is by that very fact to make a fateful and completely disabling decision against truth. Why is it, one wonders, that so many men over the course of the centuries have so often chosen to take up residence in the arid territory of skepticism in a futile attempt to escape from the truth? Was the motivation, at bottom, simply a fear of truth? Can men fear truth perhaps because they sense its capacity for exposing their elementary finitude, and that is an exposure the embarrassing consequences of which they are unwilling to face?

The phenomenon of extreme skepticism is the boldest possible stance to take with regard to truth: it denies outright that it exists. Those who take this position may be bold, but they had better be blushing as well, for their position is glaringly incoherent, and cannot be consistently maintained without contradiction. It is a perfect example of an auto-destructive position. The man who confidently proclaims that there is no truth of course expects us to take that claim to be true. He wants us to accept "There is no truth" as true, but if there is no truth then there is no basis for taking his claim to be true. It is empty of sense.

The only face-saving ploy open to him, a desperate move on his part, is to make the feeble claim that his universal assertion admits of a single exception, but by making that move he only sinks deeper into the mire of contradiction. As we know from our logic, to claim that a universal assertion (All X are Y) is true but that it admits of a single exception (One X is not Y) establishes a contradictory situation. Both cannot be true; if one is true, the other must be false. If truth is being claimed for "One X is not Y," which the extreme skeptic is doing, then "All X are Y" is necessarily and unavoidably false. To put it in plain English: By claiming that "There is no truth" (which is tantamount to saying "All statements are false"), then adding the claim that "There is one statement that is not false," the initial claim ("There is no truth") is thereby shown to be necessarily and unavoidably false. So, succinctly put, the skeptic contradicts himself by claiming (a) there is not truth ("All statements are false") and (b) there is one statement that is true ("There is not truth").

Chapter Five

The Moral Realm: Ethics

What Is the Subject Matter of Ethics?

The principal concern and focus of the science of ethics is human behavior. But could not the same thing be said of all of what are known as the social sciences? Yes, but there is an important difference with regard to ethics. What distinguishes any one of those sciences from another is the particular aspect under which it studies human behavior. So, for example, economics studies economic man, political science studies political man, sociology studies man as a social animal, and so on. Ethics, for its part, studies moral man, hence its alternative name, moral philosophy. It is possible that any one of the social sciences could study human behavior in a purely descriptive way. A sociologist, let us say, could be content simply with describing how human beings typically conduct themselves in various social settings, without necessarily feeling any need to evaluate the behaviors he describes. There is no concern with whether the described behaviors are good, bad, or indifferent, as judged from a moral point of view. This approach would be entirely different from that taken by ethics. In ethics, to be sure, we are concerned with describing how human beings behave, either as individuals or collectively, but we go beyond mere description. Ethics subjects human behavior to moral evaluation, determines whether it is good or bad according to established moral standards.

There is a tendency today in academic courses in ethics to come at the subject from the wrong end, beginning by looking at particular cases having to do with rare and extremely difficult moral problems, without first presenting and discussing the principles according to which those problems are to be assessed and then, the hope is, eventually resolved. This would be like asking someone who does not know the rules of chess to solve a difficult chess problem. Students without any systematic study of ethics in their background are confronted with a number of "hard cases," and are then unreasonably expected to be able to deal with them competently.

Case in point: You live in Germany; it is the early 1940s. Members of the Gestapo are banging on your door in the middle of the night. You open. They demand to know if you are hiding a Jewish family in your attic, which in fact you are. How are you going to handle this situation?

Case in point: You are in a lifeboat on the open sea with thirteen other people. It has been determined that there is only enough food and water for ten people until a rescue ship can be expected to arrive on the scene. It has been proposed that four of the people in the boat—two of whom are in their eighties, one a Down Syndrome child, the fourth in an advanced stage of cancer—be thrown overboard. A poll is taken of all the people in the boat to determine if this course should be followed. How would you react to a situation like this?

Case in point: You are the captain of a cruise ship sailing in Alaskan waters. The ship strikes a submerged iceberg. There is severe damage to the prow of the vessel and water is rushing into the hold. Unless you take quick action there is the real possibility that the ship will sink to the bottom with the loss of many lives. You have the option of closing water-tight bulkheads at midships, which will save the ship and the majority of the passengers, but the passengers and crew still in the forward sections of the ship will surely drown. As the captain of the ship, what would you decide to do, and why?

The Moral Framework

While it is highly unlikely that any of us will ever find ourselves in situations as dire as those just described, for which we can be thankful, all of us are faced at times with moral decisions which we find quite difficult enough, given the circumstances that attend them, and which severely test our moral mettle. How we come out of a situation in which we must make a difficult decision with serious moral implications all depends on how we enter into the situation, that is, on how well equipped we are mentally to be able to handle the decision in a morally competent manner. The decision stands the best chance of being sound if it is made by someone who has reached at least a minimal degree of moral maturity. The test of an ethical person, a morally upright human being, is that the person is able to do the right thing in the right way at the right time. This is no small order. Sound moral decisions do not come out of the blue; they are not the product of whim, or of chance. They have a foundation beneath them, a foundation made up of sound ethical principles.

A sound moral decision, even though it be quickly made and acted upon, invariably has a history of relevant deliberation and action behind it. It is made within a moral framework. When a major league baseball player steps up to the plate, he brings the knowledge of his whole baseball-playing past with him. So it is with all of us when we make significant ethical decisions; we come to those decisions informed by the knowledge of a moral code, and we make decisions according to the dictates of that code. The worth of the decisions will entirely depend on the worth of the code according to which they are made. There is even honor among thieves, as they say, but theirs is a specious honor, because it rests upon loyalty to a corrupt code.

It is not unusual to hear certain kinds of human behavior described as amoral. The term is commonly used, for example, to describe particularly egregious examples of Machiavellian machinations taking place in the world of politics, or as a reaction to especially horrific instances of "man's inhumanity to man." For all its prominence in popular usage, however, the term is a misnomer. There is no such thing as human behavior which is literally amoral, that is, behavior which is not framed within and guided by a morality. What is a morality, understood in a generic, not specifically determined way? It is simply a set of standards, be they simple or complex, be they seemly or unseemly, by which an adult, mentally competent human being assesses and guides his own behavior. Every adult human being who is not mentally impaired has a moral code, a set of moral standards, whatever be their quality looked at objectively, which determines his ideas about the nature of reality, defines what counts as good and bad for him, and sets the general pattern for all his actions.

What we usually mean when we call someone "amoral" is that he is "immoral," meaning that we judge the moral standards by which he lives to be totally unacceptable, for they are not in accord with certain basic standards of morality by which the behavior of all human beings should be guided. The only living beings that are strictly speaking amoral are plants and animals. We may have any number of indecorous things to say about poison ivy and mosquitoes, but we do not call them wicked for the negative effects they can have on our lives. The task for all of us, as moral agents, is to ensure that the moral code that shapes and governs our lives is sound, that it be one the moral standards of which are consonant with right reason, and can therefore be reasonably defended. A sound moral code provides us with a rational framework within which we can confidently direct the course of our lives. To establish whether or not our moral code is based on reason, we turn to ethics, moral philosophy; here we will find the basic principles that will instruct and guide us.

Consequential Decisions

Every decision we are called upon to make has consequences of one kind or another, and the weightier the consequences, the more serious the decision. Some decisions can be especially difficult to make for the unpleasant consequences that we expect them to have. To avoid them, we would prefer to avoid the decision. But if it is a decision that is unavoidably mine to make, to avoid it would be morally irresponsible. To be fully conscious, morally, is to have a keen sense of responsibility. We deceive ourselves if we think we can avoid consequences by avoiding making needed decisions, for failure to decide brings with it its own set of consequences, and they may turn out to be more negative than those we were trying to avoid by side-stepping the decision. Then there is this: calculating the consequences of a decision is often pretty much a guessing game, and we sometimes guess wrong. Life has its pleasant surprises as well as unpleasant ones, and on occasion the dire consequences we thought would follow our making a difficult decision do not follow. In any event, and here is a general common sense rule: seldom is it the case that failing to do something that demands to be done (e.g., making a difficult decision) will be free of negative ramifications. We dodge the rock Scylla only to be swallowed up by the whirlpool Charybdis.

We always make our significant moral moves, of whatever particular kind, within a moral framework, a morality; we never operate within what is effectively a vacuum. This morality is not something we invent; for most of us it is something we are born into and grow up with, maturing as we mature, and it shapes us into the kind of moral agents we turn out to be as adults. It gives us the moral code by which we direct the course of our lives. The quality, the moral soundness, of any particular morality is judged by comparing it with a morality that can claim primacy of place because of its antiquity and its universality. We recognize it as a moral code whose standards are so basic and so transparently integral to the race itself that they apply to and affect all human beings simply by reason of the fact that they are human beings. This is what has been traditionally known as the natural law, or the universal moral law. It is called the natural law because it applies to and is consonant with human nature. It can be identified as one of the fundamental aspects or features of our human nature because it is deeply embedded in that nature.

A Dissenting View

I will return to the very important subject of the natural law at the end of the chapter, but it would be appropriate at this point to call attention to the fact that for some two centuries now there have been philosophers who deny the existence of the natural law, rejecting the idea that there is a universal moral code. They take the position that there are no objective moral standards, no moral absolutes if you will, that apply to all human beings just as such. This position can trace its proximate origins to the eighteenth century and to the hyper-individualism it cultivated, and which, since then, has been a prominent feature of Western culture.

Existentialism, a philosophical movement that developed in France in the aftermath of World War Two, principally under the intellectual leadership of the formidable Jean-Paul Sartre, serves as a good example of a philosophy whose fostering of individualism went hand in hand with the rejection of objective moral standards. For existentialism, morality is not a given; it is something which, in effect, we construct as we proceed through life. But the theory goes even further than that: not only do we invent the moral code by which we live, we, on a deeper level, in effect invent ourselves as well. There is, according to Sartre, no human nature besides the one which is the summary effect of our actions.

Sartre recounts an incident which took place, I believe, when he was teaching in a secondary school in the northern part of France. A young man, one of his students, came to him for advice regarding an excruciatingly difficult decision he had to make. Should he go to England and join the French resistance army there? If he did, it would mean he, an only child, would leave behind a widowed mother, a poor woman, to fend for herself. How should he decide? Sartre's response was curt: "Just decide!" There were no general, governing standards to which the young man could appeal for guidance. One did not make decisions according to a code; one established the code by making the decisions. The goodness or the badness of a decision is determined by oneself. Sartre was a devout atheist who had no use for the gods, and that seemed to have led him to adopt the practice of burdening frail human beings with responsibilities which even the doughty Olympians would have found burdensome; they, after all, felt themselves subservient to Fate.

What are we to make of Sartre's advice? Presumably the young man to whom it was addressed, given the fact that he was a student in a French lycée, was quite intelligent. We should therefore expect him not to make a raw act of the will to settle a serious issue fraught with weighty consequences, that is, not to do so without long and deep deliberation before making his decision. We would hope that the young man would do that. As a result he should come to see that of the two obligations he is torn between honoring, the obligation he feels toward his country and that toward his mother, the latter takes precedence. There is no question that, given his widowed and impoverished mother's total dependence on him, he is obliged as a dutiful son to remain in France and take care of her.

The Human Act

The philosophical study of ethics, like the philosophical study of any other subject, begins with first principles. In the case of ethics, these principles form the foundation upon which rests the moral framework within which we live and act. We have described ethics as the evaluative study of human behavior, which is simply the sum total of individual human acts. We focus on the human act in order to assess it in terms of its being morally good or bad. But what is the character of an act which we identify precisely as a human act? That is the first question we need to address, for unless an act is a human act it is not a fit subject for moral assessment.

Moral philosophy attaches special significance to what it designates as a human act. In ordinary usage we take the term human act to be simply an act performed by a human being, and there would be no argument with that way of taking it. But according to the specialized meaning ethics gives to the term, we call a human act one that is (a) conscious, (b) deliberate, and (c) freely chosen. I am sitting at my desk with a book in front of me, trying to puzzle my way through a particularly convoluted philosophical argument, and in the midst of which I raise my right arm and scratch the side of my head. I did that more or less unconsciously; it is not something I thought about beforehand, and I certainly did not make anything like a formal decision to perform the act. Given its source, we say that it is an act of a human being, but not a human act, because it lacked the features, noted above, to qualify as the latter. We have two other names for a human act; we call it a moral act, and a voluntary act. Perhaps voluntary act is the best term to use, for it explicitly expresses the key feature of the act, its voluntariness. It is only when we act consciously, deliberately, and willingly that we act as full-fledged moral agents.

For any act to be unambiguously a human act, we must know what we are doing when we are performing the act, and we must be doing it willingly. It is the presence of those two factors, knowledge and will, that makes an act clearly moral, and therefore subject to moral assessment as either good or bad. If an act is assessed as good, we praise it; if the assessment of the act is negative, we blame it. If someone through his actions brings about what is, objectively considered, a clearly good result, but if he does so completely by accident, by dumb luck we might say, we usually do not shower him with praise. On the other hand, if a person is forced to do something which is objectively wrong, acting at gunpoint let us say, and we know that person would never have freely chosen to do the act under normal circumstances, we would not consider the person blameworthy, as if he had done the act in an unqualifiedly voluntarily way. In a situation such as that his voluntariness would certainly be qualified.

Motivation

What moves us to act, to do the things we consciously choose to do? It is simply the fact that we have some kind of end in mind, a purpose we seek to achieve. That end or purpose might be rather trivial, like going to the kitchen to get a drink of water to assuage one's thirst, or handing a clerk some money to buy a newspaper. Or the end or purpose pursued might be of major, life-altering proportions, as in the case of George proposing marriage to Georgia, or Martha deciding to enter medical school. Whatever the nature or quality of the ends toward which we direct our actions, be they large or small in importance, what invariably motivates us to seek those ends is the fact that we regard them as good. I mean good here as understood in a very basic and individual-specific sense. It is good as it is taken to be such by the subject who chooses to pursue it. We always act to achieve ends which we take to be, once achieved, beneficial to us in one way or another. This is a key point. We are constitutionally incapable of desiring to achieve something which we think will be bad for us, even though our chosen good, objectively considered, may in fact be bad. The suicide looks upon his death as something beneficial, therefore good; he regards the cessation of life better than its continuation. He is fatally wrong, of course, but he could not have chosen suicide if he had not tragically persuaded himself that it was a good-for-him.

One of the hallmarks of our status as moral agents is that we always act for the sake of an end; we are inveterately purposeful creatures. And because we always select our ends in the light of the fact that we regard them as good, the two terms, end and good, can be considered virtually synonymous, looked at from a practical point of view.

Are we always right in selecting the ends we set out to attain, in determining what would be truly good for us? How lovely it would be were that the case, but we all know from our own experience that the lovely does not always happen. We have gone after things because we thought at the time that they were worth going after—and we had to think that, otherwise we would not have gone after them—only to have to admit later, regretfully, that we were mistaken. Given the all too common experiences of that sort, in ethics we make an important distinction between *true goods*, goods whose attainment will really be to our benefit because they will contribute to our betterment as human persons, and *apparent* or *false goods*, whose attainment will have just the opposite effect. Zeno choosing to have a martini may have certain limited benefits for him. His deciding to have a fifth martini is not at all a good idea, especially if he intends to drive home after the party.

Happiness

Aristotle was the first philosopher to think extensively and systematically about ethical issues, so much so that he arguably can be considered the father of the science of ethics. There were thinkers before him whose writings gave much attention to ethical questions—one thinks especially of Plato, to whom Aristotle was indebted for many of his ideas—but he was the first to organize basic ethical questions and treat them systematically, thus laying the foundation for a science. In developing that science he took due note of the fact that it is the salient mark of the human agent to act *purposely*. Every conscious act that we perform has a purpose behind it, necessarily; it is purpose that defines the act. Aristotle then raised the question whether there was a single purpose that served as the end and basic explanation for *all* human acts, a single end that was the goal of all human striving. Was there one thing the pursuit and attainment of which motivates everything we do, a prize possession all of us want? He decided that there was: it is happiness. And with that he identified what was to become one of the key concepts in his ethical theory. It has much to offer us.

If we were to ask just about anyone we know, and strangers as well, what was behind all the major moves they have made in their lives or, more broadly, what now, generally, are they most looking for in life, chances are we would get responses that explicitly or implicitly had to do with the idea of happiness. And we would not be terribly surprised by this. Who, in this wide world of ours, does not want to be happy? But if there would be common agreement that happiness is the principal purpose behind everything we do, what we are always striving for, we would get a disparity of responses if we were to ask people what they meant by happiness; what was it, specifically, they were striving to achieve? Happiness could be described as a state in which people are generally content, they are in the main satisfied with their lot in life. But what is the cause of that contentment, that satisfaction?

Aristotle had his own idea as to what happiness was essentially all about, and he was acutely aware that it conflicted with several other ideas current in his day, ideas which, he believed, were radically inadequate. It was clear to him that just as we can be wrong about particular goods, mistaking apparent or false goods for true ones, so we can be wrong about happiness itself. Among the ways we can be wrong about happiness is to equate it with pleasure, or to think it consists in the possession of power, or to associate happiness with riches, or to think that honors or fame are the keys to happiness. These and like ideas about the nature of happiness, true happiness, miss the point, fail to recognize what should be the principal end of human action. Aristotle's idea of happiness will doubtless sound dissonant to modern ears, as it did to many ears in ancient Greece. I will first simply state it, then explain its implications. Happiness, for Aristotle, was a life lived in accordance with virtue. In short, a happy life is a virtuous life.

The first thing to note about happiness, thus understood, is that it is something which is under the control of the individual. Happiness is not some kind of serendipitous state that one sunny day just falls out of the sky on us, or that we stumble upon by chance, as if it were nothing more than the result of luck. Whether or not we are happy, in the final analysis, is entirely up to us; it is something for which we alone are responsible. We make it happen, and we do so by our actions, by the way we consistently behave over the long haul, throughout the course of our entire lives. Happiness, then, consists in a specific and very special way of living one's life, in such a way that is consistent with, and reflects, the key virtues of prudence, justice, fortitude, and temperance, from which all the many other virtues flow, and about which we will have more to say presently.

The Aristotelian understanding of the nature of happiness is radically human. To live a life of virtue is to fully come into our own as human beings, as rational creatures for whom mind matters most. To pursue virtue is to pursue the good, the true good, the attainment of which is not only beneficial, but necessary, for genuinely human fulfillment. A virtuous life, then, is not simply a particular lifestyle, one among many, that one can casually choose not to choose, and still continue to be serious about the question of what it means be human. Rightly understood, a happy life is simply a human life, given our nature, as it should be.

We would seem to have in the Aristotelian notion of happiness, as a life lived according to virtue, what has all the earmarks of the perfect plan for complete human fulfillment, leading to unmitigated happiness. Or do we? In the last part of his principal book on ethics, Aristotle discusses a life given over to contemplation as the culmination of a virtuous life, but even with that he expresses doubts that in this life our natural end, happiness as complete human fulfillment, can ever be realized. At this point Thomas Aquinas, Aristotle's greatest commentator, enters the discussion and makes the arresting argument that a natural desire which is as central and deep-seated as our desire for happiness cannot be frustrated. But that happiness, if it is to entail human fulfillment in the most comprehensive sense, must have two basic conditions attached to it: it must be complete, and it must be permanent. These conditions cannot be met in this world, only in the life to come.

Knowingly and Willingly

But the height of happiness to be reached in this world consists in a life that is lived virtuously; there is no disagreement between Aquinas and Aristotle on that score. This is a happiness which is one and the same with our behavior; it is the accompanying effect of how we choose to live out our lives, grounded in individual acts. We have noted that for an act to qualify as a human or moral act it must be done knowingly and willingly. How could it be otherwise? Unless a person is asleep or narcotized in some way, is not that person fully aware, while deliberately performing a given act, of what the act is all about? Well, not necessarily. Particular acts can have degrees of awareness associated with them; there can be certain ramifications to our acts which we might be quite ignorant of while performing them. I perform Act A to bring about the intended result B; unbeknownst to me, however, in performing Act A I am also bringing about result C, which I do not at all intend, and which turns out to be something definitely negative. We need an example to clarify that point.

Mr. Stevenson is the principal of Optimum High School in Upbeat, Utah. One night he continued working in his office long after the school had closed for the day, writing a lengthy report he had to submit to the district superintendent. It was ten o'clock before he was finally able to lock up and head for home. As he was walking down the hall and passing the gym he noticed through the door windows that the lights were on. He thought that strange. He knew the basketball team had practiced that afternoon, and supposed the coach forgot to turn off the lights after practice. But to make sure the gym was in fact empty he stepped inside and called out, "Anyone in here?" No answer. He waited a few seconds and called out again, a bit louder. Still no answer. With that he went to a master switch near the door, pulled it, and the gym went dark. Continuing down the hall to the exit door he grumbled to himself at the carelessness of some people, what with the size of the electric bills he has to pay. Well, at least he did his bit for the day in the cause of conserving energy.

What Mr. Stevenson did not know was that Maggie the night janitress was in a workroom at the end of a short hallway at the opposite end of the gym, filling a bucket with which she was going to do some wet mopping around the periphery of the court. Then she would finish dry mopping the court, which she had left half completed. Because of the noise of the splashing water, plus the fact that Maggie's hearing was less than it should be, she did not hear Mr. Stevenson when he called out. She was surprised when she came out of the workroom and saw that the gym was dark. Who could have shut the lights off? She was a bit irritated at that, but there was nothing to do but get them back on again. In making her way through the darkened gym she tripped over the dry mop which she had left on the court at the place where she had left off, something she habitually did. She took a rather hard fall, with her right arm receiving the brunt of the shock. Mouthing a few choice expletives, she got up, made it the rest of the way to the master switch, and once again the gym was illuminated. She managed to finish the rest of her work efficiently enough that night, but her right arm was giving her considerable pain. She decided, when she left the school at eleven, that she would drop by the emergency room at a nearby hospital and have the arm looked at. As it turned out, Maggie had a seriously broken arm, and she spent the next few weeks wearing a cast.

Now, it could be said that Mr. Stevenson was the cause, at least remotely, of Maggie's broken arm, for if he had not turned off the gym lights Maggie would have had no reason to cross the court to turn them back on again, and therefore would not have fallen and suffered a broken arm. All that is true enough, but it would be rash of us to regard Mr. Stevenson as being blameworthy for Maggie's broken arm. Yes, he had turned off the gym lights, but in doing so he was ignorant of the fact that there was anyone in the gym. He had conscientiously thought of the possibility that there might be someone there, and he took all reasonable steps to ensure that the gym was in fact empty before he pulled the master switch. Mr. Stevenson cannot be held to be morally responsible for Maggie's mishap. He was ignorant of the consequences of his act, but his ignorance was not culpable.

Not all ignorance is excusable. In the previous chapter on epistemology, recall that we identified something called privative ignorance, ignorance for which one is culpable. Jasper performed an act that had damaging consequences. In performing the act he was not aware that those consequences would inevitably follow from it. But Jasper's ignorance was culpable, for, given his position and responsibilities, he was ignorant of something which he should have known regarding the nature of his act and of its consequences. He can therefore be fittingly blamed for his act.

Because we must know what we are doing in order to be morally responsible for an act, non-privative ignorance excuses. Besides knowing what we are doing, in the way explained, we have to will what we are doing. If we are forced to do something against our will, we cannot without qualification be said to be morally responsible for the act. Physical coercion would be a clear case where the will is directly thwarted, but there is psychological coercion as well, examples of which would be a situation where one is responding to blackmail, or to the ransom demands of kidnappers. Sometimes our will may be thwarted, not because of malicious actions on the part of others, but simply because of circumstances over which we have no control. Nora cannot be blamed for missing her best friend's wedding in California, at which she was to act as maid of honor, because all the flights out of Denver were cancelled because of a major snow storm, and she had to spend a frustrating two days in an airport terminal filled with disgruntled travelers.

A basic principle needs to be emphasized here: It goes without saying that if we are not free agents, then we are not moral agents in any meaningful sense of the term. If we are not the conscious, originating source of our acts, if we do not freely choose to act or refrain from acting, if we are not responsible for our choices, then ethics is no more a science than is astrology or numerology, and we are wasting our time with it.

Conscience

As responsible moral agents, we are under strict obligation, in making and then acting upon our decisions, to follow our conscience. That is one of the basic principles of the moral life; it needs some explaining. Does it mean that so long as I follow the dictates of my conscience I can be morally assured that I will be always doing the right thing? That would be an opinion that enjoys, it seems, much currency today, but it needs to be challenged.

What is conscience? Some people entertain an idea of conscience which suggests the pseudo-mystical, conceiving it to be something like a second and wiser self, nestled snugly deep within the psyche, which is always on the ready, in tough situations, to communicate to the anxious heart, in a small, hushed voice, just the advice needed to make the right decision every time. This makes for a nicely convenient arrangement, for apparently all you have to do is be docilely receptive to what your conscience tells you, and you cannot go wrong. One can confidently heed the voice of conscience, for it is virtually infallible in what it has to say. "I cannot act in any other way than I do, for I am only following my conscience." That seemingly is to be taken as the final word on the matter.

The problem with the pseudo-mystical view of conscience is that it creates a false duality within the moral agent, between conscience on the one hand, and the acting person on the other. The two, in fact, are one and the same. Conscience is not something, it is someone, and that someone is you. To speak more precisely, what we call conscience is simply the human intellect, the mind, functioning in a significantly specialized way, that is, by making judgments as to what is the good to be done and the evil to be avoided. Clementine is properly following her conscience when, through reasoning, she makes the correct distinctions regarding moral right and wrong, and then acts according to those distinctions. There is no more mystery about conscience than that.

It is naïve to suppose that conscience is infallible. That would be like saying that a person can never make a mistake in distinguishing between right and wrong, a position which our own experiences would be unlikely to lend much support. A key point bears repeating: conscience is simply the name we give to the judgments we make regarding moral matters. We are no more infallible in making judgments regarding moral matters than we are in making judgments about things in general. Even a person who subscribes to a sound moral code and who for the most part faithfully abides by it can sometimes lapse and make an erroneous judgment, one that contradicts the code to which he subscribes. So it happens with Roland on occasion. And in response to such occasions, we, who know the man well, will say something like: Roland is going against his better judgment, acting out of character.

Now let us consider a very serious state of affairs. Our subject is Disordered Dick, who, almost from the time of his birth, has been subjected to, victimized by, it would not be an exaggeration to say, the worst possible environment conceivable in which to be raised, with regard to family life, with regard to the quality of the formal education to which he was exposed, with regard to the overall social environment in which he grew to physical maturity. By the time Dick was twenty-one he had established a working moral code for himself. The code was not very elaborate, nor sophisticated; in fact, it was rather crude. As to its particular principles, they represented a marked departure from the commonly agreed-upon standards for civilized human behavior. For example, according to Dick's thinking, stealing was not wrong, nor was lying, nor was making promises that he did not intend to keep. He had become quite good at stealing, and he found lying as one of the more effective means by which to make one's way in what he regarded as a rotten and hostile world.

In these and other ways it can be said that Dick was sincerely following his conscience; the problem was the condition of the conscience he is following. His conscience was severely bent out of shape. Traditionally, a conscience in that condition is referred to as a corrupt conscience. What does that mean, concretely, in terms of what we have said about the nature of conscience? It means that, given the circumstances in which he was raised, Dick never developed the habit of making sound judgments regarding the nature of right and wrong and the critical difference between the two. But note this, to repeat an important point: Dick always acted to achieve ends that he thought were good for him. He could not have done otherwise, for we always act to achieve ends that we perceive to be good. The trouble is that our perceptions can be quite wrong, and such was the case with Dick more often than not.

How are we morally to evaluate Dick's situation? He did not choose the circumstances into which he was born and in which he was raised. It was not his fault that he was deprived of a healthy moral education, as the result of which he did not form the habit as he was growing up of consistently making sound judgments regarding right and wrong. Does that mean that Dick should be seen as completely blameless with regard to the state of his conscience, that he is in no way morally responsible for his current situation? That would be going too far. Certainly, given the circumstances of his birth and raising, his responsibility for how he thinks and acts is mitigated, but it cannot be reduced to zero. To argue that he is not at all responsible for his present state, as some people today are inclined to argue, would be effectively to deprive him of his fundamental dignity as a human being, a rational creature endowed with free will. For one thing, it would be hard to imagine that over the course of his growing-up years Dick was not exposed from time to time to people and circumstances that would have stirred up his latent moral consciousness, enlightening him to the point where he could have at least begun to work on developing a healthy conscience, but he chose not to. That choice would have made him responsible for the wayward conscience with which he is now burdened. And there is another factor to consider, a large one, and that is the natural law. It is part of Dick's nature that he has within him something like an intuitive sense that certain things are just plain wrong. He may be adept at stealing, but he steals selectively; he would never steal from people he considers friends. And there is something else, rather interesting: every once in a while, in a pensive mood, it strikes him that he has never lied to his girlfriend Rosaline, nor made promises to her he didn't keep, and he can't imagine acting any differently towards her. That thought always gives him pause. Might we not have there the seeds for a possible moral awakening?

Should reflecting on cases such as Dick's lead us to the conclusion that we ought to amend the basic principle that we should always follow our conscience? No. The principle stands firm: we must always follow our conscience, but we must take the greatest care to ensure that our conscience is worth following. That simply means that we must be certain that the judgments we make regarding moral matters are sound, i.e., that they are in accordance with right reason. Guided by reason, we make moral judgments that are sound because, say, they reflect a moral code which is itself sound. A person with a healthy conscience is one who consistently makes the right choices regarding what is right and what is wrong.

Morality and Reason

The judgments of conscience, as noted, are acts of the intellect, and thus the products of reason. If we are to live up to our identity as rational animals, it

behooves us to act reasonably in whatever we do, but especially in the judgments we make regarding moral matters. In our study of logic we saw that
to reason well is to do nothing more than to think clearly about the way
things actually are; it is to be on consistently friendly terms with reality.
Morality and reason are inextricably intertwined with one another, so much
so that it prompted Thomas Aquinas to maintain that the essence of sin is
irrationality. To be a morally bad person is to be a radically unreasonable
person, while conversely the morally upright person is one who is known
for his consistently rational behavior. When Dick acts immorally, the first
person he is always harming is himself,

What is involved, specifically, in forging a happy fusion between morality and rationality? How do we act rationally as moral agents? It cannot be
only a matter of following a moral code, irrespective of the quality of that
code. Disordered Dick was wonderfully consistent in following the dictates
of his own moral code, but that moral code was a decidedly distorted one.
Rational moral thinking is indeed reflected in consistently following a moral
code, but that code must be sound, meaning that it must have an objective
basis to it; it must be consonant, to put the matter in the broadest terms,
with reality. How to determine whether a particular moral code is objectively grounded, is consonant with reality, is a most important question,
and is one which we shall address in due course.

Morality and Emotion

There is no major ethical system, originating in the East or in the West,
which does not lay great stress on the fact that our emotions must be governed by reason. We cannot expect to live a stable, coherent moral life if
reason does not reign, maintaining a steady monitoring watch over our
emotions lest they should get out of hand. This is an arrangement the rightness of which we can easily confirm simply by consulting our own experience. Earlier we cited the psychological principle, also readily confirmed
by personal experience, which recognizes the inverse relation between intensity of emotion and clarity of thought. In more cases than not, the more
intense an emotional state, the less capable we are of thinking clearly. Clear,
controlled thinking is important no matter the subject of our thought, but
it is especially important when we are thinking about and making decisions

about moral matters. What is at stake here is the quality of human acts, which cumulatively go to shape the history of each individual and, for that matter, of the entire human race as well. The destiny of a nation is determined by the sum total of the individuals acts of those who make up the membership of that nation.

Today there is a fair number of people, with some philosophers to be counted among them, who would take exception to the time-honored rule that reason must be the governing factor in the moral life. In fact, they would assume just the opposite point of view, arguing that emotion, our feelings, should be the governing factor in our thinking and acting. Some philosophers I have read go so far as to maintain that we should be guided by our feelings because feelings themselves are invested with a kind of reason. And they might quote Blaise Pascal's famous quip that, "The heart has its reasons that reason knows nothing of," taking "heart" to represent the emotions. The philosophers I alluded to certainly have an interesting point of view, but it does not represent sound human psychology. Our intellectual powers and our emotive powers are of two quite different kinds; we might say that they are on entirely different tracks. To be able to reason there must be the capacity to think, to generate ideas, and to be able to put ideas together constructively. Our emotions do not think, nor generate ideas, nor construct arguments; they simply emote. That is their job, and they do it quite well. The source of their power, which is considerable, is visceral, not intellectual. To be guided by our emotions is to put ourselves in tow of forces which, taken just in themselves, that is, unguided by reason, are sightless and mindless. This is not to denigrate the emotions; in Chapter Three we stressed the point that they are intrinsically good. We could not live without them. We simply would not be human without them.

But once again, our emotions must not govern, but be governed. As governed they are companionable helpmates, for they work cooperatively with reason, aiding and abetting it, and in a certain sense enriching its operations. The quality of the thought of a philosopher who takes justifiable pleasure in his thinking is for that reason, one may reasonably surmise: thought that is better than it otherwise would be.

Let us examine the question more closely, and ask why it is that emotion is unfit to be the governing factor in the moral life. It comes down to a matter of pure practicality, which is just where we want to be, for the moral life is all about practicality. For any human society, such as a political community, to be able to exist at all, there must be among the members of the society, and despite what differences may divide them on other issues, common agreement on certain basic ideas relating to the rights and wrongs of human behavior, for if there were no such consensus, and assuming that state of affairs goes uncorrected, the society would eventually simply implode. There must be a pool of shared ideas regarding morality, though these ideas need not necessarily be explicitly expressed, such as in the form of laws or regulations; their operative presence would be attested to simply by the stable state of the society itself. It is the very nature of ideas, the products of the human mind, that they can be shared; they can have a public dimension to them, so that they are recognized, understood, and agreed upon by many. It is reason, working with shared ideas, that makes human community possible.

This is something that emotion, left to itself, is unable to effect. Our emotions declare themselves with abrupt immediacy, and that is just what we would want; they come in, as it were, ahead of thought. Take the emotion of fear; it is a first response to something sensed, not thought of, as fearful. Then reason must enter the scene, which often takes the form of the cogitative sense, which tells us the nature of what we are emotionally responding to. Is our fear rational or irrational? The fear itself cannot tell us that, for it is unreasoning. Sometimes we realize, either immediately or retrospectively, that our fearful response was not warranted, that our fear was irrational; sometimes our fear is quite rational, however, and we take action accordingly. In either case fear is under the guidance of reason.

There are few things more intensely private, more individual specific, than emotion, which means that, just as emotion, it is never faultlessly communicable. We can share ideas about emotions, and we can imagine what the emotions of others must be alike because, either on the basis of what they tell us about them, or simply by observing their behavior (they are laughing uproariously or weeping uncontrollably), we compare their identified emotional states, as reported or observed, with emotional states of like kind which we have experienced ourselves. But we cannot actually participate in or share the emotion of another, precisely as the emotion of the other. I may say to a friend, "I feel your pain," and am in earnest in saying so, meaning I have genuine sympathy or, more deeply, empathy, for what my friend is experiencing. What I am directly experiencing are my ideas, or my imaginings, of what his pain must be like, again, by comparing the information I have about his emotional experiences with what I take to be like experiences that I myself have known. When I say, "I feel your pain," what I am feeling is not my friend's feelings but my own. But they are directly related to what I know of my friend's state, and they can be quite strong, causing me much distress, perhaps affecting my day-to-day life for extended periods.

The only way we can effectively get to the feelings of others, and we can— that is what sympathy and empathy are all about—is by relying on something other than feelings alone. We would be making a mistake should we suppose that a real person-to-person bond can be forged between two people, where the full personhood of each is involved, if feelings are given primacy of place, to the point where mind is minimized. In such a case there would not be the kind of meeting of minds which ensures a coming together that is fully human, personal through and through.

Let us now apply these considerations to the moral realm. If my feelings tell me that Act X is morally right, and your feelings tell you just the opposite, we twain shall never meet. So long as we are guided dominantly by feelings, we will never be able to find any common ground on which we can stand and communicate intelligibly with one another. Eventually we would have to advert to reason, if we want to live together in community. Otherwise it seems the only alternative would be to repair to the desert and live as aberrant hermits, meditating on our emotions.

Virtue

Happiness, of the kind which is within our power to achieve in this world, is a life lived in accordance with virtue. Our purpose, in studying ethics, which is much concerned with the subject of virtue, must be practical. Ethics identifies itself as a practical science, a brain child of the practical intellect. We should want to know moral theory not just to know the theory, but in order to apply the theory to our own lives. With regard to virtue specifically, we want to know its general nature, and we want to know the nature of particular virtues such as prudence, justice, fortitude, and temperance, not so that we can impress people at cocktail parties with our ethical erudition, but so that we can make those virtues an integral part of our lives. I should want to know all about justice, for example, so that I finally turn out to be a reasonably just man. Purely theoretical knowledge of ethical lore is sterile.

Let us back up a bit and begin at the beginning, with questions that lead to definitions and explanations. What is virtue, and why is it central to the moral life? Our English word virtue, like so many of our English words, has its roots in Latin, specifically in the word *virtus*, which means strength, power, ability. That information reveals the basic character of any virtue: it is a capacity, an enabling power, which allows us to act in a consistently effective way with respect to a specific kind of action. A virtue is obviously a positive capacity, so that the action it enables is ordered toward what is truly good. A virtue, once possessed, becomes a permanent part of the possessing person, and that is one of its most beneficial features. Virtues do not come and go like moods; they are permanently in place, readily available, and can be called upon as needed.

The permanency of virtues is attributable to the fact that they are habits. A habit is a fixed disposition. Dispositions, in turn, are simply the sum total of the strengths, weaknesses, talents, and propensities of various kinds with which we are naturally endowed. We are born with them, in most cases. Aristotle, you might recall, put dispositions in the category of quality. Together they compose what is commonly called one's natural temperament or personality. Because a virtue is a habit, a fixed disposition, it is not easily lost, and that is what makes it especially valuable. A just person, someone who possesses the virtue of justice, does not suddenly become unjust because on a given occasion he commits an unjust act. The exceptional ballplayer who regularly bats over .300 does not cease to be exceptional because he has a bad day at the plate and strikes out three times. If a habit is a bad one, on the other hand, it is just that much more difficult to get rid of, as we know by experience. This is as true of physical habits as it is of intellectual or moral ones.

Our natural dispositions, taking them all in all, tend to be a rather mixed bag: some are positive, in the possibilities they offer for beneficial development; others negative, for their development would not be to a person's benefit, hence they need to be curbed rather than developed. For example, one person might be naturally outgoing and industrious, while another might be naturally lethargic and overly timorous. We are not virtuous by nature; that is the bad news. The good news is that all of us, whatever the set of natural dispositions with which we are endowed, have a natural inclination, an ingrained orientation, toward virtue. All human beings, by nature, are ordered toward the good. It is our task, by our actions, to foster and nurture what is essential to our nature. Hector may not be a paragon of virtue, and in his more introspective and honest moments he does not feel particularly good about himself for just that reason. That is because he has this natural inclination to virtue, to be other, to be better, than he is right now. By not pursuing virtue as he should be doing, he is not responding positively to the tendencies of his deepest self, is not living up to his status as a rational creature.

As with happiness in general, so with virtue in particular; it is something we ourselves must bring about, through our conscious, deliberate actions. The process begins with a firm act of the will on our part; we must want to acquire a particular virtue, then we must roll up our sleeves and do the work that acquisition requires.

Consider the pattern of actions we follow when we want to acquire certain physical habits, like playing tennis reasonably well, or mastering a musical instrument. If we want to become a competent pianist, or even a proficient one, we start by becoming acquainted with the rudiments, and the rest is a matter of practice, practice, practice. The same holds true when it comes to the acquisition of the moral virtues, let us say the virtue of justice. First, we must make ourselves aware of what the virtue entails. That might require some doing when it comes to some of the finer aspects of the virtue, but in the main the first steps are easily enough taken, for all of us have a quasi-intuitive understanding of justice; it comes with our basic nature as social animals. The process is quite uncomplicated. So, as there is no other way of learning how to play the piano than by playing the piano, by the same token there is no other way of acquiring the virtue of justice than by repetitively acting in a just way. In either case, no shortcuts are available.

Initially the going can be fairly rough, especially if acting in a consistently just manner has previously not been a notable aspect of one's general behavior. Such a person would be burdened with a number of bad habits that he will need to get out of his system. He will be clumsy, will make mistakes, will occasionally revert to his old ways, as it might be with a beginning pianist, unless he happens to be another Mozart. If we are persistent and persevering in our efforts to acquire a particular virtue, eventually it will be fixed in place, will become a permanent part of who we are. Once that happy stage is reached, acting in a consistently just manner will not demand great effort of us, it will become natural; it could be positively pleasurable at times. Why should one not be gratefully pleased at being able to act virtuously?

Again, a virtue, once acquired, becomes a permanent possession. Does that mean that an acquired virtue can never be lost? No. The permanency of any moral virtue is contingent upon our continuing to practice the virtue, and with the same intensity with which it was initially acquired. Every athlete and musician knows, especially if they are professionals, that if they cease to practice or get lackadaisical or sloppy in the way they practice, they will lose their edge and performance will suffer. If they really get careless, once-loyal fans might begin to boo, and the applause at concerts will be restrained and muted, polite patter. In like manner, the moral virtues need constant, conscientious attention. It is a truism of the moral life that if we are not moving forward we are slipping backward.

The Cardinal Virtues

The four virtues that I named earlier—prudence, justice, fortitude, temperance—are called the cardinal virtues, and they are the chief, the most basic, of the moral virtues. They are called cardinal virtues because all the other virtues hinge upon them. ("Cardinal" comes from the Latin *cardinalis*, which means chief or principal, which in turn is rooted in *cardo*, which means hinge.) Of the four cardinal virtues by far and away the most important is prudence, and that is because it governs the other three. To properly understand that virtue we must first rid ourselves of what tends to be the popular view of it. According to that view, prudence is taken to be a kind of calculated, self-protective cunning. A prudent person would then be understood as one who carefully watches his step so he doesn't make any false moves, doesn't say or do anything that will prove disadvantageous to him. While that might in some cases be a very narrow application of prudence, it is by no means the essence of the virtue. Prudence, rightly understood, is the virtue that governs not only the three other cardinal virtues but one's entire moral life, and that is what makes it so important.

It is the virtue that lends to the mind that clarity of vision, sharpness of discrimination, and steadfastness of purpose which enables us to make sound judgments of conscience. A prudent person is one who has a vivid sense of the elementary difference between moral right and wrong, and acts accordingly. An imprudent person, on the other hand, would be someone who is lacking those crucial capacities; his typical state would be one of mental disorientation. Recalling for a moment Disordered Dick, we can say that his basic problem is that he very much lacks the virtue of prudence.

Justice is classically defined as that virtue by which we give to each person what is due to the person. What that amounts to, on the most rudimentary level, is acknowledging and honoring the fundamental natural and inalienable rights possessed by every human being, the most fundamental of which would of course be the right to life. Justice is the preeminent social virtue, for without its operative presence, at least at a minimal level, no society deserving of being called human could endure. The only truly human society is a just society. In a political community, once justice becomes negligible, tyranny, in one form or another, takes over. We act justly toward our neighbors on a daily basis when we deal with them openly and honestly, eschewing grossly uncivil behaviors such as lying, cheating, and stealing.

Of all the emotions that are integral to our make-up, fear is potentially the most debilitating. It must be kept under constant control, and the virtue that enables us to do that is fortitude or courage. Aristotle, in his treatment of the virtues, saw the essence of each virtue as the mean or middle ground between the extremes of defect and excess. So, in the case of courage the defect to be avoided would be cowardice, where fear is allowed to take over and govern our actions. It can never be a matter of removing fear altogether, but rather of preventing it from so affecting our mind that we are incapable of thinking clearly about what we must do in tight situations. A courageous person is not a fearless person, but one who looks fear in the face and stares it down. To be utterly without fear would be positively dangerous; a controlled fear is on our side, alerting us to the presence of real dangers and enabling us to deal with them effectively. The opposite extreme of fortitude from cowardice is recklessness. If a person debilitated by fear cannot be considered courageous, neither can the person who habitually fails to face dangerous situations rationally. The behavior of the reckless man is such that his actions are not sufficiently tempered by a healthy fear. In tight situations he can be a danger to himself and others, precisely because his actions are not accompanied by sufficient premeditated thought.

Temperance is the virtue by which we moderate and keep from gaining the ascendancy in our lives those potent sense pleasures having to do with eating, drinking, and sexual desire. It is the very potency of these pleasures that makes the proper governance of them a full-time job. All of these pleasures are good in themselves, and needless to say the activities associated with them are necessary: if we do not get sufficient food and drink, our health suffers; if man and woman do not meet, marry, and procreate, the race does not survive. But we know what happens to people who lack the virtue of temperance; they turn into sorry types: the glutton, the sot, the profligate. To be without temperance is to lose control of ourselves at a very elementary level, and that necessarily has deleterious consequences for the whole of one's life. There is no more onerous and confining kind of subservience than being a drudge to one's own emotions turned tyrannical.

Moral Relativism

Moral relativism is a specific expression of epistemological relativism, the erroneous position which denies that there are any fixed truths. For the epistemological relativist truth itself is variable and is constantly subject to change. What was considered to be true yesterday might be false today, and yesterday's falsity might turn out to be today's truth. Person A takes to be true what Person B takes to be false, and vice versa, and that represents, supposedly, an unavoidable state of affairs for which there is no remedy. Moral relativism is simply epistemological relativism as applied to the moral realm. If one sees no stability and permanency to truth in general, he would then be blind to the stability and permanency of truth as it relates to moral issues. This being the way the two positions are related to one another, if epistemological relativism can be shown to be untenable, then it would follow that a specific manifestation of it, moral relativism, is also untenable. It would be suitable to insert here a brief version of the argument.

Epistemological relativism can be shown to be untenable, in the first place, because it cannot even state its basic principle, "all truth is relative," without undermining the very position it is advocating, for the expectation is that the basic principle, when stated, is to be accepted as absolutely true.

The relativist thus turns out to be a crypto-absolutist. Secondly, anyone seriously subscribing to epistemological relativism would have to be prepared to reject, or call into question with compelling reasons for doing so, a countless number of facts that could not possibly be other than what they are, that is, simply and immutably true: Paris is north of Marseille; Washington was the first president of the United States; the whole is greater than any of its parts; if equals are added to equals the sums are equal; four is the square root of sixteen; the Detroit Tigers won the 1945 World Series, etc., etc., etc. In sum, because epistemological relativism is untenable, so is moral relativism, for it is simply a particular expression of epistemological relativism.

However, the matter must not be left at that, for there are some who, while rejecting epistemological relativism, are nonetheless insistent on holding to moral relativism, maintaining that, specifically within the realm of morals, there are no fixed and invariable truths. That point requires special emphasis. What I am calling moral relativism is the position that denies that there are any fundamental, immutable moral truths—we can appropriately call them moral absolutes—which are universal in the sense that they apply to all human beings in all places and at all times. One of the most comprehensive of such truths is that it is always wrong to do wanton harm to anyone. More specific expressions of that comprehensive truth would be: it is always wrong to murder; it is always wrong to steal; it is always wrong to lie. (Aristotle would add adultery to the list.) If fundamental moral truths of this kind were not abided by, human society would be impossible.

To condemn moral relativism, as just defined, is not to deny that there is a perfectly legitimate, and even necessary, kind of relativism that enters into moral reasoning. There are certain very general principles pertaining to the natural law that are invariably true and must be respected as such. But precisely because they are general principles, they cannot be applied indiscriminately, in precisely the same way to everyone. They must be applied relatively, that is, relative to particular persons and to the particular conditions and circumstances pertaining to them. The more particular the circumstances, the more judicious must be the application of the general principle.

The advocates of moral relativism imply that the position they defend is sound because it is based on what is simply a matter of fact. Of course they are right if all they mean is that today moral relativism is an undeniably sociological fact, and a significant one at that. In other words, there are a great many people in contemporary society who subscribe to, and pattern their behavior after the dictates of, moral relativism. But it is a large mistake to conclude that because there are many people today who subscribe to moral relativism, and guide their lives accordingly, therefore the position they represent is a rational one. Non sequitur. It is incontestably the case that in contemporary society there is not to be found anything like unanimity of agreement regarding a wide range of fundamental moral issues. People take diametrically opposed positions on a wide range of very important moral questions. There is a critically important difference to be recognized between moral relativism as a sociological fact and moral relativism as a defensible philosophical position, just as there is a difference to be noted between the fact of a Marxist government and the quality of the philosophical theory of Marxism. Citing the factual presence, even dominance, of moral relativism in a given society is no argument for its authenticity and authority as a philosophical position, nor should it lead to the conclusion that the society is in a morally healthy condition.

Moral relativism can be shown to be indefensible as a philosophical position on a purely practical level, which is precisely the level on which one would want to proceed, for ethics, after all, is a science that is principally concerned with practical reason. Imagine two people, Charles and Charlene, who are in total disagreement regarding a moral issue of the utmost importance. They are both quite intelligent, and both are earnestly desirous of resolving their differences, but what hinders them from doing so is that they are both moral relativists. They both acknowledge the distinction between moral good and evil, but they cannot agree as to what constitutes each. So, regarding X, Charles takes it to be good, whereas Charlene takes it to be evil; with regard to Y, Charles takes it to be evil, whereas Charlene takes it to be good. Neither of them are prepared to abandon their relativism with respect to the nature of good and evil. Now human beings can be said only to fulfill themselves as rational creatures, creatures who are by nature ordered toward achieving the good, only to the extent that they actively pursue the good. But one cannot pursue the good if one does not know the good. Charles and Charlene, as moral relativists on the most basic level, do not know the good, and consequently they cannot effectively pursue it, and thus they are incapable, for as long as they continue to adhere to moral relativism, to attain the end which is proper to their nature as rational creatures. Therefore, moral relativism is false.

One of the more serious problems regarding moral relativism is the deleterious effect it can have on an entire society should it become a dominant and strongly influential factor. It has been acknowledged that there are societies today in which moral relativism figures prominently. Perhaps that can be said of the societies of most of the Western countries. Let us consider a particular society in which moral relativism is rampant and in which, consequently, there is much heated disagreement over any number of serious moral issues. Now, two things are to be observed about moral issues: First, seldom are they considered to be anything but essential, rarely are they regarded as peripheral, or of secondary importance; that attests to the strength of their influence. Second, the continued unity and stability of any society depends directly on there being an adequate degree of agreement among the members of the society regarding certain basic moral issues. By "moral issues" here I mean any and all issues that have anything to do with human behavior. By "adequate degree of agreement" I mean agreement which is sufficient to preserve the unity and the stability of the society.

Should the moral relativism that characterizes the society we are considering intensify over time, that is, should the disagreements among members of the society over moral issues become more deeply entrenched and therefore less accessible to amicable resolution, the society becomes increasingly more divisive, and patterns of social isolationism develop where group sets itself against group, and benevolence towards all is replaced by animus towards "them." Given these degenerating trends, the unity and stability of the society are put in jeopardy, and if vigorous measures are not taken to reverse them, the society could eventually dissolve, the victim of moral relativism run amuck.

Moral Nihilism

I will make a few brief comments here on a phenomenon I call moral nihilism. A few brief comments are all it deserves for, as its name indicates, it is not so much about morality as the demolition of morality. We have given much stress in this chapter to the intimate relation between morality and reason. Morally righteous behavior is essentially rational behavior; to choose evil over good is a preeminently irrational act. Moral nihilism can be described as a particular attitude, point of view, egregious distortion of thinking and insult to reason, the direct effect of which is profoundly to destabilize, indeed to undermine, the very foundations of reason as it applies to morality. In more specific terms, moral nihilism can be identified as a frontal attack on meaning itself, the meaning that is inherent to and communicated by the words that constitute the basic vocabulary of intelligible moral discourse. A signal feature of moral nihilism is its commitment to the wanton mauling and manipulation of language, so that words are put in the service of utter nonsense and give no service to truth. Moral nihilism is nothing less than an assault on reality, the way things actually are; it permits the substitution of whatever someone declares to be so, for what is objectively and immutably so. To the moral nihilist, contradiction is a mild nuisance, a distraction, and absurdity makes perfectly good sense. He regards nature as entirely subservient to his fantastic determinations; central to his convictions is the belief that he can decide what he is, even though his decision runs directly contrary to the rock-solid facts of the matter. In sum, moral nihilism is a form of madness.

The Natural Law

The guiding assumption of those who advocate moral relativism, the belief that there are no universal moral standards by which human beings guide their lives, simply has no basis in fact. There are such standards, and collectively they are known as the natural law, or simply the universal moral law. In the previous chapter I cited the Universal Declaration of Human Rights as a document that might be regarded as at least an oblique acknowledgment of the reality of the natural law, for its citation of certain basic principles that were claimed to have universal applicability. There was a time, not too long ago, when most philosophers, jurists, politicians, and the general public freely acknowledged the existence and surpassing importance of the natural law. But for at least a century now general consciousness of the natural law has been drastically dimmed, and many among the intelligentsia choose either to ignore it, as if were no more than a fiction, or actively to attack it as a bad idea that for too long exerted a baleful influence on our moral thinking and was therefore fit to be scrubbed from our collective consciousness.

What is the natural law? Thomas Aquinas provides us with a telling definition when he identifies the natural law as simply the eternal law of God as it is known by human reason. But we might ask: How can we know the eternal law of God, for surely we have no direct access to the divine mind? True enough, but we can be said to have indirect access to the divine mind by looking to the effects of God's creation, the physical world in which we live. The most striking characteristic of that world is the marvelous orderliness by which it is constituted. There are two dimensions to that orderliness. There is the dimension of the physical order, which is made manifest by and we recognize in the regularities of nature, the physical laws. This order we come to know simply by observation or, if we want a deeper, more precise knowledge of it, by systematic research and experimentation.

The second dimension of the world's orderliness is the moral order, which is not as immediately obvious to us as the physical order, but which is nonetheless every bit as objective as the physical order; there are two basic ways by which we can gain access to it. The first way is analogous to the way by which we come to recognize the order of the physical universe. Comparable to the regularities of the material universe, which manifest the physical laws, there are what we may call the positive regularities of human behavior, which can be said to make manifest to us the natural law. Now, this analogy is not perfect, and an important difference must be noted. The regularities of the material universe are entirely determined, but the regularities of human behavior are of course not determined, for human beings are possessed of free will, and that explains why the regularities of human behavior can sometimes be, sadly, quite irregular. From this we need to make a distinction between the positive regularities of human behavior (behavior consonant with the natural law) and the negative regularities of human behavior (behavior which violates the natural law). The next question to ask is this: Which type of human behavior has been more frequently displayed over the course of human history? It would be impossible to come up with anything like a precise response to that question; we can only conjecture. We are all too painfully familiar with how man can abuse his free will by doing evil; history has offered us a plethora of depressing examples of the inhumane ways humans can behave toward one another. On that basis one might decide that it was the negative regularities of human behavior which have been more common. Here we will decide otherwise, and suppose that it has been the positive regularities of human behavior (manifesting the guiding presence within human beings of the natural law) which has been the more common. This cannot be proved in any strict sense, but neither can it be flatly disproved. So, both are suppositions. That does not mean, however, they are of equal weight. To maintain that the positive regularities of human behavior have been the more common over our history is, we contend, (a) a reasonable position to hold, and (b) more defensible than the opposite position. To state our position clearly: over the course of history most human beings have for the most part behaved benevolently toward one another. To state our conclusion: that benevolent human behavior is an objective manifestation of the operative presence of the natural law.

A counter argument, one against our position, could cite and emphasize all the examples of man's negative behavior over the course of history, and claim that has been the more common behavior.

Response: There is no denying such behavior, but there is no basis for claiming it to be the more common behavior. It is part of the picture, to be sure, but by no means is it the whole picture; furthermore, and to repeat, there is no reason to suppose that it is the dominant part of the picture.

The counter argument would likely continue to put much stress on the fact that historical writing is replete with examples of man's negative behavior, and bear down on the claim that it was that kind of behavior which has been the more common behavior in any given era.

Response: The counter argument insists that the abundance of the accounts of negative human behavior in historical writings proves that such behavior was the more common. To show the weakness of that claim it would be helpful to compare the kind of information we typically get from historical writing with that which we typically get every day from the news media. It is a definite characteristic of "the news" that it tends to focus on the negative expressions of human behavior, keeping the public closely informed of the latest incidents showing the multiple ways in which human beings can act contrary to the precepts found in the natural law. Because of the habitual tendency of the media to concentrate on the negative, one could think that the behavior they report on is typical, but in fact it is very much atypical. The vast majority of people today live and behave benevolently toward their fellows, and thus abide at least by certain basic precepts of the natural law. It is rare that these people make the news. We are therefore given a distorted picture of contemporary human behavior taken overall.

The same can be said of historical writings. They too have displayed a decided tendency to overemphasize negative human behavior while underemphasizing positive human behavior. The average historian favors writing about extraordinary people, and extraordinary people, as the historian identifies them, are seldom paragons of virtue. Consider how much of written history concerns itself with war, with which man has much preoccupied himself over the course of his history. Granted, historical writings do contain an abundance of accounts of humans' inhuman behavior, but it would be a mistake to take that as proof that such behavior has been the more common over the course of the centuries. In sum, because the pictures presented by both historical writings and contemporary news reporting tend to concentrate on negative human behavior while paying significantly less attention to positive human behavior, it would not be reasonable to conclude that they are giving us a reliable account of the quality of human behavior in general, as it is today, as it has been throughout the course of human history.

To sum up the argument from the positive regularities of human behavior over the course of history: Most people, most of the time, in whatever era they might have lived, in whatever clime, within whatever culture they found themselves, acting as free agents, chose to act benevolently toward their fellow human beings. From this we can conclude that they were guided in their behavior by a knowledge that was inherent and common to all human beings, knowledge which dictated their benevolent behavior. Thus we have in the positive regularities of human behavior an objective manifestation of the existence of a universal moral law, the natural law.

The second way we gain access to the natural law is quite personal. How do we come to know, as individuals, in terms of the experience we have of ourselves precisely as persons, the reality of the natural law? How do we come to grasp its reality intellectually? It is through reasoning. Recall the Thomistic definition: the natural law is the eternal law of God as it is known by human reason. So our immediate access to the natural law is through the exercise of our reasoning capacities.

What would be a productive line which our reasoning could follow in thinking about the natural law? We take an important clue from Aristotle, who reminded us that every agent, and preeminently the human agent, acts for the sake of an end. This translates into the basic truth that all the actions of an agent are ordered toward achieving what is fulfilling of the agent's proper nature. That truth is very much applicable to ourselves as rational agents. Through reflection, we come to realize that we are, by our very nature, ordered toward, "meant for" in a rudimentary way, the good. We are ordered toward the good, not only in a theoretical way, but in the most practical of ways, in terms of how we behave, according to the habitual direction of our willing. The more we think seriously, deeply, about ourselves as agents, actors, "doing" beings, we come to realize that there is only one way for us habitually to act, to do, and that is in such a way that we do what is good, and avoid doing anything and everything that is opposite to the good. With that realization, however fuzzy and vague it might be initially, we make dramatic encounter with the first principle of the natural law, the most fundamental truth of morality—that good must be done and evil must be avoided. Take careful note of that "must." Accompanying our awareness of the first principle of the natural law is the recognition that, as a law, it is something toward which we have an obligation. It is imperative, to be consonant with our very nature, to live up to it, that we be obedient to a law the reality of which we come to know as something, in its essential character, not imposed upon us from without, but as something that wells up from within, from the deepest recesses of our being as rational creatures.

Consciousness of the moral law, then, introduces into our lives the governing notion of "ought." As moral agents we are sensitive to the fact that there are things that are not just pleasant to do, not just nice to do, but which ought to be done, whether or not they are pleasant or qualify as being "nice." As rational creatures, we are naturally ordered toward the good, not only in its many particular manifestations, but most importantly in its supernal reality, the Ultimate Good. (The many particular goods we constantly seek are by no means insignificant, for if they are true goods, they gain their very character as good because they reflect, participate in, the Ultimate Good.) Recall what was stated earlier in the chapter, that though we are not naturally virtuous, we are nonetheless naturally inclined to virtue. That natural inclination to virtue is the operative presence of the natural law within us.

From the natural law's first principle and most basic truth, that good must be done and evil shunned, all the more particular truths of morality flow. The natural law is natural precisely because of its affinity to human nature, knowable to every individual who has reached the age of reason. The natural law is one, and that makes one the human nature in which it is embedded. All of us, simply because we are human beings, intelligent, reasoning creatures, know that, in our relations with others, it is right to acknowledge and respect the integrity of everyone as persons, to treat them as we would want to be treated by them. We know that it is right to help other people who are in need of help. We know that it is right to respect the property of others. We know that it is wrong to do harm to others in any way whatever. We know that it is wrong to deceive others, or deal with them in any way that takes unfair advantage of them.

We know these things quasi-instinctively, simply by keeping tuned to the foundational inclinations of our rational nature. The natural law might be described as the common moral sense which is shared by all the members of the human race. Because the natural law is the explicit confirmation of our shared nature as human beings, those who see fit to deny it are effectively denying that there is a nature that we all share, and are therefore giving sanction to racism, bigotry, and all the other tired forms of malevolent behavior that are the signs of rebellion against the very first principle of the natural law.

Yet more will be said about the natural law in the following chapter.

Chapter Six

The Social Realm: Political Philosophy

The Political Animal

Man, Aristotle wrote, is by nature a political animal. We are irrepressibly social creatures. It is simply a declaration of our essential selves that we are naturally moved to come together and organize ourselves into groups, large or small, for this purpose or that. There is little to wonder at regarding this socializing propensity of ours for, after all, we were all born into a social unit, the family, and thus knew human togetherness right from the beginning. Unlike all the other societies we know, the society which is the family would seem to have arisen as a spontaneous response to the exigencies created by the begetting and rearing of children, and on that account it could be regarded as a natural society. That is how Aristotle regarded it, as we read in his *Politics*. But he went further, arguing that, besides the family, there was another natural society, and that was the state, or political community. That he should have identified the family as a natural society is understandable enough, given its presumably spontaneous origins. Man and woman meet, they mate, they beget progeny, and with that series of significant events certain primitive obligations are created, the proper honoring of which demands a stable and enduring social unit.

It might at first hearing strike us as a bit odd that Aristotle should have also considered the state to be a natural society. It would perhaps strike us as even more odd that he should have considered the state to be a perfect society, especially in light of the kind of real-world politics with which we are familiar today. (Let me note, parenthetically, that in this chapter's reflections on political philosophy I will be using the term "state" to refer to any organized political community, be it municipal, county, state, provincial, or national. Aristotle's term was *polis,* which could mean one's city or country.)

Aristotle identified the state as a natural society because he saw it as the kind of organized unit that one would expect to be created by those who were by nature social animals. Given our social nature, it was inevitable that, sooner or later, we would have gotten around to establishing political communities. The state did not arise with the same kind of spontaneity as did the family, nor at the same time as did the family but, given human nature, it would in due season necessarily make its appearance. What did Aristotle mean by calling the state a perfect society? He certainly did not mean that the state was morally perfect. Aristotle was anything but naive, and he arguably had a more comprehensive understanding of the various political systems of his day, and of previous days, than any other living man at the time. And of course he had first-hand knowledge of the political situation in the Athens in which he lived, which situation, more times than not, was far from pretty. In calling the state a perfect society he meant that, if it was healthy and well organized, it had the wherewithal to meet all the needs of individual citizens so as to afford them the opportunity to attain complete fulfillment as human beings. This is something which the family, on its own, could not do.

We cannot adequately understand and appreciate the attitude Aristotle took toward the family and the state if we fail to see the critical importance he attached to virtue. Aristotle wrote two works on ethics, in which he focused on virtue as it applies to individual persons. It is important to note that he regarded political philosophy as an extension of ethics; it was, as it were, moral philosophy applied collectively, specifically regarding the state. It was because he was guided by the kind of thinking which gave primacy of place to virtue that led him to argue that one of the principal responsibilities of the state was to promote virtue among the citizenry. It is the task of the state to create a social atmosphere which is conducive to living a life according to virtue which, as we saw in the previous chapter, was an idea central to his moral philosophy. Need it be said that modern politicians are not especially inclined to think along Aristotelian lines in this regard?

The family might be described as the elementary school of virtue. That is where children learn the basics of the morally good life. And by that kind of formation they were being properly prepared to become good citizens, for once they reached maturity and became actively involved in the larger society which is the state, they were then in a social environment which, ideally, was nourishing of the virtuous life. But again, as "perfect," the state could provide for the individual what the family could not, in the form, say, of educational opportunities, medical facilities, art forms of various kinds (architecture, sculpture, painting, music, drama), and general intellectual, cultural, and moral enrichment. Also, at an elementary material level, the state can offer more variety in the form of food, clothing, and shelter than any one family could provide. The process of attaining complete human fulfillment necessarily begins in the family, but it sees its completion in the state. One of the more important contributions made by the state is that it creates a social atmosphere in which is engendered the peculiar kind of friendship which, as Aristotle saw things, is essential to a healthy political community.

Should the family fall short in meeting its formative responsibilities, should it fail to serve as the elementary school for virtue, then things can only bode ill for the state, given how the state was dependent on the family. There would be no worse situations than those in which children were exposed to dominantly negative influences in their formative years. It would be very difficult for any child who had been schooled in habits antithetical to virtue, who, worse, had been subjected to what amounted to severe moral crippling, later to overcome the bad habits which had been acquired so as to be able, as an adult, to walk steadily along the paths of virtue and hence be a responsible citizen. In light of how Aristotle saw how family related to state, the responsibility of the family to raise virtuous children was a heavy one, for the moral health of the state could be said to have its source in the moral health of the family.

But those guiding the formal education of children also bore a heavy responsibility, to ensure that their charges were properly schooled in those subjects which were conducive to the development in them of the virtues they would need to make them productive citizens of the state. It is no accident that in his *Politics* Aristotle gives a considerable amount of attention to the subject of education.

East meets West in the manner in which the giant thinkers of their respective classical periods looked upon the family as vitally important for society as a whole. The Chinese philosopher Confucius, who lived in the century before Aristotle's, gave much emphasis to the importance of the family, but he was not especially original in this respect, for since time immemorial the family was considered to be the mainstay of Chinese society. Significantly, to this day it is customary in China, when signing one's name, to put the family name first, before one's personal name. With regard to the matter of virtue, Confucius saw the relationships between the state, the family, and the individual to be of the closest kind. A virtuous state, he argued, depended upon a virtuous family, and a virtuous family, in turn, depended upon virtuous individuals. In the final analysis, then, it all comes down to the moral quality of the individual. This is a point with which Aristotle would have totally agreed.

The Origins of the State

The natural, spontaneous way the family came into existence does not have to be elaborated upon. The exact details regarding the formation of the state, or political community, are lost in the murky mists of prehistoric times, but the experts seem to agree that it probably all began in Sumer in the mid-fourth century B.C., with the foundation of the world's first cities. Societies that take the form of states do not come about by accident; at one level of sophistication or another, they are the result of planning. Doubtless there was something like an evolutionary process that led to the founding of the very first recognizable states. Power certainly had something to do with it, but certainly it was power with a coherent organizing purpose behind it; there had to be a plan, however crude, for the establishment of something which was stable, workable, and enduring. This would seem to call for an organizing plan of some sort, a set of rules perhaps, which initially would have had much of the ad hoc about them, rough and ready guidelines to give structure to the new-born society and to regulate the behavior of its members. If this aboriginal state was to survive, it could only do so as a more or less coherent whole, a durable unit, the foundation of which would be a set of commonly held principles, basic ideas to be subscribed to, if for no other reason than to ensure, on a rudimentary level, the material well-being and personal security of its members against both intra-societal and extra-societal harms.

The "State of Nature" Theorist

Three philosophers whose lives spanned the seventeenth and eighteenth centuries—two Englishmen, Thomas Hobbes and John Locke, and a Frenchman,

Jean-Jacques Rousseau—in speculating on the origins of the political state, broached as an hypothesis what they called the state of nature, which they imagined to be the general condition in which the human race found itself before the advent of civilization. This state of nature was one in which individualism reigned supreme, and there were no bounds to complete, untrammeled freedom. The three philosophers provided different descriptions of this hypothetical state of nature, but they were in basic agreement that it was the initial epoch in human history which preceded the creation of the political state. For Hobbes and Locke it was the unsettled and even positively dangerous conditions that prevailed in the state of nature that necessitated the eventual creation of the political state. This was brought about through the social contract, an agreement whereby individuals willingly surrendered certain aspects of their freedom in exchange for the opportunity to live within a social context that gave them order, peace, and safety. Rousseau took a more benign view of the state of nature than did Hobbes and Locke. He seemed to conceive it as having an Eden-like environment, whose state of innocence was lost, not by original sin, but by the advent of private property. Accordingly, he did not take the transition from the state of nature to civilization to be in every way beneficial for the human race, whereas for Hobbes and Locke the transition was unqualifiedly positive.

Hobbes, Locke, and Rousseau, who together set the stage for modern political thought, all regarded human nature in a fundamentally different way than did Aristotle. Because, for Aristotle, human beings were by nature social animals, the founding of political communities is something they would have naturally taken to; it was perfectly in accord with their essential nature, and that was the reason, then, that the state, along with the family, could be called a natural society. Hobbes, Locke, and Rousseau, on the other hand, regarded man as essentially an individualistic animal. Thus human beings, in submitting themselves to collective organization in order to escape from the radical deficiencies of the state of nature, as Hobbes and Locke saw it, were in effect acting contrary to their essential nature, which was individualistic, not social. They were voluntarily giving up the unlimited freedom they enjoyed in the state of nature, but this was the price they were willing to pay in order to join a society which offered peace and safety, and in which their individuality would at least to some degree be honored and protected.

The idea of the state of nature as conceived by Hobbes, Locke and Rousseau is an interesting but unnecessary hypothesis, based on a skewed understanding of human nature. Because they regarded human beings as by nature essentially individualistic, and not social, their speculations led them to conceive of organized human societies, particularly in the form of political communities, as in effect artificial, representing a mode of life that ran contrary to man's basic nature. Hobbes and Locke viewed the political state as something like a lesser evil, appreciably better than what human beings would have had to continue to face were they to remain in the state of nature. Rousseau voiced a dissenting opinion on that score, taking a decidedly gloomy attitude toward the way human history had devolved following the dissolution of the state of nature, causing him melodramatically to proclaim that, "Man is born free, and everywhere he is in chains." The chains are provided by civilization, specifically by the political state. Even so, he had to accept the way things had actually turned out, and in any event was not reluctant about offering his own theories on what the best possible political state should look like.

The term "individualistic" I employ here is intended to describe a faulty understanding of human nature. We are all, needless to say, individuals, but we are not individualistic, not, that is, isolated and anti-social automatons who are unnaturally constrained by the political communities into which we were born. Hobbes's account of the state of nature was especially bleak; for him, it represented a hellish situation where man habitually acted wolfishly toward man, and life was "solitary, poor, nasty, brutish, and short." His abiding pessimistic estimate of human nature caused him to neglect the operative presence of the virtues of justice and altruism, virtues that explain the perennially demonstrated capacity on the part of human beings, even in the worst of times, to think and act in ways that generously extend beyond narrow self-interest. Part of our nature as "social animals" is an enduring, motivating consciousness of the presence and importance of "*the other*," the one we commonly call neighbor, toward whom we are capable of feeling in many respects deeply obligated. A very large fact that all three of our philosophers tended to forget, as they speculated on a putative state of nature populated by individualists, is that human beings are born into a society; it is called the family.

Utopianism

The word utopia was a neologism created by Sir Thomas More, who was the chancellor of England under King Henry VIII, and who lost both his elevated political position and his head because he courageously refused to acknowledge Henry's self-proclaimed ascendancy as head of the Catholic Church. More wrote a book about an imagined isolated kingdom called Utopia (the name comes from the Greek and can be translated literally as No Place), the apparent purpose of which was to criticize, obliquely, various aspects of the prevailing political scene of his day. It would be a mistake to think that More was presenting the society he described in his book as an ideal model which real human societies should seek to imitate in all its particulars. There has been built up over the years, but especially since More's book appeared, a considerable body of what can be described as utopian literature, books from which we can learn the accounts of what their authors conceived to be the ideal state.

The most famous of these works in Western literature, and the one that inaugurated the literary genre, is Plato's *Republic*, a book which is surely much more widely read today than it ever was at the time it was published. Just how seriously Plato took every aspect of the state which he describes in great detail in the book is open to debate. It seems quite safe to say, though, that not many modern readers, at least in the West, would choose to be a citizen in Plato's imagined republic. The philosopher Karl Popper was so put off by the work that he branded Plato as the first totalitarian, a very harsh judgment to be sure, but perhaps not completely baseless, if one is to understand Plato as completely endorsing the kind of society he describes for his readers. Popper's judgment, however, is not entirely fair to the great Athenian philosopher, and that is because it fails to take into account all of his copious writings. The *Republic* was not Plato's final word on political philosophy. In the *Laws,* his last work, he either retracts or significantly amends many of the notions that figured prominently in the *Republic.*

There are today a number of political theorists, as well as active political operatives, who have been much affected by the ideology of utopianism. Because this ideology has been very influential in world politics over the past two hundred years or so, it is well that we give it some consideration here. What is utopianism, considered not as theory only but as praxis, the attempt to realize the theory? It is the expression of a certain designing attitude that tends to look at a particular political community as an open field for radical transformation according to a preconceived set of ideas, regarded as sacrosanct in the mind of the utopian theorist.

Now, there is not a political community on the face of the earth that could not use some improvement, but the very idea of improvement implies the recognition of something which is essentially sound and stable. In more cases than not, the utopian does not think in terms of improvement; he does not want to bolster a standing edifice but wants to raze it entirely and start from scratch. The utopian is a revolutionary of a special kind. History shows us that many revolutionaries are activated dominantly by negative impulses; they have a clear idea of what they dislike and want to demolish, but seldom think fruitfully and in detail beyond that stage, having no clear idea of what is to replace what they have demolished. The utopian revolutionary, for his part, usually has an elaborate plan for the new regime which is to replace the old one. In the case of Marxist utopianism, which was monumentally influential over the course of the twentieth century, the plan was assigned supreme significance by those souls who felt themselves called to be its faithful executors. This plan was like no other, for its source, Karl Heinrich Marx, was to be numbered among the great sages of all time. If a political community, or for that matter the whole of the world's population, were to be governed by this plan, the utopian designers devoutly believed, the human race would happily discover itself to be living, at long last, in the culminating Golden Age of history.

Utopianism is an ideology, and although the connotations surrounding the term today tend to be negative, an ideology need not necessarily be a bad thing, for it can be taken to refer simply to a set of ideas, usually having to do with things political, and it can be either good or bad, depending on the quality of the ideas that compose it. (I recently came across a definition of ideology which struck me as rather pointed: "a philosophy plus a moral imperative.") The ideas that go together to compose the ideology of utopianism are, uniformly, quite bad, and that makes it a bad ideology. The term "ideologue" is almost always used as a pejorative, and that is how I use the term in describing someone who subscribes to the ideology of utopianism.

An ideologue is someone who is so thoroughly caught up in and captivated by a theory, a set of bad ideas, that he is no longer capable of seeing things as they actually are; he is blind to the root realities of the human condition. An ideologue is that peculiar kind of believer who continues to believe in ideas that can be shown, and in fact repeatedly have been shown, to be highly questionable, if not entirely false, and eminently dangerous because they are false. The utopian ideologue is not given to seriously critiquing the theory to which he is committed, nor to giving serious regard to the disastrous history of the various attempts at implementing it. His theory occupies a semi-celestial sphere where the principle of contradiction does not apply, and he sees his single-minded obligation to be its faithful proselytizer and promoter, his unblinking eyes fixed steadily on revolution. Many utopian ideologues in modern times have taken their cue from the philosopher Karl Marx, for whom the principal task of philosophy was not to understand the world, but to change it, to completely reshape the basic structure of human society. But to embark upon the ambitious project of changing the world, beginning with this or that country's political system, it is necessary to have power, and once the utopian ideologue succeeds in having in his grasp the reins of power, he can prove to be a singularly dangerous person. The twentieth century was turned into a veritable moral wasteland because of the number of madcap utopian ideologues who gained power in key countries and were thus able to put their utopian dreams in effect, with nightmarish results—Vladimir Lenin, Josef Stalin, Adolf Hitler, Mao Ze Dong, Pol Pot, to name the most notorious of the lot.

The erroneousness of utopian ideology consists fundamentally in the fact that it is totally materialistic and horizontal in its mode of thinking. It lacks a transcendental dimension, meaning that it is systematically committed to the thesis that there is nothing at all which is superior to and encompassing of the human. But there is a costly paradox in that position, for if you deny that there is anything superior to the human you end up not elevating the human, but degrading it. A humanism which stops at the human invariably turns out to be less than human. The utopian ideologue finds it almost impossible to think in terms of the individual person; he is a rigid collectivist whose way of reasoning runs most comfortably when he is thinking mainly in terms of faceless abstractions—the people, the rich, the bourgeoisie, the masses, the proletariat, the party. The individual person gets lost in the constant shuffle of the political agitation demanded by his fervid imaginings, and woe to anyone who would have the temerity to stand in the way of the progressive process of transforming a society according to the dictates of the utopian dream. The lives of uncooperative individuals are to be dispensed with by scores, by hundreds, by thousands, by millions if need be. What counts is the Idea, the theory, the grand plan for the future.

But the future that is envisioned by the utopian ideologue never arrives, the dream is never realized, and that is because the dream, for everyone except for the utopian ideologue himself, is a nightmare. The dedicated utopian ideologue may go down to defeat, as invariably he does, but he leaves behind him a scorched earth.

Government

No organized community of any size can be self-governing, if by that is meant that all its members have an equal share in the running of the business of the community. Every community, if it is to maintain its integrity as a coherent whole, if it is to fulfill its proper ends, needs to have one or more of its members whose full-time task is to care for the overall welfare of the community—leaders, administrators, governors, whatever they might be called. Even the smallest of human societies, the family, has its governors and providers in the form of father and mother. It is abundantly clear that a political community could not do without government. But what kind of government, for there is a variety from which to choose? And among the various forms of government, are they all qualitatively pretty much the same, or are some better than others? Is there any one form of government which can be claimed to be the very best?

Those are the kinds of questions that have been batted about for centuries by political theorists and philosophers. In Plato's *Republic* we have proposed to us a government of a most rare kind, for it is made up of philosophers, that is, men who are exemplary for their wisdom and virtue. The philosopher king was Plato's ideal candidate to fill the role of governor of the *polis*, the political community. It is an interesting proposal, but philosopher kings are hard to come by. How many singularly wise and virtuous men would, in any age, be available for the job?

Aristotle, who studied at Plato's Academy for almost twenty years, wrote one of the great classical works on political philosophy, the *Politics*. In this work he surveys various forms of government, real and ideal, judges the ideal forms proposed by Plato in the *Republic* and the *Laws* to be inadequate, and recommends as the best form of government a middle way between the rule of the rich (oligarchy) and the rule of the poor (democracy), a system in which the middle class will have the responsibility of governing the state. For Aristotle, whatever the form of government, the supreme ruler must not be men but law, *just* law. Law is just if it serves the common good; the common good is realized if happiness is the hallmark of the state; happiness, for Aristotle, as we have seen, is a life lived according to virtue.

In the thirteenth century Thomas Aquinas proposed monarchy as the best form of government, but the form of monarchical government he proposed was of a very special kind, the kind which he would be willing to endorse. Monarchy, for Aquinas, is the best form of government only if a very stringent requirement is met: the one who occupies the throne must be someone of outstanding moral goodness, a virtual saint in fact. Should that fail to be the case, which would happen more often than not, then monarchy became potentially the most dangerous form of government, for if the monarch turns out to be vicious rather than virtuous, the throne is occupied by a tyrant, and with that injustice becomes institutionalized in the realm. But not even a virtuous monarch can manage on his own, for the responsibilities of government are too weighty and complex for one person to handle effectively. The king is therefore to be assisted by a number of subordinates who, besides being competent administrators, must themselves be, like the king, renowned for virtue. Because he did not favor hereditary monarchy, Aquinas specified that kingship should be an elected position, and the people of the realm should do the electing.

What Aquinas proposes, then, is a form of government which is partly a kingdom, in that there is one person who is the principal authority and makes the final decisions (Aquinas saw this as superior to any other arrangement simply for its practical efficiency; with many heads there are conflicting voices); partly an aristocracy, for there were a number of persons, subordinate to the king, who share in governance; and partly a democracy, for the rulers are not only chosen by the people, they are chosen from among the people as well. All in all, it is a rather impressive set-up and, with a change of a name or two, it would be much like the basic structure of many governments in the world today that identify themselves as representative democracies. For monarch substitute president; for those subordinate to the monarch invested with ruling power substitute parliament, congress, state, provincial, and municipal governments; as for people, no substitution is necessary, composing as they do the sum total of a political community.

There can be no argument against the Aristotelian notion that government, be it the supreme government of a political community, or one having subordinate status within that community, must be governed by law, and that law, needless to say, must be just. Everyone within a state must be governed by law, very much including those who do the governing. In a healthy state the authority and power with which a government is invested, and without which it would not be able to govern at all, is granted to the government by the law. But if in the actual practice of governing it should operate outside the law, effectively bypassing the law, the poison of injustice would then seep down through the various social layers and eventually infect the whole society. No government can effectively govern without the requisite power, but it is well to be mindful of Lord Acton's telling reminder of the potentially deleterious effects of power, especially political power. Acton maintained that power corrupts and absolute power corrupts absolutely. There is something about having a controlling influence over many aspects of the lives of large numbers of people that can derange what previously appeared to be a well-balanced mind. One begins to hanker after even more control, so as to be able to shape the citizenry according to one's own pet conceptions of how they should live their lives. Here is where bad ideology could enter the picture and become a dominant factor.

How often it happens—there is a depressingly repetitious pattern to be detected in this regard—that central governments, even in self-identified democratic countries, become increasingly more autocratically centralized, ignoring the principle of subsidiarity, and usurp powers that rightly belong to subordinate governmental bodies, thus depriving them of their legitimate autonomy. The result of this pattern, which often has its source in an incipient utopianism, is that the people have less say in public affairs, and the state as a whole becomes gradually more ideologically homogeneous. With that it is set on a course which, unless altered, could well lead to outright totalitarianism. This sad drama has been played out in more than one country in recent times.

The Principle of Subsidiarity

The basic idea of the principle of subsidiarity can be concretely expressed by a naval example: if an ordinary seaman and an admiral can perform a given task equally well, the admiral, except in extraordinary circumstances, should leave it to the ordinary seaman to take care of it. Now to delineate the principle in more theoretical terms: we begin by noting that in any human society, be it as small as the family or as large as the state, there is necessarily a given order which is based upon degrees of authority and differences of function, accompanied by the power to exercise the different functions. Within the family that order is relatively simple, founded on the natural subordination of children to parents. The order is naturally more complex in more complex societies, such as the state. In the United States, for example, the federal government with its various branches exercises supreme authority, and is invested by the Constitution with various powers by which it is able to efficiently exercise that authority. Subordinate to the federal government there are state governments, county governments, municipal governments, and within the municipal governments of large cities, even smaller governmental units; each subordinate government has the authority, power, and responsibilities proper to it.

Broadly stated, the principle as applied to the family would make for a situation where parents would not do for children what children are able to do and should be doing for themselves. As applied to the state, the principle ensures that whatever can be efficiently done by a subordinate form of government would not be done by a higher form.

With regard to the family, it is part of parental responsibility that they should educate their children in such a way that, as they advance in age, they should become gradually more self-sufficient and self-reliant, so that when they arrive at physical maturity they are intellectually and emotionally mature as well, making them fit for responsible citizenship within the political community and making them feel confidently at home in society at large. Overly protective and exaggeratedly solicitous parents who, at any particular stage of their children's development, insist on doing for them what the children should have learned to do for themselves, do their children a grave disservice by possibly fixing them in states of arrested development of one kind or another. A family in which parental behavior of this sort regularly takes place would not be meeting its responsibility to serve as a foundational support for the larger society; the children of such families could reach adulthood in a condition where, let us say, they are emotionally still adolescents, and as such their ability to be positive contributors to the larger society would be severely hampered.

Political philosophy attaches much importance to the principle of subsidiarity, especially as it applies to the state. The principle is duly honored within a state if no higher form of government would intrude upon or seek to usurp the authority and power proper to a lower form of government, and where each level of government would be left free to exercise without interference the powers and responsibilities which are constitutionally proper to it. That is how it should be, but things are not always as they should be.

In recent decades we have witnessed a practice which has become increasingly more prevalent, whereby central governments, often grown to ungainly proportions, have regularly invaded the governmental territory of lower forms of government and have taken upon themselves tasks and responsibilities that can and should be met by these subordinate forms of government. In more cases than not local governments are not only capable of performing certain tasks, but they are much more proficient at doing so than the central government, and this for the obvious reason that people on the scene have a much better sense of what needs to be done, and how best to do it, than do legislators, judges, and bureaucrats in a capital that is far way, not only physically but temperamentally as well.

There is a distinctly moral dimension to serious and systematic violations of the principle of subsidiarity, particularly when they take place within a democratic republic, for they have the gradual effect of infecting the citizenry with an enfeebling lethargy with regard to all things political. The sense of individual responsibility that a citizen should feel toward the political community is dampened, or it may be effectively suppressed, so that in the end citizens succumb to a numbing passivity, allowing their lives to be shaped and managed down to the details by a government in which they play no meaningful participatory role. The very notion of self-government eventually fades from their mirco-managed minds. The fundamental purpose behind the principle of subsidiarity is ultimately to preserve and protect the legitimate freedom of the individual. Besides not infringing upon the powers and duties of subordinate governments, the central government should not attempt to marginalize or drive from the public square socially beneficial nongovernmental organizations, but recognize and appreciate the valuable contributions to the common good which have traditionally been made by private and volunteer associations. Often what these associations do is done with more efficiency and more economically than what is done by government organizations, which have shown themselves at times to be masterfully inefficient and egregiously wasteful. All that having been said, it needs to be emphasized that the fundamental purpose of the principle of subsidiarity is to preserve and protect the legitimate freedom of the individual. In the final analysis, it is the freedom of the individual that suffers most from the violation of the principle. Every individual is perfected, brought to a state of genuine human fulfillment, principally by his own activity. If political authorities systematically curtail that activity, or place major obstacles before it, the individual gradually loses citizenship in any meaningful sense. The healthy independence, the self-sufficiency and self-reliance of the individual, goes by the board; estrangement from the larger social milieu sets in. Man the political animal becomes alienated man.

Bureaucracy

Bureaucracy can not only become a problematic phenomenon for any state; should it become a fixed and dominating feature of a representative democracy, it is a positive danger to that particular form of government. Let us start at the beginning, spelling out the obvious and unproblematic, and work our way methodically to the kinds of problems which will be the focus of our discussion in this section. A bureau is simply a government department or division, to which is assigned mainly administrative tasks. Bureaucrats are simply people who are employed in a bureau; they are government officials who take care of those routine housekeeping chores related to the smooth running of a government. Bureaucrats can be appointed to their positions by elected government officials, either directly or indirectly; in some cases they are hired by established bureaucrats, senior members of a particular bureau, who had themselves been hired to fill the bureaucratic ranks. However their membership might be renewed and increased, there is a tendency of government bureaus to be self-perpetuating. Once a bureau is in place, it can assume the permanency of a Mount Everest. Former U. S. Congressman James F. Burns once appositely quipped, "The nearest approach to immortality on earth is a government bureau."

No government of any appreciable size could do without bureaus and those who work in them, because of the nature of the tasks they perform. It may be possible to take the terms "bureaucrat" and "bureaucracy" in an entirely neutral way, but today that would require some effort, for the fact is that both terms have borne, for some time now, decidedly negative connotations. Bureaucrat and bureaucracy may not exactly be dirty words, but they have been deeply tarnished. The Oxford English Dictionary defines "bureaucrat" as "one who endeavors to concentrate power in his bureau," and "bureaucracy" as "government by bureau." Bureaucracy has come to refer to a form of governmental usurpation, where a subordinate section of government, a bureau, takes on and exercises powers, and assumes ranges of influence, which far exceed those which were intended for it or are proper to it. This practice first became prominent in Europe (in the nineteenth century Thomas Carlyle made reference to "the continental nuisance called Bureaucracy"), but it has now sunk deep and tenacious roots on this side of the Atlantic, where it has become, in too many instances, much more than a mere nuisance.

That a democratic republic, a form of government which is based upon the premise that the source of its power is the citizenry at large, exercising its power through elected representatives, should harbor within its bosom a large cadre of unelected officials who establish and implement rules and regulations that directly impinge upon public life, and do so in a manner which effectively skirts the democratic process, is to create a situation which is, to say the least, paradoxical. The result of the legislative efforts of these bureaucratic activists is what is called administrative law, that is, law that is improperly promulgated by government administrators, and not enacted by duly elected legislators.

The tenure of the average bureaucrat in office is often life-long, and the effects of this kind of professional longevity can be, upon the bureaucrat himself, significantly mind-altering, engendering within him the world view of the self-assured "expert," one who supposes that he knows what is best for his society, and who, given what he takes to be the prerogatives of his position, can exercise considerable formative influence upon that society, anonymously and virtually autonomously, without being inhibited in any way by a pesty electorate. Government bureaus can quickly be the breeding grounds for ideologies of various sorts, with the result that what the bureaucratic expert knows to be "best" for a society is not necessarily the result of original political thinking on his part, but something which has been derived from a set of basic ideological propositions which were the foundation of his education, to which he is committed, and which he actively seeks to give practical implementation. From the bureaucrat's point of view, the ideas and principles which are reflected in the rules and regulations he imposes upon a society do not have to have beforehand either the approbation or the authoritative sanction of the people, hence the democratic process is rendered nugatory.

An important task of government bureaus is to administrate the laws enacted by the legislative branch, as well as the directives coming from the executive branch. However, what is now happening with increased frequency is the proliferation of administrative law, rules and regulations formulated and promulgated by non-elected and non-accountable government bureaucrats, and often enforced, by the bureaus themselves, with dictatorial stringency, and leaving those who are affected by their rules and regulations with no choice but non-negotiable compliance. Because these bureaucratically imposed rules and regulations have the operative force of laws, what we have here is a clear case, on the part of the bureaus, of the usurpation of a power not legitimately theirs, as they arrogate to themselves a responsibility which is the exclusive domain of the legislative branch.

That bureaucracy is a serious danger to the very integrity of a democratic republic should be self-evident. In a healthy, properly run republic, laws are enacted by the legislative branch, whose members are elected by the people, so that the people, albeit indirectly, have a say in the formulation of the laws by which they are to be governed. When bureaucracy gains the ascendency in a democratic republic, laws come from an illegitimate source and the voice of the people is stifled, if not eventually silenced altogether should this form of governmental mismanagement continue unabated.

Majority Rule

Let us accept, for the sake of argument, that a representative democracy is the best form of government now going. We will grant that it is not a perfect form of government—its flaws and limitations are on constant display— but it must be said, whatever the advocates of utopianism might have to say about the matter, that there never has been nor will there ever be, a perfect form of government, and that for the uncomplicated reason that the human beings who form and run governments are themselves manifestly, we might say congenitally, imperfect. It might be reasonably maintained that, over the centuries, we have succeeded in perfecting imperfection.

Whatever might be the quality of any particular representative democracy, all of them are devoted, with one degree of earnestness or another, to the principle of majority rule. It is a good principle so long as it is understood and applied in sound logical terms. It would be to succumb to a monumental fallacy to suppose that the majority view, simply because it is the majority view, is always and invariably the right view. The majority may have the final word on any given issue, but the word itself can be the wrong one. Only in athletic contests can mere numbers, as represented by the final score, decide an issue beyond further argument. In matters of public policy the relevant question is not how many people hold a certain opinion, but what is the nature and quality of the opinion they are holding. That is a rather elementary point, plain common sense in fact, but it is remarkable how often those who are sincerely devoted to a democratic form of government can let it slip from their memory, or decide deliberately to forget it out of pure expediency. The critically important qualification to be applied to the principle of majority rule is this: the voice of the majority should rule in any political community only insofar as the voice expresses the truth, what is objectively right because it is consonant with the common good of the community. The final test must always be truth.

The Common Good

It is not unusual to hear today references to the common good, especially coming from political theorists, and even on occasion from active politicians, and they are speaking of something which they usually agree should be a principal concern of any government. They are certainly right in this, but because there is considerable confusion of thought regarding the nature of the common good, it is important for us to cast some clarifying light on the matter.

A standard misunderstanding of the common good, as it applies to a political community, is that it is the sum total of the material goods that are available to the individual members of the community. This is to interpret the principle in purely economic terms, and is therefore altogether too narrow. This is not to say, however, that economic considerations play no part in the common good. All the members of a polity must have available to them the material goods, in the form of requisite food, clothing, shelter, and more, which are necessary to enable them to live lives which are consonant with human dignity. But there is a much deeper level to the notion of the common good than that. A government should establish and maintain a general state of affairs, an abiding social atmosphere, in which all citizens are able to realize, as fully as possible, their status as rational creatures whose identity and destiny cannot be summed up in, or reduced to, materialistic terms. The common good is a present reality in any state where each citizen can freely follow the admonition of the ancient Greek poet Pindar, "Become what you are!" that is, become fully human, live up to your essential selves as rational agents. How does the state ensure that a genuine common good is operatively in place? First and foremost, by the enactment and enforcement of just laws, for it is only in a just society that individuals can live and strive in a truly human way. In a healthy polity, Aristotle reminds us, it is not men but law that must rule. Truisms of that sort easily trip off the tongue, but how strictly are they abided by in any given society?

It is impossible to separate the notion of the common good from the notion of civic virtue, to which Aristotle, as we know, attached so much importance in his political philosophy. As he saw things, quite rightly, the very rationale of the common good was to guarantee the happiness of the citizenry. But what was happiness, true happiness? It certainly was not to be equated with materialistic hedonism. Genuine happiness consisted in living a life according to virtue; it was, putting it plainly, being a good person, a credit to the human race and, more particularly, to the political community to which one belongs. Think in terms of a particular virtue, *the* social virtue, and therefore the one governing political life—justice. The common good is precisely common in the sense that justice is the identifying mark, not just of individuals, but of the society as a whole of which they are members. If a genuine common good reigns in any political community, the isolated, alienated individual, who was the favorite pet of the existentialist philosophers, would be a complete anomaly.

Ideally, the good of the individual and the good of the state are, in an important sense, one and the same, and they support and reinforce one another. Both are dedicated to the good life, understood in the most serious and elevated sense, a life of virtue, involving what is most essentially human, and which therefore extends beyond the merely human. Now, looked at from the point of view of the state, and notwithstanding the fact that the good of the individuals composing the state and the good of the state itself, that is, the body politic as a whole, are not in conflict, there are certain circumstances where the good of the state can take precedence over the good of the individual or, to put it figuratively, where the good of the whole, and that which is for the sake of the whole, supersedes the good of the part. The individual citizen who is inspired by civic virtue is prepared to acknowledge this fact and act upon it. I have in mind a situation where the state is put in jeopardy, say by the military invasion of a foreign aggressor or, what is not entirely uncommon these days, by inimical forces within the state that seek to disrupt its order and tranquility by violence, and the individual feels obligated to come to the defense of the state. This is an obligation which the conscientious citizen is willing to meet, even if by doing so he puts his own life in danger, and this is because he feels duty-bound to come to the defense of the common good, with which his own individual good is inextricably bound up. Just as he would come to the defense of his family were it to be threatened, he does the same with regard to the state, which he is inclined to regard as a larger family to which he belongs. At one level of consciousness or another he is aware that, without a common good, individual goods are rendered null and void. In situations less serious than the ones just described, in normal circumstances any time private citizens involve themselves in activities which are beneficial to the society as a whole, perhaps in a self-sacrificial ways, they are recognizing the precedence of the common good over individual goods and are willing to contribute to it in any way they can.

The above commentary is not to be construed as meaning that the individual, as a conscientious citizen, should look upon the state as absolutely the most important factor in his life, to which he is entirely subservient and to which he owes, in every respect, complete and unquestioning obedience. Far from it. That is the kind of attitude toward the state advocated by philosophers like Jean-Jacques Rousseau and Georg Hegel, an attitude which informs the marching orders of every dedicated totalitarian. Looked at from the point of view other than the state and its common good, there is another, higher point of view according to which the individual takes precedence over the state. The state, in comparison to the human person, is an abstraction, whereas the person is a concrete reality, a substantial entity of intrinsic value and with a transcendent orientation and destiny. The individual citizen looks up to the state, but looks beyond the state as well.

In our discussion of the principle of subsidiarity, above, we stressed the point that its fundamental purpose was to preserve and protect the freedom of individuals. In this we can see how closely related that principle is to the common good, given the fact that genuine individual goods and the common good are bound up with one another. It is only by the rational exercise of his freedom that the individual can meaningfully contribute to the common good.

Law

No political society is possible without law, and no society capable of fostering a genuine common good is possible without just law. Actually, "just law" is a redundancy, for if a law is not just it simply does not qualify as law, a point which we will attempt to make clear as we proceed. Law can be defined as (a) a rational ordinance, (b) intended to serve the common good, (c) formulated by a proper authority, (d) and which is promulgated. Some brief comments on each of the parts of that definition are in order. That is the definition of law provided for us by St. Thomas Aquinas.

A law is a rational ordinance. An ordinance is a rule of action, intended to regulate a certain type of behavior within a political community, such as, for example, traffic laws intended to regulate those who operate vehicles on the public roadways. A law must be rational, which means, in the first instance, it must be addressed to people who are recognized as being rational agents. A rational law is one which is recognized as reasonable by a citizenry that is making a proper use of reason and therefore can recognize the difference between the reasonable and the unreasonable. A proposed law would clearly be irrational if it would violate any natural human right, such as the right to life, or the right to private property. A law would be irrational if it would prove to be unduly burdensome to those expected to abide by it, such as in a case where a government would proliferate laws unnecessarily, with the purpose of micromanaging every aspect of a citizen's life.

The purpose of law is to serve the common good, which is to say that it must be for the benefit of all who compose a body politic. A law is clearly unjust if it favors only part of the population, while at the same time imposing undue burdens on another part. Law must not play favorites; it must be fair to all.

A law must be formulated by a proper authority. Not every person or body in a duly established political community is entitled to make laws, but only those persons or bodies that have been designated to do so by a nation's constitution. In Great Britain that would be the Parliament; in the United States it would be the two houses of Congress. We have seen earlier that the administrative law that comes out of government bureaus would lack legitimacy in a healthy democratic republic, because it originates from an improper authority.

Finally, and obviously, a law must not be kept secret; it must be promulgated, made public. Citizens can scarcely be expected to adhere to a law of which they have no knowledge, much less prosecuted for disobeying a law that a legislator has not promulgated.

Looked at from a purely practical standpoint, we can say that the purpose of law is to regulate public behavior, allowing certain types of behavior, while prohibiting other types of behavior. In a way, law hems us in, curbs our freedom, but we readily accept that fact because we realize what the consequences would be were there no regulation of public behavior. The term law and the term order are commonly coupled together, and appropriately so, for without law there would be no order, and without order human society would be impossible. Imagine if there were no traffic laws, for example. Vehicular chaos would ensue. Driving a car would require a good deal of bravado, not to say a spirit of devil-dare, and pedestrian paranoia would be a national mental health problem; crossing a street would

have the character of a suicide mission. Laws, we have said, in order to quality as laws, must be just.

Let us review some of the criteria that must be met if laws are to qualify
as just: generally, they must be reasonable; they must not violate natural
human rights; they must not be burdensome. A basic point to be emphasized here is that there must be something above civil law itself by which it
can be evaluated. Is not this a point on which we could reasonably be expected to have common agreement? Sometimes reasonable expectations go
begging.

There is a theory of law, enjoying some currency today, which would
take exception to the idea that there is a law superior to civil law; it is called
legal positivism. According to this theory, civil law, the law made by any
particular state, is self-justifying, which is to say that once a law has been
enacted by a duly established legislator or legislative body, there is no appeal
that can be made beyond the law itself. Consider this situation: Law X has
been enacted by the political community, the state, of which I am a member. In being informed of the particulars of that law, I am deeply troubled
by it. I determine, after calm, rational reflection, that what the law is man-
dating is simply not right, and therefore I decide that I cannot consent to
it, I cannot obey it. I ask, why should I obey Law X? The answer I get to
my question from legal positivism, loud, clear, and cold, is: "Because it's
the law!" That is the first and the last word on the subject. I am informed
that for me to wonder whether the law is just or unjust is to engage in idle
speculation; my considerations and second thoughts are simply irrelevant.

Legal positivism represents a totally wrong-headed understanding of
the nature and purpose of law. We have already acquainted ourselves with
attitudes toward law that conflict with the position taken by legal positivism. Recall the positions put forward by Plato, Aristotle, and Thomas
Aquinas, arguing that the purpose of law, most especially civil law, is to
make those who are subject to it virtuous, to perfect them as human beings,
to bring them to the point where they measure up to their identity as rational agents. But law can only do that if it is just, and the justice of any
law cannot be established, as legal positivism claims, simply by reference
to the law itself. That would be like a situation where I claim that $2 + 2 =
5$, and when someone calls me out on that errant arithmetical claim, asks
me why I say that is so, I respond, "Because I say it is so. Next question."

A certain action, a certain type of behavior, might be entirely legal in the minimal sense of the term; it is on the books; it is sanctioned by the state, no penalties or punishment is attached to acting in accordance with it; indeed, it might carry with it certain material benefits. But these are mere sociological facts; they tell us, just in themselves, nothing about the intrinsic rightness or wrongness of the action or behavior in question. Do we need to remind ourselves that it was once perfectly legal in the United States of America for one human being to own another human being? Would anyone be prepared to say today, as many might have said in the pre-Civil War nineteenth century, "It's the law!" and that was all that needed to be said in order to justify slavery? In a later time in our history there was a national law that effectively made it a criminal act to nurse a bottle of beer or sip a glass of wine, much less to be found harboring some of the more potent alcoholic beverages. Among other things, this was an astonishing example of the federal government taking militant punitive action against a range of honorable and innocent culturally diverse customs. And it was all perfectly legal.

Back to the Natural Law

There must be something above civil law itself that can be appealed to in order to be able to judge whether any given law is just or unjust, that is, to be able to determine whether it is a genuine law or merely something that happens to be on the books. Besides the particular criteria already referred to, there is one major, overriding criterion or standard against which the quality of any human law is to be determined: the universal moral law, otherwise known as the natural law, which we discussed at some length in the previous chapter. If a human law faithfully reflects what is contained in the natural law, then we have assurance that it is a just law; if it is a direct violation of the natural law, then it does not even have the status of a law. Such were the laws sanctioning slavery, which were once in effect in this country.

William Blackstone, the eighteenth-century British legal scholar and jurist, whose *Commentaries on the Laws of England* was for years the virtual bible for legal education and consultation in English-speaking countries, stated unequivocally that if a civil law contradicted the natural law it then simply is not law and therefore could be summarily ignored. Whether or not Blackstone was aware of the fact, Thomas Aquinas had made precisely the same argument some six centuries earlier. If there are no standards that transcend human law and by which it can be judged, then the demagogues, tyrants, and dictators of the world have the final say as to what is right and wrong, and to dissent from what they give legal sanction to is, as history attests, in some cases to forfeit your life.

Such was the case in ancient Thebes, ruled by the tyrannical Creon. He at one time mandated that anyone who rebelled against him and was killed in battle should be left unburied, his body the prey of jackals and vultures. A young woman named Antigone had a brother who fought against Creon's partisans and was killed in battle. Antigone defied Creon's ruling and buried her brother. Creon had her brought before him and before condemning her to death he berated her for having the unspeakable audacity to disobey his mandate. By what authority did she presume to do so? Her answer, appealing to the natural law, resonates down through the ages: "I did not think that your pronouncements were so powerful that mere man could override the unwritten and unfailing laws of heaven. These live, not for today and yesterday, but for all time."

Justice

If the abiding concern of the government of any political community should in fact be the virtue of the members of the community, then the virtue on which that concern should be concentrated is justice. Justice is the preeminent social virtue; it is the other-oriented virtue, the virtue of concentrated neighborliness. The three other cardinal virtues— prudence, fortitude, and temperance—are directed toward the moral betterment of the individual. I am properly focused on myself when I think about the need to be prudent, courageous, and temperate. But when I think about the need to be just I am looking outward, concerned with how I behave toward other people. Do I begin with a basic respect for them simply as persons? Do I consistently deal with them fairly and squarely? Justice forces us to get out of ourselves, to think about others first, to gauge their welfare to be as important, and perhaps in some cases, even more important than our own. If everyone in a political community were to be a paragon of justice, that political community would be a veritable earthly paradise.

There are three ways in which justice operatively manifests itself in any body politic; accordingly, we identify three basic kinds of justice: distributive justice, legal justice, and commutative justice. Distributive justice has to do with the actions of those who have the responsibility of governing a political community. Legal justice, sometimes called social justice, is manifested in the way ordinary, non-office holding citizens contribute to the common good, to the welfare of the community as a whole. Commutative justice is justice as it operates on the horizontal level, in the manner in which all the citizens behave toward one another as they strive, the hope is, regularly to abide by the Golden Rule.

Distributive justice demands of those who have been chosen by the people to govern them that they do so in such a way which, first of all, serves to preserve and protect the stability and integrity of the state. This would entail the government's conducting domestic affairs in such a way that care for the common good is its principal concern. The government would follow a foreign policy that was aimed at establishing mutually beneficial, non-exploitative relations with other nations. The chief means through which a government governs is through the laws it enacts, and it goes without saying that the demands of distributive justice can be met only through the enactment of just laws. Foremost among the responsibilities of a government is to ensure that the inalienable natural rights of the citizens are studiously honored and protected; these have been given classical summary statement in the triad of the rights to life, liberty, and property. Thomas Jefferson, in writing the Declaration of Independence, substituted "happiness" for "property." Given that alteration, nothing prevents us from interpreting happiness in Aristotelian terms as a life lived according to virtue.

Legal or social justice is fruitfully practiced within a society when a critical mass of citizens are animated by a deep-seated sense of responsibility toward the society of which they are members. All of them feel they have a role to play, however minor and inconspicuous it might be in some cases, toward the maintenance of the common good. This sense of responsibility on the part of the citizenry toward the general welfare of their society can take any number of concrete forms—regularly and conscientiously exercising their franchise, dutifully (if painfully) paying their taxes, responding to the call to serve on juries, promoting volunteer organizations that serve to

meet pressing social needs, and in general demonstrating a practical awareness of what is going on in the political arena, and recognizing its import,
positive or negative, for the society as a whole. To nurture a systematic in-
difference toward the political community to which one belongs, to gladly
receive but begrudgingly to give, is completely antithetical to the spirit of
legal justice. If enough people in a society entertain an indifferent attitude
of that sort over a prolonged period of time, the door is opened to the arrival of ambitious demagogues and aspiring tyrants.

Commutative justice is what was described above as justice at work
horizontally, represented by the daily dealings of citizen with citizen. A society displays commutative justice when its citizens are genuine neighbors
toward one another. They honor and respect one another as persons, unique
and non-duplicable individuals who are possessed of intrinsic worth. For
all the ways they may differ from one another, they habitually treat one another, on a basic level, the level of the simply human, as equals.

Equality

Equality, understood as describing the condition in which human being properly relates to human being, is one of the focal ideas of modern political
thought and, as ideas go, it is a fairly modern one, taking into account the
full sweep of recorded history. A good many of the key ideas of Western philosophy are traceable to the very beginnings of that philosophy, which took
place in the Greece of the sixth century B.C. And the idea of equality? One
will not find in the fragmentary writings that have come down to us from
the philosophers who lived in that century any developed notion of human
equality. And the two giants of ancient Greek philosophy, Plato and Aristotle,
would perhaps have been quite baffled by the earnest attention we today give
to the concept of equality. If we were to ask what is our understanding of
human equality today, and how it figures in our political thought, the question would likely trigger a jumble of disparate answers. The fact of the matter
is, though the term is given high rank in our vocabulary and is much bandied
about, there is considerable confusion over the understanding of equality and
its practical applications to political communities.

We will begin our discussion with a simple assertion: All men are equal.
Is that true? The only reasonable answer to the question is yes and no. On

one level, we will call it the level of the non-essential, nothing is more blatantly obvious than the fact that human beings are not equal. Confining ourselves to adults alone, we observe that they are not all the same with regard to sex, height, weight, eye color, skin pigmentation, in what they eat, in the language they speak, in their religion or lack thereof, in their musical or athletic talent, in their proficiency in math, in their age, their economic status, the state of their health, the football team they choose to root for, and on and on and on. What we cannot help but see when we survey the race as a whole is not equality but rampant diversity, or inequality. If all human beings were equal on the non-essential level, among other things, it would make for a very dull world in which to live. Human interrelationships would lack spice, would be bland and boring. And consider the agonizing problems that would be created for professional sports if all men were equal on the non-essential level. If all males between the ages of eighteen and thirty-five were equal in height, musculature, and athletic ability, they would all be possible candidates for lucrative jobs in the National Basketball Association. The competition would be ferocious. And all the male fans sitting in the stands watching a game would resent the fact that they were not down there on the court.

So, the first and obvious answer to the question that asks if we are equal is No. But the inequality that we called attention to in the remarks above, once again, has to do with non-essentials. There is a deeper level, however, the level of the essential, and if we ask the question with that level in mind then the answer to the question is an emphatic Yes. We take it to be an axiomatic truth of political life that everyone is equal before the law. In the eyes of the law no one citizen is to be considered superior or inferior to any other citizen; all are to be treated equally. But what is the warrant for supposing that such equality really exists? Is this idea of equality before the law no more than a social convention? If so, like other social conventions, it is liable to change over time. Is its basis the fact that it has been proclaimed in a positive law? If so, the equality in question would be as tenuous as the positive law that proclaims it; positive laws change.

In his memorable Gettysburg Address, Abraham Lincoln made a statement that no one in his audience would have taken exception to. He said that the United States was founded on "the proposition that all men are created equal." There we have the only logically defensible basis for the political position which holds that all citizens are equal before the law. Here we have a principle relating to human law which does not have its roots in human law itself, nor in mere convention. We take it to be true that everyone is equal before the law because everyone, on the most basic level, is in fact equal in terms of origins. It is a matter of our essential equality. All human beings share in the same essential nature; they all have the exalted rank of rational agents, of persons. In sum, then, the bold claim that all men are equal is, at the deepest level, perfectly and permanently true.

Given the essential equality of all human beings, it should be among the chief priorities of government, especially the government of a nation that identifies itself as democratic, to do everything in its power, motivated by the obligations of distributive justice, to reduce, if not entirely eliminate, the inequalities that exist among the citizenry regarding material goods. If there is any portion of the citizenry that is so materially deprived, through no fault of their own, that they cannot fend for themselves regarding the basic necessities of life, there can be no question but that the government should come to their assistance, not entirely on its own, however, but along with those outstanding non-government organizations which have shown themselves to be remarkably efficient over the years working in the field of social welfare. It is important that there should be full cooperation between government and non-government organizations in these efforts and, as we stated earlier, by no means should government do anything to frustrate or curb the legitimate activities of non-government organizations. The principle of subsidiarity should be scrupulously abided by in these matters. If a private enterprise or a volunteer organization can perform a task just as or more efficiently than government, then it should be given to them to handle, and if local government can match or exceed what central government can do, it is local government that should take action.

Every political community should strive to establish only the kind and degree of equality which serves to enhance the human spirit of each and every member of the community, being mindful of the psychology of individual differences. A social atmosphere should be created in which all citizens have the freedom and the wherewithal to develop to the maximum degree possible whatever natural potentialities with which they have been endowed, thus enabling them to contribute maximally to the common good.

How, more precisely, should we understand the human equality that is advocated by that account? I want to suggest that it would be helpful to think of it as analogous to what is revealed to us by mathematical proportions. Consider the following proportions: 2 : 4, 3 : 6, 4 : 8, 5 : 10. That series could be extended indefinitely. Notice that each of those proportions is composed of different natural numbers, and they are clearly quite different from one another. (Aristotle maintained that each number represents a separate species, a judgment adopted by Thomas Aquinas.) Each proportion, we could say, is unique, starkly individual, because it is composed of numbers which are different from the numbers which compose the other proportions. And yet, despite those differences, they all have something very basic in common. They are all the same by reason of the fact that they reflect identical proportions: the first number is half of the second, the second number is double the first. Now, let us say that each of those proportions represents a human being, a member of a political society, and the first number represents the individual's potential, i.e., natural talents and abilities, and the second number represents the full realization of that potential, something that could only come about if the individual lives in a social environment which not only allows for that realization to take place, but actively underwrites it. Given that relation, between individual potential and opportunity to realize it, I would contend that any political society, including its government, is doing what needs to be done to ensure equality if it provides that opportunity. A social context is created in which all citizens will have available to them the freedom and wherewithal to become fully human according to the potential with which they are naturally endowed. The only thing that would hold them back would be personal moral limitations, such as lack of will. In this way a political society would be treating all its citizens equally, while at the same time respecting the natural differences that exist among them.

In the example of the series of mathematical proportions I want to stress the point that while in one sense no two proportions are the same, because they are made up of different numbers, they are nonetheless the same in the sense that they all represent exactly the same proportion: half to double. Again, taking each of the proportions to symbolize a human individual and a member of a political community, the different numbers in each proportion can together be taken to represent the non-essential differences among human beings, while the fact that they all represent the same proportion will serve to represent the fact that all human beings, despite their differences, are essentially the same.

Rights

In contemporary political thought, the concept of rights looms very large. As with equality, there is much talk about rights, but not all the talk is luminously intelligible. When there is dissonance regarding the meaning of terms, it is always a good idea to start with definitions. What is a right? The first thing to be noted is that the idea of right is inseparable from the idea of justice. Justice, the preeminent social virtue, is that by which we give to others what is due to them, in a word, what we owe them. One of the most basic things we owe to others is an acknowledgment of and respect for their rights. A right is a personal possession which allows and enables a person to act in certain ways. If I have a right to X that means that I am entitled, in justice, to exercise X. Others honor my right to X, negatively, by doing nothing which in any way hinders or prohibits me from exercising X. One of the most glaring omissions in all the fervid talk we now hear about rights is that there is scarcely a mention made of duties. Let it be loudly proclaimed that there is no genuine right that does not come accompanied by an inseparable duty. Rights and duties are correlative. If you have a right to X, I have a serious obligation to acknowledge that right and honor it.

We distinguish between natural rights and artificial rights. Natural rights are those founded upon the natural law. They are the rights which we possess by nature; they are simply a permanent part of who we are as human beings. Natural rights are inalienable, meaning that they cannot be taken from us. An oppressive governmental regime can deny the exercise of one's natural rights, but no human power can deprive any person of natural rights. What cannot be granted by the state cannot be taken away by the state.

Unquestionably the most basic and the most important of our natural rights is the right to life, which belongs to all human beings from the moment they begin to exist as human beings. This is the right that preserves personhood, preventing any person from being treated as if they were no more than a thing, and thus being regarded as potentially disposable. One of the fundamental principles of the natural law is that we should never do wanton harm to others, much less put their lives in jeopardy. By abiding by this principle we are respecting people's right to life. Two other basic natural rights are the right to liberty and the right to private property. All of us, by nature, have the right to be free and unhindered in our actions so long as we are acting within the framework of justice and do not irrationally interfere with the freedom of others. One of the things that is owed to every human being is the right to own things, to have material things and real property to which we can confidently lay claim. We are by nature possessive creatures, and while that aspect of our nature can get out of hand (there we have the origins of greed), in itself it is perfectly healthy. I have the natural right to have things I can call exclusively "mine," things which I possess through honest labor or by way of gift, and which I can use and dispose of as I see fit. One of the erroneous ideas propagated by the philosophy of dialectical materialism was that there was something intrinsically wrong with the idea of private property, a rather paradoxical stance to be taken by a philosophy that claimed the only reality to be material reality. Both Aristotle and Thomas Aquinas defended the positive need for private property within any society, arguing that it is only when people own things that they take proper care of them. If all property were public property no one would feel any responsibility for it, and it would thus be routinely neglected. The "let George do it" attitude would prevail, and the result would be an unsightly, trashy environment. The habitual litter bug seldom litters his own yard; it is the public park which is the favorite venue for his careless deposits.

Artificial rights are so called, not because they are sham or counterfeit (they are genuine rights), but to distinguish them from natural rights; they are the products of human artificers. Civil rights, which have their basis in the positive law laid down by the state, would be the most prominent example of artificial rights. I do not have a natural right to operate a motor vehicle; this is a right granted to me by the state in which I reside. In order to acquire that right I had initially to take a written examination and a driver's test; after successfully passing both I was granted a license, which I must renew every five years. Because my right to operate a motor vehicle is not a natural right, it is alienable. Having been granted it by the state, the state can, for just reasons, take it away from me. If I turn out to be a reckless driver, accumulating a number of tickets for moving violations, if I am so irresponsible that I have a habit of driving after overindulging in martinis, the state would have the right, the duty really, for the sake of the common good, to relieve me of my right to drive. There are any number of other artificial rights granted by the state, such as the right to fish or to operate a pleasure boat in public waters, the right to hunt, the right to fly an airplane, and the right to set up and operate a radio station.

Rights go hand in hand with responsibilities. My right to drive a car carries with it a raft of responsibilities associated with safe driving. In general, I must exercise any right, natural or artificial, in such a way that does not harm the common good or violate the rights of others. Practically speaking, we properly respect the legitimate rights of others by, at the very least, doing nothing to hinder the free exercise of their rights. Notice I referred there to legitimate rights. That suggests that there are illegitimate or so-called rights. I said just above that an artificial right is not to be thought of as a counterfeit right; it is genuine. There are, however, counterfeit rights; they are the bane of any political community that has serious aspirations for maintaining its communal health; it does this by not kowtowing to the irrational claims of people with hyperactive self-serving imaginations, who conjure up rights out of thin air, with no regard for the common good.

An illegitimate or counterfeit right can be falsely legitimized simply by passing a law that declares it to be a right, thereby legitimizing it in a purely technical sense. The illegitimate laws that allowed for slavery came accompanied with any number of pseudo-rights supposedly belonging to the slave owner. But one might ask: Because the legitimization of counterfeit rights puts them in the category of artificial rights, does not that give them a kind of respectability? No, because nothing prevents any artificial right from being illegitimate. States are liable to create counterfeit rights, just as they are liable to enact bad laws, or what are in effect non-laws, because they run counter to the natural law. A circumstance of that kind accentuates the great difference between natural rights and artificial rights. The former, because they are not of human origin, have permanent and inviolable legitimacy. The latter, being the products of human making, are subject to all the limitations and imperfections that can accompany human artifacts. A just law depends entirely on the justice of the lawmaker. A specious right that is legitimized is comparable to an unjust law. It may be on the books but, again, its status as a right is purely technical. The "right" to own human beings as slaves was a counterfeit right, meaning that, in reality, it was a non-right, a pure fiction, and that is because it contradicted the natural right of every human being to be free. A counterfeit twenty-dollar bill might pass as the real thing, but it is not the real thing.

There are three criteria that enable us to identify a counterfeit right. First, it clearly violates the natural law, which encompasses such basic natural rights as the right to life, to liberty, and to private property. Second, it imposes undue burdens on some or all the members of a political community in which it is allowed to be exercised. We saw that this is one of the identifying characteristics of an unjust law. Third, it clearly infringes upon or violates the legitimate rights of others. A prominent example of a counterfeit right, which blemishes the pages of American history, was the "right" to own slaves.

E Pluribus Unum

United we stand, divided we fall. This maxim has special application to political communities; unity is an absolutely necessary condition for their very existence. But the necessity of political unity is matched by its fragility; political unity is like a delicate plant that requires constant, assiduous attention, otherwise it will take sick, wither, and die. We learn from *The Federalist Papers* that the founders of the United States were much concerned with the dangers of what they called factionalism. They were convinced that if people aspire to unite themselves in a viable political community, nothing would more surely thwart that aspiration than their not being able to get beyond the stage where there was nothing but a loose gathering of exclusionist groups that could not agree among themselves upon a common end which all would be willing to strive to achieve. This critically important political unity, without which no durable polis would ever be possible, is given concrete expression in a society where there is a genuine common good. The common good can be thought of as the soul, the life principle, of the body politic. It reflects the singleness of mind and purpose that binds individuals together, giving them the secure and satisfying sense that, for all the differences that may exist among them, they are essentially one. From a political point of view, what they share is foundational, the rest is incidental. Together, they make up a distinct "people."

"Things fall apart; the center cannot hold." In that memorable line from a poem by William Butler Yeats, if we take "the center" to stand for the common good, we have a poignant description of what brings about the dissolution of a political community. It is when the political unity that is embodied in a genuine common good is fractured that things fall apart. A people disintegrates into peoples; what once was one now is many, and the chances of the many ever being one again are not promising. The various disunited groups become increasingly alienated from one another, and often what serves as the strongest unifying factor for any single group is the animus its members harbor towards the other groups. The field of "we" has been appreciably diminished, and "they" is given more extended employment in the standard vocabulary. The ultimate outcome of this political falling apart would be, not "one nation under God," but multiple nations under a cloud of mutual suspicion if not outright hatred.

There are two kinds of unity that a political community can display, the kind which is imposed from above, e.g., by a totalitarian government, and that which rises up from the spirit of a people who are capable of distinguishing the essential from the non-essential, who are keenly sensitive to the human sameness that undergirds the human differences. The first kind of unity is completely stultifying; it is the gray unity of despotic and tyrannical regimes, the unity which, in modern times, has commonly been the masterwork of utopian ideologues. It results in a society of bland, spiritless homogenization, where individuals can survive as individuals only by going underground and there do what they can to bring about the restoration of a sane society.

A genuinely free society, one in which individuals can seek goods that are truly perfective of them without being unjustly hampered from doing so, is anything but a blandly homogenous society. Differences abound, as is only natural, but they do not separate, subsumed as they are under the encompassing umbrella of unity. The good which dominates in the minds of the citizenry is the good which is regarded as common to all. Today there is much talk of diversity, but the discourse often shows insufficient awareness of basic social realities. This is the case when people take the position that diversity is something that must be actively promoted. There is no need for this. A healthy diversity will take care of itself; it always has. Political unity, on the other hand, will not take care of itself; like freedom, it can be lost by careless inattention. There is something potentially quite dangerous, for the preservation of political unity, in the active promotion of diversity, for it can be driven by ideological agendas under whose promotional impetus diversity tends to degenerate into divisiveness. Differences are accentuated and cynically exploited for political purposes, while the commonly held ideals and purposes that lent unity and coherence to a political community are denigrated and come under attack.

Then there is the notion of multi-culturalism, also much discussed today, but not always with the kind of balanced perspective that an intelligent treatment of the subject requires. There is no gainsaying the fact that it should be an aspect of public education that children and young adults should be made aware of, and learn to appreciate, cultures other than their own. That has always been thought to be an integral part of what we call a liberal education. What is the relation between culture and political unity? That is the question that needs to be seriously addressed. It is not possible to have genuine political unity without a common culture, one that is shared by all the members of the political community. This is not to say that there cannot be vibrant sub-cultures which thrive within the ambit of a single dominant culture. These sub-cultures would not detract from the unifying influence of the common culture, insofar as its members see their loyalty to the sub-culture as subordinate to their loyalty to the common culture, with which they fully identify. Should any sub-culture within a political community so gain the ascendency that it is effectively a rival to the common culture, then political unity is put in jeopardy.

The common culture which supports and sustains political unity cannot be artificial, in the sense that it is imposed upon a people. Again, we must refer to the critical notion of the common good. It would be difficult to imagine the operative presence of a genuine common good within a society that does not have a common culture. There cannot be a disparity between the two. This common culture would have an organic quality to it, in that it is something that was the natural outgrowth of a people who have lived and worked and worried together on the same stretch of geography for a lengthy period of time, and who have therefore built up a rich and varied complex of shared experiences, of shared convictions, desires, and aspirations, of fears. They have a shared history which knits them together as a people. They are not foreign to one another. They are friends, in the sense that Aristotle thought that the members of a healthy political community very importantly must be.

As noted above, the common good serves as the animating source, the soul, of the unity of a political community. A key aspect of the common good is that it reflects the unifying consciousness of the members of the society that it governs. They see themselves as essentially of one mind as to what the community to which they belong is at bottom all about, its reason for being. They are committed to a common political ideal, an ideal which perhaps will never be realized in all its amplitude, but which, for all that, is not one they are prepared to abandon, because they recognize that the unremitting striving after its realization in itself lends dignity and meaning to their lives. Constantly to strive to be "one from many," not to allow the inessential to take precedence over the essential, is the prescription for preserving the health of a political community.

Chapter Seven
Foundational Principles: Metaphysics

The Queen of the Philosophical Sciences

Metaphysics has traditionally been known as the queen of the philosophical sciences, the principal reason for its having been accorded that regal title has to do with the depth and the scope of the science. It is the salient mark of philosophy in general, as previously noted, that it strives to get to the bottom of things, to ferret out and identify the most basic truths about reality. Metaphysics does this in a sharply focused way, with the intention of coming to terms with those principles, those foundational truths, that have universal application, that, in other words, apply to being as such, to whatever actually exists. Because of the universal application of what it focuses on, metaphysics is the most comprehensive of the philosophical sciences. It could also be called the most ambitious of the philosophical sciences, for it makes bold to take into account nothing less than the sum total of reality.

The Latin phrase by which the subject matter of metaphysics has traditionally been described is *ens qua ens*, which may be translated literally as "being just as being," the more expanded meaning of which tells us that metaphysics concerns itself with whatever exists in whatever way it is possible to exist. Metaphysics is magnanimously inclusive; it leaves nothing out which qualifies as being.

There is nothing more basic than being, nothing more total, for apart from being there is simply nothing. The human mind, as we saw in our discussion of epistemology, was made to know, and the proper object of the mind, that towards which its knowledge is directed and of which it is constituted, is being. Being as an abstraction? No, being as it manifests itself, in the first instance, in the form of concrete material objects—this coffee mug sitting in front of me on the table, the table itself, the floor on which it rests, the house of which the floor composes a part. Metaphysics starts on a level as homely and prosaic as things like that, everyday things with which we are quite familiar, but it does not end there. It moves beyond reflecting on things like coffee mugs, tables, floors, and houses, and reflects on the phenomenon of existence, the act of existing, however it might manifest itself. The melancholy Hamlet pondered over the elementary question of "to be or not to be." The "not to be" is of interest to metaphysics only insofar as it makes reference to the negation of being, the absence of anything the mind could give its attention to; it is that infinitely fertile "to be" that commands the science's fullest attention.

The Three Degrees of Abstraction

Metaphysics is often described as a highly abstract science, and that is true enough, but it is not unique in that respect. No science could make any progress as a science if it did not engage liberally in abstract thinking. We commonly recognize three degrees, or kinds, of abstraction, each of which serves to identify a specific scientific realm. Before we get into describing the particulars of those three kinds of abstraction, we need first to take note of what is common to all three. What, in general, is abstraction? What does the mind do when it abstracts, and why does it do it? Whenever we endeavor to understand a subject which is large and complex, a subject which we would not be able to take in entirely in a single intellectual gulp, so to speak, we have to break it down mentally and deal with it one piece at a time. The process of taking away one piece at a time, while leaving the other pieces behind, is the heart of the process of abstraction. It is the eminently practical procedure by which we select out one part of a complex object, give it our focused, undistracted attention so we can master our knowledge of it, and then, having done that, go on to study other parts of the object, one by one, until we have exhausted them all. The systematic analysis of any particular object and the process of abstraction go hand in hand; in fact, the two are in effect one and the same thing. (The Greek word which is the root of our "analysis" means "to take things apart.")

Now we are ready to take a close look at the three degrees of abstraction, which are: physical abstraction; mathematical abstraction; metaphysical abstraction. Physical abstraction is the form of abstraction which is employed in the empirical sciences, those sciences dedicated to the understanding of physical reality, the world of material being. The philosophy of nature, which we studied in Chapter Two, leans heavily on physical abstraction. We will take the example of a zoologist who has decided to study a rare type of animal, let's call it a sheebo, which he happened upon by accident while exploring the jungles of the Amazon. Once having made that discovery, he sets himself the goal to be recognized one day as the world's premier expert regarding all things pertaining to the sheebo. He thus embarks upon a lengthy and extensive research project, the purpose of which will enable him to tell everything that can be told about the sheebo, its physical features, pertinent distinctions between male and female, its general habitat, its mating and feeding habits, and whatever other information can be gathered about the sheebo so as to provide an exhaustive and accurate account of the creature. He cannot of course take on everything at once, so in his investigations he employs abstraction, focusing on one aspect of the sheebo at a time, say, starting with its feeding habits, until, carefully studying one sheebo after another, he is eventually satisfied that he has studied a sufficient number of them all together to ensure that he has recorded every significant feature of the animal and its behavioral habits.

He necessarily spends much time observing many individual sheebos, but as a zoologist he is not interested in individuals just as such, that is, he is not concerned with recording what might be unique and limited to a particular individual. It might be, for example, that a given individual is a physical sport, a freak of nature, which would make it atypical; his concern is with the typical, with what is common to sheebos as a species. His aim is to formulate accurate generalizations that can be reliably said of all sheebos. In this sense he can be said to abstract from the individual.

The second degree of abstraction, the mathematical, declares by its very name the field it is limited to. While physical abstraction remains within the material realm, when we think mathematically we can dispense with material considerations. As we reflect on the square root of 36, or try to figure out the area of a rectangle whose sides measure respectively 22 and 14 inches, we are not thinking, in the first case, of 36 apples or oranges, or, in the second case, of a rectangular slab of marble, but simply of the number 36 and of rectangularity, abstracted from matter of any kind. We can dispense with material considerations when we think mathematically, but we never leave matter behind entirely, and that is because, despite what some

Platonically-inclined mathematicians are wont to think, all of our ideas, including our mathematical ideas, are rooted in the soil of sense experience, and sense experience has only to do with material being. Man may conceive the idea of a geometrically perfect circle, but the germ of that fetching idea was planted, way back when, as, let us say, Cal the caveman stared wondrously at the geometrically imperfect but nonetheless lovely circle of a full moon glowing quietly white over the eastern hills.

Mathematics abstracts from matter, leaving it behind, but what it takes away is quantity, and quantity, we remember from our encounter with the philosophy of nature, is a property of matter. Whatever is material has quantity or is extended, and whatever is extended is measurable. The mathematician does not have to bother about *what* is extended, but can be content with meditating on extension just as such, as abstracted. But if there were no extended matter to begin with, abstracted extension would be inexplicable.

The third degree of abstraction is the metaphysical, the one with which we will be principally concerned. Notice that in the first two degrees of abstraction we moved, in our thought, away from being considered in exclusively material terms. In physical abstraction we remain very much in the material realm, but selectively so. We are not concerned with individual material things as such, but with the common characteristics of groups or classes of individual material things. It is the abstracted aspects of material things which, taken together, provide the basis for the idea of type or species. We set aside considerations of the individual material beings which were the source of those aspects. When we rise to the second level of abstraction and think mathematically we can operate quite efficiently without any direct reference to the material realm, although, because mathematics has its roots in that realm, we never completely sever ties with it. (It is because mathematics is so closely tied to the material realm that explains why it can be so easily applied to that realm.)

Through the abstraction that we exercise in metaphysics we can set aside the consideration of being in exclusively material terms. Here we can, if we want, consider being as completely separated from matter, although we must remember that the basic principles that we are dealing with in the science apply, in almost every case, to both material and immaterial being. Metaphysics, whose subject is being just as being, whatever really *is* in whatever way, very much allows for the possibility that there are real beings, actually existing substances, which have nothing of the material in their composition. Metaphysics wants to make sure that it misses nothing, excludes nothing, from the all-embracing realm of being, and this is why, when we think philosophically on the level of metaphysics, we deal with principles that are so basic that they are universally applicable, covering the full range of reality, having reference to all real being, transcending the distinction between material being and immaterial being.

Ours is a realist metaphysics; its inquisitive gaze is directed outward, toward the objective and the shared. Its principal focus is not on the mind, on the ideas that make up the contents of the mind, but on things in the external world to which those ideas refer and without which they would be void of content. The abstract thought in which metaphysics typically engages does not have the effect of distancing us from reality; to the contrary, it carries us to the very core of reality.

Substantial Being

We introduced the idea of substance in Chapter Two, as an important part of our discussion of the philosophy of nature; now we return to it. Aristotle, who wrote the first systematic work of metaphysics, saw it as a science which just as well could be called wisdom, because it is especially dedicated to getting to the bottom of things by discovering "first causes," that is, the most elementary explanations for what we find in the world in which we live, and "such a science," he says, "will be about substance." Later he writes, "if the universe is of the nature of the whole, substance is its first part." What is it about substance that makes it so central for metaphysics? Think of it this way: the ambitious task we have assigned to ourselves is to come to terms with being, not, please note, as a mere idea to which we attach the word "being," but as that which really is, "out there," in that wide and immeasurably rich extra-mental world. When it comes to being, existence, it is with substance where it all begins and ends. We identify substance as that which "exists through itself," meaning independently. It has been given existence as a gift (it cannot call itself into existence), but the gift once given, it owns it fully. A substance is the paradigmatic individual, and as such each has a specific nameable identity. When Aristotle says that substance is the "first part" of the universe, what he means is that we cannot come to know the universe as a whole, however imperfectly that necessarily must be, except through substance, through this or that material existent, for the universe is no more than the sum total of those individual existents. We get at least some inkling of the whole through study of the part. The extent to which we will ever be able to penetrate the mystery of sheer existence, the act of be-ing, will come through our encounter with substance, for the act of existence is seated in every substance, no matter how humble it may be.

Essence and Existence

In discussing material substance in Chapter Two we emphasized the fact that all material substances are composed of matter and form, the form in this case being substantial form, that which puts a precise identifying mark on matter, determining it to be a specific kind of substance, inanimate or animate—a chunk of silicon, a cactus plant, a golden retriever. The distinction between matter and form, which goes under the title of the hylomorphic theory, obviously applies only to material substances, and in metaphysics our interest is not limited to them. However, calling attention to material substances here is useful, for it allows us to point out that they are composed in a yet more fundamental way than by matter and form. At the most basic level, all substances, be they material or immaterial, are composed of essence and existence.

The distinction between essence and existence applies universally, then, to every created being. It is a real, not just a logical, distinction, which is to say that it is an actual, inseparable aspect of every substance. The human mind does not impose this distinction upon things, it discovers it in them, as something which is intrinsic to them. The basic import of the distinction is that it serves to call attention to the real difference between *what* something is and *that* something is.

The real existence of a substance rarely fails to declare itself to us in bold, unmistakable terms. Under normal circumstances we can confidently trust what our senses are telling us about the external world. But consider this situation. I am out on the open prairie and I see an object in the far distance. From my vantage point I cannot clearly make out what it is and, as bad luck would have it, I left my binoculars at home. I am puzzled as to the identity of this object, but there is no doubt in my mind that there is really something out there, whatever it might be. Urged on by curiosity I decide to trudge over there and investigate. As I approach the object, keeping a steady eye on it, I think it might be a buffalo but, if so, I wonder about its solitary condition and its immobility. Finally, I get close enough to see that it is nothing but a large boulder which, at least from a distance, had a deceptive buffalo shape to it. What did my investigating trek reveal to me? Not the existence of the thing, for I was sure of that right from the outset. It was its essence I had discovered, its identity precisely as a boulder.

We do not have to be a great distance from an object in order to be puzzled over what it is; sometimes it can be in full view right in front of us, as was the case when I was at the zoo recently staring at an animal I could not identify. Now of course I was not in a state of complete befuddlement. After all, I was in a zoo, and therefore knew I was dealing with an animal, but I was quite ignorant as to what *kind* of animal it was. It was only when a knowledgeable bystander politely informed me that I was staring at an aardvark that the lights went on and I had the right idea about the creature. You will recall from the chapter on psychology that when we have a sound idea of any object, we then have, encapsulated within that idea as it were, the essence of the object. The words that express the ideas which tell us the essence of things provide the answer to the key question, What is it? When the common language of philosophy was Latin the word *quidditas* was coined to serve as a synonym for essence. The *quidditas* or "whatness" of a thing is its specific identity, its nature, which we identify with a precise name—aardvark, buffalo, boulder, whatever name is the proper fit for the thing.

The essence of a thing is its basic meaning, everything we correctly understand about it in and through the various ideas we have of it. Does the basic meaning of a thing, anything at all with which we are acquainted or have been acquainted, include the fact that the thing should necessarily exist? To rephrase the question: does the essence of a thing necessarily entail existence? If that were so, then it would be impossible for that thing not to exist, and that is because the essential meaning of the thing would be "to exist." But of course we know that is not the way of the world as we know it. Everything with which we are acquainted is what we call contingent; it actually exists here and now—there can be no doubt about that—but we may know of a time when it did not exist, and we can imagine a future time when it will not exist. The neighbor's garage, built just this summer, was not here last summer; it can be reasonably conjectured that in 500 years it will not be here. Such is the nature of a contingent thing, that-which-does-not-exist-by-necessity. Not here yesterday, here today, gone tomorrow. It is not of the very essence of contingent things that they should exist; if it were, they would never cease to be. Existence is not one and the same with essence; they are really distinct.

For anything that actually exists here and now, essence and existence are absolutely inseparable. We cannot have an essence that does not actually exist; that would be like supposing there could be a real thing that was not real. A chimera of that sort would be like the little man upon the stair, a little man who wasn't there. On the other hand, it would be just as senseless to suppose that there could be pure existence, detached from any essence. There is no such thing as existence just as such; there is only and always *things that exist*, substances. We can only know existence through the things that have it. On a very basic and most personal of levels, we know existence because we are, as it were, actually doing it. The Hamlets of the world can muse about being and non-being because they actually are; they are securely ensconced in the realm of being.

We can get a vivid sense of the real distinction between essence and existence because we can conceptualize essences which right now have no extra-mental existence. Let us say that when you were a kid you had a pet collie named Cookie. You remember when your father brought her home as a cuddly little puppy. Over the years Cookie became very much part of the family, living to the advanced canine age of fourteen years, after which she went the way of all flesh and is now no more. But your memories of her are vivid, and you think about her often, having a rich store of ideas pertaining to her, and ideas, recall, encapsulate essence, so in those ideas you retain the essence of Cookie, an essence which is now separated from existence.

There is more: we can grasp the essence of individuals which never existed and never will exist, as we do when we think about the likes of Macbeth, Hamlet, Scrooge, Huck Finn, and the Wicked Witch of the West. Our imaginations can create very elaborate ideas of any number of things, some perhaps quite fantastic, whose only existence will be as ideas in our minds.

Actual Being, Potential Being

In Chapter Two we introduced the distinction between act and potency, between actual being and potential being, between what is right now and what is possible to be tomorrow. We now bring that distinction back into the conversation, for it plays a very important part in metaphysical reasoning. Metaphysics, as we have said, is comprehensive in its concerns; it deals with being however it might manifest itself. The distinction between act and potency, like that between essence and existence, has universal application to being, material or immaterial, though it has more direct application to material being.

Some brief reminders will be in order here, apropos of what we have already learned about the distinction between actual being and potential being. Common sense makes us readily aware of the reality of this distinction. Actual being refers to anything that really exists, here and now, as something that is separate from and independent of any mind that might be thinking about it. When we say that a thing, a substance, is "in act" (*in actu)* we simply mean that it is actually there. Actual being is foundational with respect to potential being; it stands to reason that there must necessarily be an actually existing thing, a subject of change, before any change can take place, say, from how it is right now to how it might be tomorrow. Actual being is here-and-now being; potential being is future being, what is not the case today, but what could really be the case tomorrow. When we say something is invested with potentiality of this or that kind we are talking about realizable possibilities for that thing. The important point to keep in mind about the difference between actual being and potential being is that they are both instances of *real* being; they both really *are,* although obviously in quite different ways. There is no question but that the scruffy-looking kitchen chair that I now turn my head to glance at is really sitting over there in the corner, and there is really a possibility, right now, that the chair on Saturday will have a new coat of paint—if I finally get around to that already long-delayed project. Potential being is as real as our rational expectation that certain things have the inherent capacity to be different from the way they are right now; with those considerations in mind, we can confidently make reasonable predictions about the future. The water in the tea kettle is now cold; it is also, now, I muse to myself in a metaphysical mood, potentially boiling, as I put the kettle on the stove and light the burner.

The reality of actual being, for the most part, speaks for itself, although sometimes it speaks in languages that have to be carefully translated. But potential being, that real being which has its roots in actual being, is especially intriguing to think about. We are all thoroughly immersed in the reality of potential being. We could not carry on as stable rational creatures without its occupying a constant and prominent place in our consciousness. If we were without the commanding awareness of potential being we would be locked into a drab, immovable now, anticipating nothing, hoping for nothing, planning nothing. If perchance we should on occasion look in the direction of the future, we would see only an impenetrable wall, high as the sky, wide as the horizons.

When we talk about potential being we of course do not have in mind something that exists independently, as if it were a substance of some kind. Potency's mode of existence is dependent or accidental, as a quality that inheres in an independently existing substance; what is *in potentia* is always founded in what is *in actu*, that is, in an actual existent. Put plainly, potentiality is not a thing, but an aspect of a thing. However, it is an inseparable aspect of a thing; we will never find an actually existing substance in the created world that lacks potency, for if we could imagine such a substance, it would be incapable of changing in any way whatever. It would be immutable. (In the next chapter we will see that there is only one being of which that can be said.) The essence of change, remember, is the transition from potency to act. If there is no possibility for change there obviously can be no change that ever takes place.

Potentiality is more readily associated with material substances in particular, for it is the very nature of matter that it bears the deep and ineradicable mark of potency. But, again, in metaphysics, because we are generously inclusive in our regard for being, we take into account the existence of immaterial beings as well. What are we to make of such beings with respect to potentiality? As immaterial they certainly would not be invested with the array of potentialities that are part and parcel of material being. They thus would not be subject to all the ways of changing as are material beings, such as, for example, motion or change of place, for the very notion of place involves extension, a property of material being, whereas immaterial being, by definition, is without extension. Furthermore, these immaterial beings would not be subject to quantitative changes such as augmentation or diminution, for what is without extension cannot increase or diminish in size. As purely immaterial beings they would be intellectual substances, pure minds as it were. But minds, as we know from our own experience, are anything but static; they change, most notably by the process of learning, gaining more knowledge. And that would represent an instance of qualitative change. We may conclude, then, that immaterial beings are possessed of potentiality in at least that very important respect; they have the capacity to change qualitatively.

We need to call attention to a distinction within the distinction between actual being and potential being, and that is the distinction between active and passive potential. Active potential is the capacity to bring about changes; passive potential is the capacity to be receptive of changes that do not originate in the substance itself. Active potency and passive potency always go together; you can't have one without the other. Think of the difference between the active and passive voice in language, in which one makes sense only in relation to the other. If there is a pusher, say, then there must be someone or something that is being pushed; and if someone or something is being pushed, there is necessarily someone or something doing the pushing. There is active and passive potency in all of us and both of them are always on call. When we bring things about in the world in which we live, for example, by my finally getting around to giving that scruffy-looking kitchen chair a new coat of paint, I would be demonstrating active potency. If you manage to change a friend's mind regarding an important issue through your eloquent and cogent arguments, you would be doing the same thing. Passive potential is the capacity to be affected, to be changed in one way or another. This receptive capacity is an integral part of our make-up, the importance of which cannot be minimized. The friend who was persuaded by your eloquent and cogent arguments was displaying passive potential. Active and passive potential—what we do and what we allow to be done to us—can both have positive and negative ramifications. One of the most valuable ways we can manifest passive potential is through the process of learning, disposing ourselves to being docilely receptive to new truths. But notice that the exercise of passive potential need not be completely passive, if it is to be constructive rather than destructive for the person involved. There is a definite active aspect to the learning process; we have to do our part. In learning a foreign language, for example, a good deal of memorization is necessary, and that requires concentrated effort.

We have been discussing potentiality in general, but in point of fact potentiality always has to do with something quite particular. In the case of active potential, for example, it always refers to a specific kind of actualization which can be precisely named. This kid, we might say, has the potential to be a first-rate shortstop. Nancy has the potential to excel at playing the ukulele. Bernie has the potential to act more responsibly if he would only put his mind to it.

The whole purpose of potentiality, we may say, is actualization, the bringing about of that critical transition from possibility to actuality, but that transition is not always made. Of course, some potentialities should not be actualized, such as the potential to do evil, but we are thinking here of potentialities that are positive in every respect. If a particular potentiality is genuine, then by definition there is a real possibility that it can be actualized; the contemplated goal is really reachable. But the fact is, when one considers the full range of being, many potentialities go unrealized; what really could have been never came to be. How many acorns, potential oak trees, make it to oak trees? Within the human realm the fact of unrealized potential takes on a special significance. We talk often of untapped potential, or wasted potential. Sometimes a person's potential goes unrealized due to circumstances that were entirely beyond the person's control. But sometimes the fault lies with ourselves; we know we had the capacity, perhaps even the responsibility, to bring about some real good, and we did not follow through on it. If situations of that sort become a pattern in a person's life, we might have the makings for tragedy. When it is a case of a person who is clearly possessed of great potential to do much good for many, and that potential is squandered, we who bear witness to this sad spectacle, Aristotle might be inclined to say, would be moved by fear and pity.

As contingent beings we are ever changing. In terms of everything we have had to say about the distinction between act and potency, one might conclude that we are ever-changing beings because we have a seemingly inexhaustible capacity to change, and in any number of ways. And if we show a habitual passive receptivity to our natural inclination to virtue, those ways of changing could only be for the better.

The One and the Many

Again, as metaphysicians we are concerned with whatever exists in whatever way it is possible to exist; that points directly to substantial being and accidental being, for those are the only two ways anything can actually exist. When we think in terms of substantial being we have in mind individuals—specific, independently existing beings. In terms of numbers, we would be referring to what is beyond counting, so staggeringly many are the substances that constitute the physical universe. Over the course of the years there have been philosophers who have been so struck by the multiplicity of being that they failed to see any cohering principle in it, any principle, that is, which would have the effect of giving unity to what seemed to them to be hopelessly disparate. It was not just a matter of the unimaginable number of beings, but their variety as well. In the inorganic realm, there are elementary particles, atoms, molecules, rocks, planets, stars, galaxies, and gatherings of galaxies. In the organic realm, moving from microbes to man, the numbers and differences to be observed are stunning. Entomologists estimate that there are millions of species of insects on the face of the earth which have yet to be identified.

In view of all this mind-boggling multiplicity, these philosophers concluded that there was no unifying theme to the whole assembly, and therefore we have to resign ourselves to the fact that what we are dealing with is effectively chaos, that is, a cosmic "many" with no discernible order to it. We will call this point of view pluralism.

Though understandable to a degree, pluralism is an inadequate point of view, and metaphysics rejects it. What we are dealing with in this section is what has traditionally been known in philosophy as the question of "the one and the many." The pluralist position is so fixated on the many that it cannot see the one, that is, any kind of unity. There is obviously no denying the many, the fact that the physical universe is composed of innumerable individual beings, but nonetheless in a real sense the many are one, and in the most fundamental of ways, for they are all united together by what has felicitously been called the great bond of being—the common factor of shared actual existence. The many are one in the unity of real being. The commonality exists at the most elementary level only, the level of sheer existence. Above that level the differences between any two substances, *in the way they exist*, may be of monumental proportions. Consider Vincent, who is standing and looking down fixedly at a single grain of sand resting in the palm of his hand. Vincent has a philosophical bent, and the thought he is turning over in his mind is that this tiny grain of sand, insignificant though it might be thought to be, is in fact wondrously significant for the simple fact that it actually exists; it is fixed at an immeasurable distance from non-being.

There is also a psychological factor that should be taken into consideration here. The human mind is so constituted that it will not accept multiplicity as just multiplicity. We have a natural propensity to mentally gather together multiple things so as to compose wholes which, as such, are more intelligible to us. This does not mean, however, that the unity of being is to be explained in purely psychological terms, as if we were only projecting a mind-manufactured unity on the extra-mental world which is in reality chaotic. The human mind comes to recognize the true unity of being, seeing it as substantiated by the act of existence shared by each and every individual being The many are one by reason of the community of real existence. There is, however, another important unifying factor regarding the multiplicity of being, and that is relation. All material being is in caught up in a grand, dynamic, intricately woven web of interrelationships. It is those interrelationships which lend special significance to the notion of the great bond of being.

Opposite to the extreme and erroneous view of pluralism there is the extreme and erroneous view of monism. If pluralism is blind to the unity of being, monism is blind to the diversity of being. A realist metaphysics recognizes the existence of countless individual substances; the most radical monist would want to push his argument to the point where he is prepared to claim there is only a single, cosmic substance, of which all of what are supposedly individual substances are really no more than features of that single substance. The basic problem with monism is that it is burdened with a debilitating aversion to making critically important distinctions. The various forms of pantheism are expressions of the monist way of thinking.

Philosophical materialism, which I will discuss at the end of this chapter, can be regarded as a form of monism.

Being Is One, Is True, Is Good

All being is one, in the way we just explained. But each individual being is also one, and each individual being is also true and good. Unity, truth, and goodness are three of what are called transcendental attributes of being. The term "transcendental" calls attention to the fact that these attributes, or characteristics, apply universally to each and every real being.

Every being, every individual existent, is one in the sense that it is unified, not divided, is singular in its existence. It is a specific this or that to which a definite name can be correctly assigned. Peter the rabbit is a self-standing unit, and is not to be confused with Percy the rabbit, much less with any chipmunk, squirrel, or ferret. It is precisely because any particular being is one that its various parts go together to compose an integral whole. If every being were not a coherent unit it would have no proper identity; it would cease to be a definitive "it." Thomas Aquinas, among other philosophers, was of the mind that the most accurate way to characterize the unity of being is negatively, as "that which is not divided." That deceptively simple statement goes right to the ontological heart of the matter, and has its confirmation in the principle of contradiction. The most direct way to identify that which is unified is to see it as the contradictory of that which is not unified. The unity of a being means that all of its parts compose a single, coherent whole. The lack of that unity does not mean there is a defective being, it means there is no being, no one thing, at all.

In claiming that every being is true we do not have logical truth foremost in mind (the truth that is established by the relation between ideas in the mind and things in the world), but ontological truth, the truth of being, of actual existence. A particular being is said to be true, then, in the elementary sense that it is truly *in* being. It is because of its actual existence that we can come to know it through the ideas the mind forms of it. Thus ontological truth, the truth of being, is the basis for logical truth. "The elm is a deciduous tree," "whales are mammals" are examples of ontological truth. Ontological truth can also be expressed negatively: "That's pyrite, not gold," "that twenty-dollar bill is counterfeit." One way of expressing the truth of any particular being is to say it fully expresses its proper nature. The foundation of the truth of being in general, all created being, is its relation to its creative source.

Every particular being, simply by reason of the fact that it exists, is good. Just as, with regard to the truth of being where we distinguished between ontological and logical truth, so here we distinguish between ontological and moral goodness. It is the former we have in mind when we refer to the goodness of being. Ontological goodness is the goodness which is concomitant with the very act of existence. The pregnant notion of the goodness of being can become more immediately accessible to us if we were to reflect on the multiple choices we make in our ordinary everyday experiences. Whenever we are attracted to any particular thing, to the point where we want to possess it, it is because we recognize in that thing, no matter how dimly, its essential goodness, a goodness which is rooted in the rudimentary fact of its existence. Being speaks to being. Your being is drawn to its being by the gravitational pull of its ontological goodness.

The Causes of Being

The definition of a science that we provided early in this book stated that it was an organized body of knowledge, based on first principles, and which sought the knowledge of causes. The dedicated commitment to discovering the causes of things stands out as a key feature of any enterprise that is deserving of the name of science. Philosophy and most particularly metaphysics is very much concerned with exploring the whole realm of causality. Aristotle, in what many commentators would consider his most important work, the *Metaphysics*, made the pursuit of all the pertinent questions relating to causality among his principal occupations. "Wisdom" was one of the names he gave to that work, and, for him, the whole project of wisdom, the mark of anyone we would be inclined to call wise, was "to deal with the first causes and the principles of things." He is not referring to two different subjects in that statement. A principle (from the Latin *principium* = beginning, origin) is that from which something proceeds in any way whatever. A cause is a particular kind of principle, noteworthy for its especially rich and trenchant explanatory value. Principle is the larger category, and embraces causality. Not all principles are causes (January 1st is the beginning of the year, the principle from which all the rest of the days follow, but the first day of the year does not cause the following days), but all causes are principles, in that they have the character of a source, an origin. The hen is the principle and the cause of the egg. The concern which metaphysics has for causes and principles shows that philosophy, in this its chief sub-science, is living up to its commitment to "get to the bottom of things."

Note that Aristotle made reference to "*first* causes." The wisdom he advocates endeavors to identify the most fundamental causes, those which apply universally, for they would then provide us with the most complete account of things. If we want to explain, in causal terms, the new building that recently went up on Main Street, we could cite a whole array of agents, carpenters, bricklayers, glaziers, plumbers, electricians, and so forth, but if we want to trace it back to where it all began, to the first cause, we would name the architect who designed the building. Or consider a causal series, where A causes B, and B causes C, which in turn brings about D. Now, let us say that it is D that really interests us; we want to gain as full a knowledge of it that we can. To know that C is the immediate cause of D provides us with important but not entirely adequate information; the same can be said of the knowledge that C was caused by B. But when we learn that B was caused by A, and that A is where the whole process began, then with that knowledge we have the ultimate explanation for the existence of D. A qualifies as a first cause.

If our common sense assures us of anything, it is that things don't just happen; they are made to happen, that is, they have causes behind them. One might ask why we should bother out heads over knowing the causes of things, but that would turn out to be an embarrassingly unphilosophical question, and would display besides a remarkable ignorance of the basic inclinations of human psychology. The fact is, we cannot help but bother our heads over knowing the causes of things; that's the way we are made. We are almost never satisfied with knowing simply *that* X is the case (the simple fact that X exists); we want to know *why* X is the case. What is the explanation for the existence of X? To ask the question Why? is to open the door to the whole realm of causality.

Usually when we think of causality it is efficient causality we have in mind. The efficient cause is the agent or agents that bring about a particular effect. You turn on the news and you hear a report of a major fire that occurred earlier in the day. A news item of that sort typically ends with a statement like, "The cause of the fire is still under investigation." The cause referred to here would be the efficient cause. Was it a lightening strike that caused the fire, an arsonist, defects in the building's electrical wiring? One of the marks of Aristotle's singular ingenuity was his discovery that causality was a broader phenomenon than what is expressed by efficient causality alone. As we have learned, besides efficient causality he identified three additional causes: the material cause, the formal cause, and the final cause. These are three additional, and very basic, ways by which things can be explained. To refresh our memory of those four causes, I will use an example modeled on the one Aristotle himself used.

Let us consider an ordinary object, a wooden kitchen chair. The material cause of the chair is the wood out of which it is made. To be thorough regarding the material cause we should also mention the screws and glue that bind the various parts of the chair together. The formal cause of the chair is its form, its shape, which makes it immediately recognizable as a chair. But there is a deeper meaning of the formal cause, and that is its embodied idea, its essential identity, its chair-ness if you will, which is given concrete expression in the external shape of a chair. The material and formal causes are called intrinsic causes because they pertain to, are internal to, the chair itself.

The efficient cause of the chair is the woodworker who designed and made it. There is a close connection between the efficient cause and what I referred to just above as the deeper meaning of the formal cause, its embodied idea. That idea began in the mind of the woodworker, and he gave it concrete expression in the chair which he made. The final cause has at least two distinct dimensions to it. Looked at from the point of view of the chair-making activity of the woodworker, the final cause would simply be the chair itself; that is the end or the purpose of his activity. The final cause of any productive activity is the product that results from that activity. Looked at from the point of view of the completed chair, the purpose of the chair is to provide seating; that's what chairs are for, to sit on.

Final causality has a significant motivating aspect to it. In the example above, it was the desire of the woodworker to make the chair that spurred his chair-making activity. We can suppose that the immediate impetus for the woodworker's action was his intention to make the chair; we will call that his principal intention. But he may have had additional intentions behind his chair-making activity. Let us say that he is employed by a furniture company and he wants to make the chair, along with other pieces of furniture, so that he can earn his salary and with that support his family. Or consider an entirely different possibility; a particular woodworker, skilled artisan that he happens to be, designs and makes a chair, not because he wants to gain any money by doing so, but simply for the sake of creating something out of the ordinary, that could be called beautiful. In this case, his final cause, what principally motivates him, is the desire to produce something that is an expression of beauty.

The Material Aspect of Material Substances

We introduced the distinction between matter and form in Chapter Two, where we saw that those two principles represent the two foundational aspects of any material substance. The material aspect, or what we should now feel comfortable in calling the material cause, is easy enough to determine: it is simply the matter of which that substance is composed, however that matter might be specifically identified. Apropos of the kitchen chair analyzed above, we identified wood and some metal and glue as its material cause. But in saying as much, has our analysis gone far enough? Since the very dawn of philosophy there have been thinkers who have argued that the various material substances that we see all around us, such as wood and metal and glue, are actually compounds that are made up of more basic material substances; these they called elements. In ancient Greece there was a philosopher by the name of Empedocles who concluded that there are four basic elements: earth, air, fire, and water. These were taken to be the elementary constituents of all material things. Those four elements were to have a long run in Western scientific thought, right up to the modern era. Lest we might think the ancients were hopelessly naive and simplistic in what they took to be the four basic elements of matter, we might consider how they can be compared with what modern physics regards as the four basic forms of matter: earth (solid); air (gas); fire (plasma); water (liquid).

Two other ancient Greek philosophers, Leucippus and Democritus, who lived a bit later than Empedocles, came up with the first atomic theory of matter, and maintained that all material substances where composed of tiny (invisible to the eye) particles that were different in size, homogenous in make-up, and infinite in number. Today modern physics still thinks of material substances as composed of more basic elements, but instead of settling for four of them, it lays claim to 109 known chemical elements. Modern physics is firmly committed to the atomic theory of matter, but the atom itself was discovered to be not truly elementary, for it is a complex structure which is composed of yet smaller elements, making it quite unlike the atom as conceived by Leucippus and Democritus, which was perfectly simple, not a composition. According to the latest count, physicists estimate that there are some seventeen truly elementary particles, that is, instances of matter which are not composed of yet smaller parts; in that respect they qualify as being simple. Has modern physics completed its analysis of the microcosmic world? Time will tell.

In light of what modern physics has to tell us about the basic structure of any material substance or compound, made up as it is of molecules and atoms, should we not, for the sake of completeness in identifying material causality, think ultimately in terms of molecules and atoms as the smallest parts of molecules, or even push our analysis farther and talk about the elementary particles of which atoms are composed? There might perhaps be some merit in pursuing our analysis to that length, in the philosophic spirit of getting to the bottom of things, but we must not allow ourselves to get so carried away by a preoccupation with parts that we lose sight of the whole, the composed thing—substance. There is a kind of reductionism which is a notable feature of contemporary thought to which the old saw about missing the forest for the trees has application. We can reason about material things—chairs, tables, the human body—in such a way that presumptuously supposes that the smallest material elements of a material substance are somehow more real, represent what is more essentially informative about the substance, than the substance itself, regarded as a whole. The parts are given precedence over the whole, and this effectively degrades its status as a substance, a coherent, independent unity. This is to look at things in such a way that, paradoxically, has the unfortunate effect of overlooking the things themselves. There is simply no logical basis for assuming that the composing parts of a material substance rate a higher ontological status than the substance that those parts go together to compose. A part is intelligible, as a part, only as it relates to the whole of which it is a part. It is the whole that should be the focus of our attention.

The Function of the Formal Cause

In the example of the kitchen chair we used above, the first step we took in discussing the formal cause was to identify it as simply the shape of the chair, its physical contours. That makes sense because the most immediate knowledge we have of any material substance is sense knowledge, so in this case the visual image we have of the chair is that of a piece of furniture displaying a distinct and characterizing shape, or exterior form. The external form of the chair is technically known as its accidental form. But then we went on to say that we must not stop at the exterior form, for that does not give us the complete picture regarding the formal cause. The external shape of any material substance is the extrinsic expression of something very important which is intrinsic to the substance, and that is what we want to get at. Were we to stop at the exterior form we would end up with a superficial understanding of the formal cause.

Let's think again of chairs. The world is full of them and, taking them all in all, we can easily imagine that the variety to be found among them, in terms of their external forms, would be very great indeed. Now, let us imagine that you have the rare opportunity of attending the International Chair Festival in Geneva. There are thousands of chairs on display; you have never seen so many chairs in one place in your life, and the variety they display is amazing. But despite the great number of chairs, and the amazing variety they display, you have no problem in recognizing all of those pieces of furniture as chairs. How is that? Because, despite the wide range of differences in their external form, you are aware of a common factor that underlies the differences, and that is the form which is deeper than the external form. We will call that the very essence of chair, the basic structuring principle that makes all chairs just what they are, chairs, however they may differ superficially, and which sets them apart clearly and unmistakably from tables, beds, and book cases.

There is a way in which the formal cause might be regarded as the most important of the four causes, or at least the most informative of them; this would be on account of what it is capable of revealing to us, which is, we recall, the very essence of any substance that we are encountering and endeavoring to know. The formal cause is the answer to the question, What is it? It is nothing other than the substantial form that we learned about in Chapter Two, that principle in and of a substance that determines it to be precisely what it is. In natural substances such as plants and animals, the substantial form is given by nature, thus accounting for the difference between, say, a lily and a leopard. In artificial substances, such as chairs, we have something analogous to natural forms, and these are provided, for example, by the the woodworkers who make chairs.

The Extrinsic Causes

The two causes we have just discussed, the material and the formal, are called intrinsic because they are inseparably part and parcel of any particular substance. The material cause does not apply universally, but only to material substances. The formal cause, for its part, is applicable to non-material causes, understanding the formal cause to be that intrinsic principle that determines an existing being to be just the kind of being it is. We might think of the formal cause to be the principle which establishes precise identity. As for the two extrinsic causes, the efficient and the final, they both apply universally, for nothing in the natural world is the explanation for its own existence, hence the need for an efficient cause external to a substance to explain its existence. And as we shall presently show, the action of every existent in the natural world is marked by finality; that is, its action is directed toward specific ends. In the course of our discussion we will come to see that though the efficient cause and the final cause are quite distinct, they are inseparable, and as such mutually explanatory.

The Efficient Cause

An efficient cause is that upon which things depend either for their very existence or for the manner in which they are existing at any given time. That succinct and precise definition is provided by St. Thomas. We will now analyze it. An efficient cause expresses its efficiency in the most fundamental way—we will call it the primary way—when it brings something into existence which did not exist previously. The woodworker who made the chair we were discussing earlier would be the efficient cause of the chair in that sense. Any human agent who is responsible for bringing into being an artifact of any kind would be the artifact's efficient cause. Sometimes the efficient cause is a single person, as with the woodworker and his chair. But when it comes to putting together complicated things like automobiles and houses, there would be many efficient causes behind them. And we would not want to leave out, in the case of the automobile, the engineer who designed the car or, in the case of the house, the architect who laid out the plans for it; they too would be efficient causes. When we move into the realm of animate being, parents can be designated as the efficient causes of their progeny in the primary way, for they literally brought them into being.

The secondary way in which an efficient cause manifests its efficiency is by modifying the state of an already existing being in one manner or another. We return to the woodworker and his chair. Let us say that after he has finished making the chair he decides to paint it white. By doing so he alters the way the chair exists, from an unpainted chair, with its natural wood color, to a white chair. Or consider the young mother who goes to the crib where lies her new-born baby, Scarlatta Jane, picks up the child and carries her to the living room. Not at all an unusual act, but nonetheless nicely illustrative of how the young mother acted as an efficient cause in that she altered the mode of her daughter's existence, from being at rest in a crib to being in motion in the arms of her mother. Any change or alteration that is brought about in any existing substance (animal, vegetable, or mineral) which is effected by an agent other than that substance, would be an instance of the secondary way in which efficient causality is exercised.

If we can account for the very existence of a being, its origins, our knowledge of it runs deep, and with that in-depth knowledge we have before us the two principal players in the drama of causality—the cause itself, and its effect. An elementary conclusion we can arrive at by reflecting on a particular cause, A, and its effect, B, is that A had to have, in the first place, the potential to bring about an effect which is just the kind represented by B. The operative principle here can be expressed by the common-sense observation that "something can't give what it doesn't have" (*non dat quod non habet*, as the Latin more pointedly puts it). Another elementary conclusion we can arrive at is that there are always obvious similarities between cause and effect. The relevant principle here is that every efficient cause brings about effects which in one way or another reflect the nature of that cause. A given cause leaves its peculiar imprint, its personal signature as it were, on the effects it produces. This information turns out to be very valuable when it comes to the discovery of causes previously unknown, which is an ongoing project in just about every human endeavor you can name, but especially so in the empirical sciences. A researcher may have on hand any number of problematic facts he is trying to make sense of. He knows that facts do not explain themselves; these facts are the results, the effects, of some cause, but it is just that cause, or perhaps set of causes, that he is ignorant of and wants to pin down. He will be much aided in his efforts if he gives very close study to the effects, the problematic facts he has ready to hand, for because of the similarity that exists between cause and effect, he will find tell-tale clues in those facts which, with persevering study, will lead him to their cause or causes. Like father, like son; like mother, like daughter. The idea behind those homely observations could be helpfully kept in mind by our researcher. Like cause, like effect.

The way some efficient causes exercise their efficiency is so obvious and quotidian that no labor has to be expended in discovering them; all we have to do is observe. The motion of the eight-ball rolling over the green sward of the pool table is explained by its having been struck by the cue ball, but efficient causality extends far beyond the range of the operations of physical forces. Dave aims an insulting comment at Larry who, in response, unceremoniously punches Dave in the nose. The efficient cause of Larry's intemperate anger was Dave, or, more immediately, the words that Dave addressed to him. Analyzing the embarrassing situation more closely, we can say that Larry's anger was the cause of his ungentlemanly advertence to physical violence. Our emotions generally can be the causes of any number of effects within ourselves, but our emotions, in turn, have causes, as in the case just described.

Our imagination can be a cause of fear or anxiety. On the positive side, we can be deeply moved, even fairly transported at times, by the beauty we see in nature or which is brought to us through the medium of art. In sum, we are immersed in a veritable sea of causal activity, for its incessant workings are ubiquitous.

The reality of efficient causality at times can be very personal, for we are all causes, and exercise our causative powers, consciously or unconsciously, countless times over the course of any day. The effects we bring about as efficient causes, either in the primary or secondary way, may at times be not all that consequential, but even so it is a remarkable fact that we can bring into being something that, without our agency, the light of day would never have illumined. The omelet you made at breakfast this morning may not have been a culinary masterpiece, but it did not exist before you made it. Consider the way you may have influenced people for the better, in big ways and little ways, over a period of just a week, perhaps without your even realizing it. There are a couple of lines from Ralph Waldo Emerson's poem, "Each and All," that come to mind: "Nor knowest thou what argument/ Thy life to thy neighbor's creed has lent." What else is influence but a form of causation, and in some instances, a very potent form at that? The words "affect" and "effect" are very closely allied in a more significant way than the manner in which they are pronounced. When we affect people we have an effect on them.

There have been some philosophers who have expressed skepticism about efficient causality, maintaining that we have reason to be doubtful that it is really operative out there in the external world or, if it is, that we can never know of its real existence, because it is one of those secrets of nature that the human mind is incapable of penetrating. Philosophers who spend too much time in their armchairs, lapsing into the kind of idle speculation which sitting in that particular piece of furniture for prolonged periods seems to generate, need to get out into the fresh air more often and take the empiricism to which they are supposedly dedicated more seriously. Consider this: a little girl, Suzanne Luella, is pulling a wagon down the sidewalk. To most unprejudiced observers, the cause of the movement of the wagon, B, is the fact that Suzanne Luella, A, is pulling it. But the skeptical philosopher would have none of that. He would admonish the observers for their rashness in making such a judgment, telling them that it may indeed appear that there is a real causal connection between A and B, but all we can say with any kind of certainty is that there is a conjunction between the two but no connection, thereby citing a difference in words which no English dictionary will allow to represent a difference in meaning. What are we to say to this? At least this much: though philosophy is not reducible to common sense, it departs from it at its peril. Once that departure is made, philosophy becomes a parlor game which might serve to alleviate the boredom and mistiness of mind brought about by too long a string of rainy days, but otherwise is best left alone.

First Cause, Secondary Cause

We now reintroduce two important distinctions pertaining to efficient causality, that between (a) first cause and secondary cause, and that between (b) principal cause and instrumental cause.

A first cause is the ultimate explanation for any effect. In an example I used earlier, I referred to a series of causes, A, B, C, that together account for the effect D. In that series, A would be the first cause in that it is the origin of the entire series, and the causes B and C would be secondary with respect to A, not simply because they come after A, but because they are subordinate to A with regard to their very capacity to act as causes. If it were not for the causal activity of the first cause, A, the subordinate causes, B and C, would have no causal efficacy.

Secondary causes can be subordinate to the first cause in two ways, essentially and accidentally. A secondary cause is essentially subordinate to a first cause if it is exercising its causal efficacy at the same time as is the first cause, and only when the first cause is doing so. In other words, the two are acting simultaneously, and the subordinate cause can act only because the first cause is acting. Picture a hockey player moving the puck down the ice toward the goal. The puck is moving in front of him because it is up against the moving blade of the hockey stick; the hockey stick is moving because the hockey player's arm is moving; his arm is moving because he is moving. We designate the hockey player as the first cause; the hockey stick and the hockey player's arm are secondary causes, which account for the puck moving over the ice. Neither the moving hockey stick nor the moving arm could cause the puck to move if the hockey player, the first cause, was not also moving. So for that reason they are essentially subordinated to the first cause.

We will go from a hockey player to a baseball player to illustrate causes accidentally subordinated to the first cause. Babe Barna is at the plate. The pitcher pitches; Babe swings and powerfully connects, sending the ball rocketing skyward. Our attention is upon the moving baseball, which is now in motion because of all the motions Babe went through to set it in motion.

He is the first cause. Now, after Babe completes his swing he lets the bat fall to the ground, drops his arms, and stands motionless for a moment as he watches with no small satisfaction the ball sail over the left field fence. The moving baseball is accidentally subordinated to all the movements which caused its own movement because its own movement can continue while the causes of its movement are no longer moving. The moving baseball does not need the movement of Babe, the first cause, to continue in motion. We will have more to say about the notion of first cause in the next chapter.

Principal Cause, Instrumental Cause

The relation between a principal cause and an instrumental cause is comparable to what obtains in the relation between causes that are essentially subordinated to the first cause. Unless the principal cause is acting, the instrumental cause lacks all causal potency and cannot function as a cause at all. Consider tools or musical instruments. Both a hand saw and a hammer are very efficient instruments, but only if they are in the hands of someone who is skilled in using them; violins and clarinets do not play themselves. Unless the carpenter picks up the hand saw or the hammer and transmits his power to them, they are powerless; unless the musician plays the clarinet, it has no music to offer us. In each case, the carpenter or the musician is the primary cause; the tools or the clarinet are the instrumental causes. We give the generic name of musical instrument to clarinets and violins because it is through their instrumentality that music is made.

The relation between the musical instrument and the instrumentalist, the musician who is the primary cause, gives rise to some interesting observations. One can have the best musical instrument that artistry can make and money can buy, but if there is no musician to play it, it remains little more than a museum piece. The instrument is the absolutely essential means by which the musician makes music, but the musician is the source of the music, not the instrument. However, let us say that we have an instrument of peerless quality, but a musician who is not especially competent who plays it; in that case he will not be able to get out of the instrument all that it is capable of giving, and that is because he does not have all that much to give to the instrument in terms of his musical talent and skills.

Now let us turn things around and think of a situation where we have a world class musician, a real virtuoso, who is asked to perform but because of circumstances has no choice but to use an inferior instrument in doing so. He resigns himself to his fate, takes the stage and gives a performance with which he himself is not satisfied but nonetheless earns him a prolonged standing ovation. The moral of the tale is that the musician, because of his superior talent, was able to get more out of the inferior instrument than would a less gifted musician. If violins could emote, this one would be very surprised at how lovely it sounded that evening. In the final analysis, the quality of the effect depends chiefly on the primary cause.

Final Cause

For Aristotle, nature, the physical universe, would be completely unintelligible without final causality, for, like efficient causality, it is ubiquitous. The final cause is "that for the sake of which" any agent acts. An agent is the source of action, which results in individual acts. An act is completed, end-oriented movement. Motion just as motion might be regarded as an incomplete act, on its way to completion; it becomes a complete act only when it arrives at a specific terminus. We may observe a physical body which is in motion, such as one of the planets of our solar system orbiting around the sun, but that movement or action is not an act as we are defining it here, and that is because the movement of the planet has no completion; it has revolution but no resolution. The planets are just going around in circles, well, in near circles. (One might argue that the end of circular motion is the perpetuation of the motion, which is a point worth considering.) Note that the description of any act unavoidably includes the point of the act, the end or purpose toward which it is directed: kicking a football, baking a cake, writing a letter, taking an oath, the ends of which acts are respectively the airborne football, the cake, the letter, the oath. In sum, an act is a doing which results in the done; it is a process that terminates in product.

The fact that we can all act as efficient causes implies that we are all necessarily caught up in final causality. The two are inseparable, a point I will elaborate upon in a moment. We are rather special causal agents because we are conscious agents; in most cases we know what we are doing and why we are doing it. Unless we are simply idling away our time by engaging in actions that are going nowhere in particular, like twiddling our thumbs, whenever we take action it is in order to accomplish something definite, although the accomplishment in any given case, such as going to the refrigerator to fetch an orange, may not be of great moment. We may generally describe intelligible activity as activity that is ordered toward achieving a specific end; it is not helter-skelter or haphazard activity. As conscious, rational agents we are by nature purposeful people.

The Pervasiveness of Purpose

When Aristotle observed that final causality was operatively present everywhere in the physical universe, he was in effect saying that our universe was fairly awash in purposefulness. In saying as much he did not have in mind only the actions of conscious agents, human beings in particular, but he included the actions of all material agents, be they humans, or animals, or plants, or even inanimate material substances. This might strike us as not a little odd, for we are normally inclined to associate purposefulness with conscious agents only. But if we understand purposefulness as not necessarily involving conscious choice on the part of an agent but as simply another way of describing the end-orientation of agency of any kind, its inherent proclivity to direct its action toward a definite resolution, then we can readily see that purposefulness is indeed a universal phenomenon. We live in a universe which is structurally framed by purpose, and that accounts for its order. Without that purpose we would not have a universe, a cosmos, an ordered whole.

That we human beings, as conscious, rational agents, act purposefully, is beyond question; that is something which is unequivocally attested to by our personal experiences. We are goal-oriented creatures, our actions are aimed at accomplishment. Final causality is manifestly an operative reality in animal behavior. Animals act to achieve specific ends, some of which, the results of their constructive activity, are marvels to behold, such as the sturdy dams of busy beavers, the castle-like structures of termites, the nests of the weaver bird, the geometric perfections which are the cells of honey bees. The higher animals are certainly conscious of the ends they pursue, although we can only guess at the quality of that consciousness. In most of their actions they are guided by fail-safe instinct, but in certain instances they seem to display something analogous to on-the-spot decision making, making deft adjustments to quickly changing circumstances. But even the most simple and primitive members of the animal kingdom, those possessed only of the tactile sense, when they move toward sources of nourishment or away from perceived dangers show that they act for the sake of an end, self-preservation in these two cases.

The most obvious manifestation of end-oriented action in the plant kingdom takes the form of vegetative growth. Every species of plant begins with seed, within the sometimes quite tiny scope of which its future mature state is enclosed. The defining act of every plant commences with the germination of the seed and culminates when it reaches full maturity; the plant's maturity is the end toward which every stage of its vegetal action is directed. Its growth is purposeful, not random.

Does purposefulness cease when we exit the realm of animate material being and into the realm of the inanimate? It does not. We repeat: we are dealing here with a phenomenon which is a principal feature of the entire natural world. Let us consider a remarkable series of substantial changes that take place quite naturally in the inorganic realm. The natural element uranium, by the process of radioactive decay, passes through a series of transformations into, first thorium, then protactinium, then radium, until it finally ends up as lead. What we observe in that process is an ordered, predictable progression, a successive action that terminates in the natural element which is lead. The lead is the final cause of the action, the end toward which it was directed, and precisely because of the finality which characterizes the action, we can call it purposeful. This does not imply of course that there was any consciousness involved on the part of the agents, as if one day the uranium underwent an identity crisis that made it so dissatisfied with its current state of being that it decided to decay its way to becoming lead.

When a chemist combines in his laboratory the gases of hydrogen and oxygen in certain proportions and under set conditions, the predictable outcome will be water. If I am holding a brick in my hands and let it drop, taking care that my bare feet are not in the way, the predictable outcome will be that the brick will fall to the ground, having had interrupted at that point its inherent inclination to proceed on to the center of the earth. The ubiquitous operative presence of final causality in the physical universe is what makes scientific prediction possible, for all we are doing when we make scientific predictions is simply reminding ourselves of the finality of a given act, calling attention to how it is ultimately going to turn out. We can go further and say that without final causality there would be no science; it is the business of science (here I mean the empirical sciences, principally physics) to take note of and measure the ordered regularities of nature, but the explanation behind those ordered regularities is final causality. To claim that without final causality there would be no ordered regularities is to imply a larger, more comprehensive claim: without final causality there would be no nature, no cosmos, only chaos.

Skepticism Regarding Final Causality

We noted earlier that there have been philosophers who were skeptical regarding efficient causality. How about final causality? No less a philosophical figure than René Descartes, the universally acknowledged father of modern philosophy, although he accepted the reality of final causality, nonetheless maintained that it was beyond the capacity of science to deal with intelligently. The rather remarkable explanation he gave for this was that we cannot know the mind of God. What he meant by that is that the human mind cannot discern the purposes God had in creating the physical universe. Now, that point can be readily enough conceded, but it is a rather odd one for someone like Descartes to make. He believed that God had indeed created the physical universe, and he certainly believed that the universe was an ordered whole, a genuine cosmos, and it was a major project of his philosophy to identify the particulars of that order.

What was M. Descartes missing? Granting that God did indeed create the physical universe, we can, using terminology we are familiar with, identify God as its efficient cause, and the universe as the grand effect of His causative action. Now, recall something we said earlier about the cause/effect relation: that the cause, to one degree or another, leaves its imprint on the effect it produces, so that by studying the effect we can learn something about the cause. We do not need to have access to the mind of Michelangelo to be able to form some reliable ideas about the purposes he had in creating his "Moses." His purposes have been given concrete expression in the statue itself. By the same token one may argue, and Descartes should have been able to argue, that God, as the efficient cause of the physical universe, could be said to have incorporated his purposes in the very fabric of the universe, and those purposes are expressed first and foremost in the order that constitutes the universe and, more particularly, in the ubiquitous operative presence of final causality that accounts for that order.

Many moderns, philosophers and especially scientists, would have little patience with that whole line of reasoning, and that is because not a few of them are professed atheists. But that is an issue the consideration of which we will postpone until we get to the next and final chapter of this book, where our subject will be natural theology. I would venture to say that the clear majority of empirical scientists today, whatever might be their religious beliefs or lack thereof, see no relevance at all of final causality to the work they are doing. We have come a long way, not only chronologically but conceptually, from the physics of Aristotle to modern physics. Aristotle saw final causality everywhere; the moderns seemingly see it nowhere. If modern thinkers, beginning in the nineteenth century, saw fit in a more or less wholesale manner to dispense with final causality, it was commonly for not very carefully thought-out philosophical reasons; in more cases than not it was a concession to practicality. The physicist, for example, simply saw no need to appeal to a final cause as something that added any explanatory weight to his analysis of physical reality. He could reasonably manage by relying principally on material and efficient causality.

One may dismiss final causality as inconsequential, supposing it to be little more than a fiction made up by bemused metaphysicians, but for all that it sturdily and steadily remains what it is—an integral and central feature of the physical universe. A scientist may not want to accept it, but in spite of himself he cannot avoid it, and that is because it is inseparable from what he does accept, and unquestioningly, namely efficient causality. No scientist, or for that matter no one at all who pays any attention to how the world works, would deny the reality of efficient causality, which provides us with the foundational explanation for all change. The efficient cause, we remind ourselves, is that cause that brings a thing into existence, or alters in one way or another an already existing thing. The very concept of cause, we know, is unintelligible unless conjoined to the concept of effect, so we say that the two, cause and effect, are correlatives. Now, the effect is nothing other than the end or the finality of the action of the efficient cause. In other words, the effect is simply the final cause, and thus a more elaborate way of saying cause and effect are inseparable is to say that efficient cause and final cause are inseparable. We live in a richly purposeful universe, there is no escaping it.

Materialism

In introducing the subject of metaphysics we described it as a philosophic science whose subject is exhaustively inclusive, dealing as it does with whatever really exists in any way it is possible to exist. Metaphysics, as we have stressed, in its concern with and focus upon real being, is not limited to material substances but includes immaterial substances as well. Metaphysics, then, acknowledges that the realm of being, of real existents, is divided between material being and immaterial being.

On this point we could expect that there would be vigorous protests coming from the camp of philosophical materialism, a camp which today is occupied by legions of foot soldiers. There would be protests, denials, some of them doubtless quite passionate, but revealingly, there would be no arguments. That is an important point to which I will return, but first it would be fitting to do a little history. Philosophical materialism, the position that holds that the only reality is material reality, would seem to be almost as old as philosophy itself, although it did not really come into its own as a dominating position until modern times. The pre-Socratic philosophers Leucippus and Democritus (fifth century B.C.), who gave us the first atomic theory, were arguably also the first dedicated materialistic philosophers. The Greek philosopher Epicurus, who lived roughly a century after Leucippus and Democritus, adopted their materialistic philosophy wholesale and incorporated it into the philosophy which he developed and which came to be known, aptly enough, as Epicureanism. That philosophy was to be given memorable publicity by the Roman poet Lucretius (c.95-55 B.C.) in his *De Rerum Natura*, "On the Nature of Things," the popularity of which reflected the fact that Epicureanism was a significant presence in the Roman empire in the last century before the Christian era. Lucretius's classic work, after centuries of slumber, was revived and became quite popular during the Renaissance, which suggests that there was as well a revival of the materialistic outlook which took place during that period.

The eighteenth century, the "Age of Reason" that engendered the Enlightenment, was a significant turning point for materialistic philosophy in the West, as many among the intellectual elites began to succumb to it, implicitly if not explicitly. But it was in the nineteenth century that materialistic thinking blossomed and could be said to have come into its own as a dominant factor in Western thought. This was attributable in great part to the influence of Charles Darwin's thoroughly materialistic theory of evolution, introduced by his *The Origin of Species*, published in 1859. Darwin's ideas, and the world view that fathered them, swept over Western culture like a tidal wave. By the twentieth century materialism had become firmly established as a prominent, if not in certain circles a dominant, philosophical point of view. Today many philosophers and scientists adhere to that point of view, with varying degrees of conviction.

At this point it would be helpful to insert a note on terminology. "Materialism," "positivism," and "naturalism" refer to basically the same point of view, and without danger of serious confusion can be used interchangeably. The point of view or philosophical position to which all three terms refer can be generally described as a form of reductionism which simplistically and arbitrarily seeks to limit the scope and the richness of reality. "Materialism" is the term I will favor in what follows.

One of the hallmarks of materialistic philosophy is its peremptory dismissal of metaphysics. In the mid-twentieth century the British philosopher A. J. Ayer published a book called *Language, Truth and Logic*, the first chapter of which was significantly entitled, "The Elimination of Metaphysics." Ayer was echoing the opinion of many positivist thinkers of his day when he branded metaphysics as "nonsense," a dismissive designation he believed it fully deserved because it dealt with matters, purported immaterial realities (i.e., immaterial beings), which could not be verified according to the criteria laid down by the empirical sciences, and that provided proof positive that immaterial realities simply did not exist. Ayer was committed to the belief that the only reality was material reality, those things whose existential status could be verified by sense experience—whatever can be seen, heard, smelled, tasted, touched, and which lend themselves to precise quantitative measurement. Because metaphysics gives attention to what it supposes to be real entities, but which are not subject to empirical verification, the materialist believes that whatever metaphysics has to say in so much of its literature simply makes no sense, and therefore is not worth being taken seriously. Note where the emphasis is being put: because metaphysical thinking does not restrain itself and operate within the proper boundaries established by the empirical sciences, it cannot be taken as a serious and worthwhile intellectual enterprise.

More than once I have referred to materialism as a philosophical position, which is an accurate enough way of identifying it. But is materialism a reasonable philosophical position? A reasonable philosophical position is a defensible position, that is, one which is capable of offering cogent logical arguments that terminate in conclusions which, if not compelling, at least achieve some degree of persuasiveness. Materialism has never been able to do that, a point I made in passing just above. Materialism can protest the position of metaphysics, can deny its viability, can call it names, but it lacks the wherewithal to demonstrate that the position of metaphysics, which accepts the real existence of immaterial being, is for that reason an untenable position. Materialism cannot take even the first step toward doing that because of the narrow intellectual terrain to which it voluntarily limits itself.

Consider the problematic situation the materialist would face should he attempt to prove that metaphysics is nonsense. He would have to prove, to demonstrate, the non-existence of immaterial being. But the severely self-limiting position that materialism imposes upon itself necessarily involves acknowledging that the only legitimate truth-discovering method of intellectual enquiry is the empirical method, or what is loosely known as the "scientific method." And the empirical method, by definition, is limited to the investigation of material being. Where does that leave the materialist who wants to prove the intellectual illegitimacy of metaphysics? So long as he chooses to remain encased in the epistemological straightjacket in which he has garbed himself, he cannot even take a first steady step toward proving that the only reality is material reality. His sharply curtailed mode of thinking does not allow him to get outside of the realm of the material.

But that gives him no warrant whatever for claiming that there is no "outside" to the realm of the material; in other words, he has no rational basis for claiming that the only reality is material being.

The situation of the materialist in this respect would be somewhat like that of a philosophic ice fish who lives his entire life in the gloomy depths of the Antarctic Ocean. The only world he knows is a water world, and on the basis of that knowledge he confidently and complacently claims that the only world is a water world. He thereby commits a very primitive kind of fallacy: refusing to allow for the existence of something that is not an element of one's own knowledge.

Both the extraordinary philosophic ice fish and the materialist are in situations which limit the way they think about reality, but the grand difference between the two is that the materialist's limiting situation is voluntary. He has chosen to adopt an attitude which deliberately curbs his thinking, confining it to a world and reality which has not been discovered by untrammeled enquiry, but which rests entirely on presupposition. He ends up by accepting as really existing only what his ideological commitment permits him to say really exists. In this sense materialism can be considered to be a form of idealism.

The only remedy for the materialist, if he is willing accept the challenge of trying to debunk metaphysics in an intellectually reputable way, is for him to agree to become, if only temporarily, a metaphysician, or a least a more generous and expansive philosopher. To summarize our reflections to this point: so long as the materialist remains committed to the intellectually confining notion that empiricism is the only road to truth, he can never reach a destination which will allow him to make any reputable (i.e., logically sound) claims about metaphysics. He has disallowed himself the kind of reasoning that would permit him to argue (in the strict, logical sense) issues of the kind about which he can now only make unfounded assertions, the kind of reasoning that is common not only to metaphysics but, it should be emphasized (and this is something the materialist should know), is common as well to sound philosophy generally, to logic, and to mathematics. The value of empirical verification is not to be minimized, but it is important to recognize that it is the most limited kind of verification.

Earlier in the chapter I identified materialism as a type of monism. Clarifications are now in order. Materialism can be identified as an ontological monism, in the sense that it allows for only one reality, material being. It can also be called an epistemological monism, because it will acknowledge only one path that will lead to the truth and that is the path of empiricism. As is the case with other forms of monism, the materialistic forms of it are not the results of long and laborious intellectual enquiry, but simply unfounded, arbitrary declarations regarding the objective order of things. They are not facts of the objective order, but projections of the subjective order.

If materialism, as a philosophical position, is incapable of offering reasonable arguments on its behalf, how is one to explain its pervasive presence in contemporary society, especially among those whom we choose to identify as the intelligentsia? The answer is that materialism is at bottom simply a belief system, a natural faith; it certainly is not a sound philosophical position, nor is it a reputable scientific point of view. The object of the materialist's faith remains entirely within the natural realm. From its very beginning materialism has been very closely allied with atheism. It would be a rare fellow indeed who identifies himself as a dedicated materialist and at the same time claims to be a theist. His god or gods would necessarily have to be material beings, and therefore much like the Olympian deities of ancient Greece. To deny the reality of immaterial being is to be a confirmed naturalist, one who has no time for the transcendent, that which stands above the natural order and governs it. To be a dedicated materialist is to be not so much a rigorous reasoner as a true believer.

Everything that can be rightly said of materialism reveals it as a severely delimiting view of the world and reality. It impoverishes, intellectually and spiritually, every society which it has infected. But it damages most the individuals who succumb to it. The materialist might be willing to accept the classic definition of man as a rational animal, but his understanding of human reason, its nature, its purpose, its capacities, is profoundly wanting in every respect. The attitude he takes toward the human intellect is not only shallow but also degrading, for he is blind to its elevated purpose and limitless potential. In nurturing this attitude he of course in the first instance does a serious disservice to himself, diminishing the value of his own mind by not acknowledging that toward which it is naturally ordered. The human mind was made to know being, not selectively, as does the materialist, but totally. The irony of his placement in the confining condition in which he has freely chosen to put himself is that it prevents him from ever coming to know, in the deepest and fullest sense, material being itself, which he erroneously supposes to represent the sum total of being. This is because we cannot arrive at anything like an adequate understanding of material being if we do not see it as but part of a whole and not the whole itself; if, specifically, we do not see how material being necessarily and subordinately relates to immaterial being. In sum, adequate knowledge of material being depends on knowledge of immaterial being. This means that the materialist will only arrive at a sufficient understanding of the material world when he abandons his materialism.

Materialists are fond of thinking of themselves as hard-core realists, having no time or patience for the kind of nonsense with which metaphysics chooses to preoccupy itself. The fact is, however, that materialists are not nearly realists enough, for the kind of selective realism they indulge in, accepting only material being as real, will never satisfy the human mind or heart. The materialist has habituated himself to stopping short, not exercising the special kind of daring which is needed in order to continue on ahead and confront being in its bountiful totality. He does not advance beyond the point where being, in its material manifestations, immediately and concretely manifests itself to us, having sadly convinced himself that at that point he is dealing with the totality. He thus burdens himself with a spirit-sapping intellectual poverty. For all his perhaps otherwise brilliance, he remains a thinker who has confined himself to what are only surface realities, depriving himself of a transforming encounter with the fathomless depths of being.

As we shall see in the next chapter, metaphysics takes on some of the most formidable questions that the human mind has posed for itself: Does God exist? Can his existence be ascertained by relying on human reason alone? What are we able to say, relying on human reason alone, of the nature of God? In dealing with questions of this weight and import, metaphysics seeks to fulfill its most elevated and demanding obligations as a philosophic science.

Chapter Eight
Ultimate Questions: Natural Theology

The Culmination of Metaphysics

The subject of this final chapter of our compendium of philosophy will be natural theology, which has traditionally been regarded as an integral part of metaphysics. As the material contents of metaphysics expanded over the years, and became a standard course in the academic curriculum, it seemed expedient, for pedagogical reasons, to split the science into two separate sub-sciences, the first of which was usually called General Ontology (the subject of the previous chapter), the second Natural Theology. Keep in mind, then, that while we now engage ourselves with the specifics of the latter subject, we are still working within the realm of the larger science of metaphysics. Aristotle, the ground-breaking pioneer in these matters, believed that the concerns with which natural theology is occupied should be those toward which metaphysical reasoning in general is directed, representing its proper culmination.

To begin, we need to reflect a moment on the title of our science, "natural theology." It explicitly identifies itself as a theology, which is a science unto itself, and whose subject matter has been succinctly described as "God and everything that pertains to God." But careful note must be taken of the qualifier in the title, "natural." What does that imply? It tells us that ours is a strictly philosophical science, and therefore it is to be distinguished from what is commonly known as sacred theology, or dogmatic theology. What the two have in common is the same basic subject matter, "God and everything that pertains to God." What importantly sets them apart is the markedly different points of view from which they approach and deal with their common subject matter. The professional theologian, one who pursues sacred theology, studies that subject matter from the point of view of divine revelation, that knowledge about God which—and this is an integral part of his belief—God himself has revealed to man, the particulars of which revelation have their principal source in the Bible. The philosopher who makes a study of natural theology does not rely upon divine revelation, but seeks to determine what can be known about God, including the question of his very existence, by relying entirely on human reason. The natural theologian may be a man of faith, but the authority he attributes to his faith does not enter into the type of reasoning he engages in while pursuing this philosophic discipline. The principal authority in natural theology derives from human reason alone, and whatever arguments it can formulate by way of giving foundation and intellectual substance to the discipline.

There is another philosophical discipline, the philosophy of religion, which is an important field of study and which today receives a good deal of lively attention; it is not to be confused with natural theology, however, for the two have distinctly different aims. But this is not to say that the developed concerns of the philosophy of religion cannot be of great benefit to natural theology for, after all, religion is the larger phenomenon, of which theology, sacred or natural, is a particular part. Historically, religion precedes theology, if by the latter one means the organized, systematic study of the contents of religion.

Origins

Though "natural theology" is the title by which our science is commonly identified, it does at times go by another, "theodicy," a name we owe to the German philosopher Gottfried Leibniz (1646-1716). It is a neologism of his own invention, and he used it as the title of his book on natural theology, which was published in 1710. As to the origins of natural theology, the classical scholar A. E. Taylor argued that it all began with Plato, in the pages of his *Laws*. There we find, in Book X of that formidable work, the first argument for the existence of God to be found in Western philosophical literature. It is an argument based on motion, or change, a type of argument about which I will have more to say in the pages that follow. If Plato can be called the founder of natural theology, Aristotle, who studied under him for some twenty years, followed in the footsteps of his great mentor in that he too, as noted above, made the concerns of natural theology a central aspect of his philosophy, regarding it as the capstone of metaphysics.

Given the aims, accomplishments, and overall import of Aristotle's greatest work, the *Metaphysics*, he is deserving of being recognized as the founder of the discipline, although, interestingly enough, the title by which we know that work is not the one he gave to it, for he gave it none. Apparently he was undecided about the matter. In the text of the work itself, however, he offers no less than three names which he thought aptly described the kind of philosophy he was developing: "first philosophy," "wisdom," and, significantly, given our concerns here, simply "theology." What he was practicing was "first philosophy" because it had to do with the most important questions philosophy can deal with; it was "wisdom" because it was devoted to ferreting out and coming to know thoroughly first causes and principles, the fundamental explanations of things, and to do that is the mark of wisdom. And "theology"? The word itself is a compound of two Greek words, and it can be translated as "the study of God." In the first book of the *Metaphysics*, he explains why he believed that study to be very much the business of philosophy: "God is thought to be among the causes of all things and to be a first principle, and God is the sole or chief possessor of this sort of knowledge." (*Metaph.* 983a, 6-10) In the same passage he goes on to say that in comparing metaphysics with all the other sciences, it is found that "none is more excellent." In the *Metaphysics* Aristotle offers an argument for the existence of God, whom he identifies as the Prime Mover. A different version of what is essentially the same argument appears in his *Physics*. Of the two, the one in the *Physics* is, in my view, the more fully developed and compelling.

The Principal Undertaking of Natural Theology

The hallmark of natural theology, the undertaking by which it is principally distinguished, is the formulation of arguments for the existence of God. This singular philosophical endeavor has a long history behind it. As noted, it all began with Plato, then came Aristotle. Among the major thinkers who contributed to the array of arguments for God's existence subsequent to those ancient Greek philosophers, the following deserve special recognition: St. Augustine, who offers an arresting argument based on mathematics; St. Anselm, whose "ontological argument" is as much discussed and debated today as it was in the eleventh century when it was first published, and which we will discuss later in the chapter; St. Thomas Aquinas, whose famous "Five Ways" of proving God's existence provide the foundation for the arguments I will feature in this chapter; René Descartes, the father of modern philosophy, provided two proofs for the existence of God, which he considered essential to his philosophy, and which are basically variations of St. Anselm's ontological argument; the most compelling argument offered by Gottfried Leibniz may generally be described as an argument from order or design; in modern times, the French philosopher Jacques Maritain, the English literary scholar C. S. Lewis, and the American philosopher Mortimer Adler have offered arguments which, each in its own way, are novel and thought-provoking.

The Nature of Proof or Demonstration

The principal task of natural theology, we have said, is the formulation of arguments that seek to prove the existence of God. That is no small task. What does it involve? At this stage we need to make some crucial distinctions, and the first one is that between metaphysical and moral arguments for the existence of God. The arguments put forward by natural theology are metaphysical arguments, which means that they are to be taken as demonstrative, or proofs in the strict sense of the word. The moral arguments, on the other hand, are not proofs in the strict sense. I have chosen to abide by the names traditionally given to the two types of argument, "metaphysical" and "moral." To be clear about what distinguishes the two types, think of them respectively, with your logic in mind, as demonstrative arguments and probable arguments. What the two types of arguments have in common is the fact that both are genuine arguments, which is to say— remember what we learned in Chapter One—they are examples of a linguistic discourse which is composed of two distinct elements, premises (the supporting data) and a conclusion (a statement which is accepted as true on the force of the data supplied in the premises). The difference between an argument which is demonstrative (a genuine proof) and one that is not is that in the first the conclusion follows necessarily from the premises, whereas in the second it does not. In a demonstrative argument, if the premises are true, and if its structure is valid, then the conclusion must be true. If I understand the premises of the argument, recognize them as being true, see how they logically relate to the conclusion, I would acknowledge the conclusion to be unavoidably true.

The conclusions of non-demonstrative arguments for the existence of God, which are called the moral arguments, do not follow necessarily from the arguments' premises. We are not logically compelled, on the basis of what the premises tell us, to accept their conclusions as true. Here we are in the realm of probability rather than certainty. Non-demonstrative arguments can vary greatly in their capacity to compel. Some are more persuasive than others; it all depends on the quality of their premises, how they are developed, and the support they lend to their conclusions. This is not an unusual circumstance for argumentation in general. Most of the arguments that we are presented with on a regular basis, as well as those which we ourselves develop, dealing with a wide variety of subjects, are non-demonstrative. If they "prove" anything, it is only in a loose sense of the word. The best examples of truly demonstrative arguments come from mathematics, such as those gems of lucid reasoning found in Euclid's *Elements*.

Point of Departure

For any argument, whatever its subject, to be successful, that is, to have a strong persuasive effect on the audience to which it is addressed, it must begin with a point of departure that is clearly understood and accepted by that audience. Any argument—and this very much includes an argument which sets out to prove the existence of God—must begin in the public sphere, in the sense that it starts by presenting facts, circumstances, a state of affairs, which are accessible and immediately apparent to all parties concerned. In the technical language of logic, the major premise or starting point of the argument must be self-evident, its truth must be manifest and incontestable. Recall the classic argument we considered in Chapter One.

> All human beings are mortal.
> All Greeks are human beings.
> All Greeks are mortal.

The major premise or basic starting point of that argument, "All human beings are mortal," is obviously true. Because the argument starts by making a statement with which everyone would agree, it has a sound basis and it can confidently take off from that point of departure. Unless its starting point is manifestly true, an argument can never get off the ground. Earlier we mentioned that the very first philosophical arguments for the existence of God, those composed by Plato and Aristotle, were based on the phenomenon of motion. They began by calling attention to the fact that things move, they change. That was a very sound starting point. Could anything be more obvious than the reality of motion?

More needs to be said about arguments whose specific intent is to prove the existence of God. Consider motion again, as the starting point for such an argument. The motion in question is not simply the idea of motion, not a theory about motion, but the actual motion of actually existing physical bodies in the external world, bodies which we are acquainted with through sense knowledge, through what we see, hear, smell, taste, and touch. The argument starts with what is generally most immediately familiar to us and concerning the reality of which we have no doubt—the material world in which we live and of which, as material beings, we are an integral part. We are attempting to prove the existence of a being that is entirely immaterial, but in doing so we start with the material.

But if we are trying to prove the existence of God, do we not run into a problem right at the outset which would seem to undermine the whole project? What problem do I have in mind? Let us say that I am genuinely ignorant regarding the question of whether or not there is a God. In that case would not any argument I attempt to formulate be aimless, for I would not know what I am trying to prove? This is a hoary problem, or pseudo-problem, that Plato tangled with centuries ago. There were certain philosophers in ancient Greece who argued that we can never arrive at knowledge that is entirely new, can never, in other words, make genuine discoveries regarding things about which we were previously ignorant. Their argument went this way: Either (1) we already know what we are looking for, in which case there is no need to look; or (2) we don't know what we are looking for, in which case any search on our part would be futile. I think you can see why I called this a pseudo-problem, the kind that one susceptible to committing the fallacy of the false dilemma would bring up.

If what it claims were true, empirical science would be impossible. The physicist may not know precisely what he is looking for, but he is not groping blindly in the dark, given the specific context within which he is conducting his research; he has ready to hand any number of firmly established facts, and on the basis of those facts, he hypothesizes the existence of a further fact. Given the existence of facts A, B, and C, which are the effects of a cause of which he is ignorant, he argues, on the basis of what he knows about the nature of those facts, that they point to the existence of D, which would be their cause. On the basis of the knowledge he has of A, B, and C, through his close scrutiny of them, he can make intelligent surmises about the nature of their putative cause, D.

The same general mode of reasoning is at work with respect to arguments for the existence of God. Clearly, before an argument is begun, one need not have a precise idea of what "God" means, but one must have some kind of idea, however vague, a working notion of sorts of what it is you are attempting to prove. It is sufficient to begin with a nominal definition of God, the kind of definition dictionaries give us. St. Augustine suggests how we might start when he writes that we "call that reality God which has nothing superior to it." So, we are trying to prove the existence of that kind of reality, something we could call "the Supreme Being," or "the Ultimate Reality," or "the Absolute."

Is God Possible?

There is a foundational principle of logic and metaphysics against which any argument for the existence of God, or for the existence of anything else for that matter, must be tested right at the outset if it is to have any legitimacy at all, and that is the principle of contradiction. That principle, we remind ourselves, tells us that it is not possible for something to be and not be at the same time and in the same respect. This is the principle which sharply divides the possible from the impossible, and is the touchstone for all sound reasoning. If I were to set out to prove that there could be a perpetual motion machine I would be embarked upon a futile venture, for the laws of physics tell us that a perpetual motion machine is impossible. Well, how about the existence of a supreme being, an eminently superior being, a being than which there is none greater? Is the idea of the possibility of such a being inherently contradictory, utterly and unavoidably irrational? If we give calm and unprejudiced reflection to the question, we see that there is no contradiction involved here; it is within the realm of possibility that such a being could exist. It does not fly in the face of rationality to suppose that there could be such a being. But does that mere possibility prove anything? It does not. There are some philosophers who have thought otherwise, arguing that the sheer possibility of God's existence somehow proves God's existence. But that is limp reasoning, violating as it does one of the basic principles of logic, which tells us that it is illicit to infer actual existence from possible existence. Common sense tells us as much. The fact that little five-year-old Patricia is remarkably adept at playing the violin and that we think it possible that she will be another Sarah Chang, does not permit us to conclude that she will one day be performing in Carnegie Hall.

A Realist Approach

We approach the challenging task of proving the existence of God from the point of view of a realist philosophy, in contrast to the point of view taken by an idealist philosophy. What does that mean, concretely? We have already declared our realist position in what we had to say above about the starting point of our argument: it is the factual world "out there," external to the mind and independent of the mind, the material universe. The idealist philosopher would have the tendency to begin his argument by looking inward rather than outward, specifically, by making his point of departure an idea of God. This was essentially the approach taken by St. Anselm in his "ontological argument," to which we referred earlier. St. Anselm based his argument on an idea of God as a being "greater than which cannot be conceived," and he saw in that idea the necessity for the actual existence of such a being. We need not here go into the particulars of his argument; suffice it to say that, though it might have considerable force as a moral argument, it falls short as a demonstration of God's existence.

Some five hundred years after St. Anselm wrote, René Descartes was to adopt basically the same approach in his arguments for the existence of God. Descartes, as is common with idealist philosophers, relies heavily on ideas. Whereas the realist philosopher maintains that all of our ideas have their origin in sense knowledge, and therefore have their roots in the external world, the idealist, on the other hand, who like Descartes would be skeptical of the reliability of sense experience, nurtures the belief that we have ideas in the mind that are innate to the mind. Where do these ideas come from? For Descartes, they come from God, and the most prominent and commanding of those ideas is the very idea of God. Descartes claimed, remarkably, that he had an idea of God before he had an idea of himself. This idea of God is that of an infinite being, and on that account, Descartes reasoned, he could not be the origin of the idea. Why not? Because he was a finite being, and the mind of a finite being could not conceive of an infinite being; only an infinite being, God, could be the origin of such an idea. Thus, Descartes took the fact that he held in his mind the idea of God as an infinite being as proof of the actual, extra-mental existence of that being.

There is a certain attractiveness to Descartes' line of reasoning, but it does not have the effect he envisioned for it. The argument is non-demonstrative. How so? What is wrong with basing purported proofs for the existence of God on ideas we have of God? We must keep in mind what was emphasized above, that an argument must begin with self-evident premises; its very first step must be taken in the public sphere, presenting facts that are accessible to all and knowable by all. Now, there is nothing less public, more private, more individual-specific, more strictly limited to ourselves, than our ideas. The idea of a being "than which a greater cannot be conceived" is a very sophisticated idea, but what if I do not share it, what if it is quite foreign to me and I have trouble understanding it? Or, apropos of Descartes' argument, what if I can in no way honestly claim that I have in my mind an overwhelming idea of God as an infinite being, which he took to be innate to his own mind? The simple fact of the matter is that I may not share other people's ideas of God, or of anything else, but I am certain that I see physical objects in the world, and I observe that they move, and I feel confident that other people have the same experiences as I do in that regard.

Objections to Our Project

Before we can proceed in presenting our proofs for the existence of God we must respond to two standard objections to the project. The first objection maintains that there is no need to prove the existence of God. The second objection maintains that no such proof is possible. We have, then, the "no need to do it" and the "can't do it" objections.

The objection that holds that there is no need to prove God's existence comes from the theist camp, from people who firmly believe in the existence of God. Their position is straightforward and uncomplicated: you do not have to prove the truth of something you already know to be true. Their contention is that all human beings, by reason of the fact that they have been created by God, have firmly rooted in the depths of their consciousness a sure knowledge of the reality of God. Knowledge of God's existence, then, simply comes naturally to man as an entirely reliable intuition and, in effect, as an accompaniment of one's self-awareness. Some who adopt this position maintain that they have a firm conviction of the existence of God because of distinct personal experiences they have had, sometimes accompanied by strong, even transporting emotions.

As to the principal point, that all human beings have a built-in, intuitive knowledge of the existence of God, this would seem to be belied by the full sweep of human history and the findings of cultural anthropology. It seems to be the case that human beings, ancient and modern, do in fact have a deeply rooted sense of the transcendent, of a reality that is above and quite other than what we find in the purely natural realm. But this sense has manifested itself, down through the course of history, and in different cultures, in a variety of different and often quite incompatible ways. Some human beings have thought in terms of a single, supreme, spiritual being; some have thought of such a being as material; some have thought there to be a plurality of gods; some have thought the gods to be benign and solicitous of all humankind; some have thought the gods demanded human sacrifice; some have thought nature itself to be divine and full of numberless animating spirits; and so on. In sum, if we can say that human beings have an intuitive sense of the divine, of the supernatural, it is an obscure and confused sense, and not much to be relied on if one is looking for clarity and specificity; it does not consistently suggest a reality that would answer to the name of Supreme Being.

As to the point that some people claim to have had deeply moving personal experiences that convince them, not simply of God's existence, but of his love for them, this is not something that any of us have a right to deny, much less to make light of. I might say that while I admire people who have such experiences, even envy them for those experiences, they are not part of my own experiences. In this sense such experiences are comparable to ideas that one might have of God; they cannot serve as starting points for demonstrative arguments for the existence of God because they are not experiences that could be shared, of the kind everyone would have access to.

Among those who contend that it is not possible to prove the existence of God one would find, unsurprisingly, many atheists, but this position is not limited to atheists. The stance taken by the atheist is unambiguous: one cannot prove the existence of something that doesn't exist, and God doesn't exist. And that's the end of the discussion. While one might admire the clarity of the atheist's views on this matter, his logic is faulty. The bold assertion of the non-existence of God is only that, an assertion, a conclusion not preceded by anything like convincing premises. The non-existence of God needs to be demonstrated, and as shown in the previous chapter, so long as the atheist restricts his reasoning to the empirical mode of enquiry, maintaining it to be the only legitimate way of reasoning, he is unable to do so. He is like someone who claims there is only one road to Peoria because he knows only one road that will get him to the town, and refuses to investigate the possibility that there may be others.

A much more interesting, and challenging, articulation of the "can't do it" objection to our project comes from theists, and one of the most interesting personages to hold this view was the eminent philosopher Immanuel Kant. He maintained that there were three fundamental truths which for stability of mind and heart we must adhere to—that there is a God, that human beings have free will, and that the human soul is immortal. But none of these can be proved; they simply must be accepted as postulates, allowing us to live a genuinely human life, just as we must accept the postulates of geometry, allowing us to make progress in mastering that mathematical science.

Kant took no stock in the projects of natural theology because he saw metaphysics, of which natural theology is an integral part, as pretty much a dead letter. If one disregards metaphysics, as traditionally understood and practiced for centuries, one is not going to give any credence to natural theology; if the whole is unacceptable, so is the part. What was Kant's complaint against metaphysics and, concomitantly, natural theology? We have seen that metaphysics, which takes into account the full range of being, argues that beginning with material being, which is immediately accessible to us through sense experience, we can, through reasoning, make our way to immaterial being. Not so, says Kant. He was adamant in insisting that the human intellect, given its limitations, was incapable of arriving at a realm of reality which transcends the world we know through sense knowledge. He did not deny the existence of such a realm, he simply maintained that it was inaccessible to human reason. In his famous and immensely influential work, *The Critique of Pure Reason*, he set out to show that (1) metaphysics was inherently self-contradictory, and (2) the classic arguments that purport to prove the existence of God do not work. To offer here a detailed critique of Kant's arguments in defense of those two theses would take us too far afield. Both sets of arguments are quite impressive in their way, but they do not achieve the effect he confidently assigned to them. His attempt to show that metaphysics is inherently, indeed inescapably, inconsistent falls short of the mark, and the same can be said for his attempts to show that certain classic arguments proving God's existence do not work. One of the problems with how he handles the classic arguments, no small one, is the eccentric twists he gives to them. He does not present them with the clarity and precision that they have traditionally been presented. In all, despite Kant's earnest and highly stimulating efforts to undermine the integrity of metaphysics and natural theology, they emerge unscathed from his concentrated critiques of them.

An attitude very much like Kant's was adopted in more recent times by the Austrian philosopher Ludwig Wittgenstein. His guiding principle was that we should remain silent about those matters about which we cannot speak intelligently, and that concerns the entire realm with which metaphysics concerns itself. He maintained that philosophy cannot prove the existence of God, or speak intelligently of a realm that transcends the natural order, not because he denied the existence of either God or the transcendent, but because he believed that the only road to them could be taken, not by the philosopher, but by the mystic.

The General Character of the Arguments

The arguments begin with and are solidly based upon fundamental facts about the material world which are obvious to everyone. That is a critical feature of all of them, something to which I have already given much stress. Their point of departure is the material world; their point of arrival is the immaterial world. The basic thrust of each argument, its central line of reasoning, is this: what we discover about the nature of the material world, the physical universe, is such that logic demands that we move beyond the confines of the material world in order to have an adequate explanation for the material world itself. We give careful attention to what we know immediately through sense knowledge, regarding the reality and nature of material being, and that leads us, necessarily, beyond the limits of that knowledge. The arguments are all dedicated to the pursuit of ultimate questions, with the intent of finding adequate answers to those questions, answers that will satisfy the inquiring philosophical mind. The existence of material being is self-evident; what is not self-evident, and what concentrated philosophical inquiry seeks to make evident, is the ultimate explanation for the existence of material being. The physicist is content to know the "how" of material being, the ways it is made up and the ways it works; the philosopher seeks to know the "why" of material being.

The arguments are metaphysical, not in the caricatured sense that they consist in nothing more than airy speculations, having no connection with how we commonly think about things when we think about them seriously, but because they rest upon and are structured by the most basic of philosophical truths, those truths which allow us to make sense of the world all around us; and because they abide rigorously by the rules of logic. Metaphysics is grounded on the proposition that the world is intelligible to the human mind; it can be understood by us, even to its very depths.

An Argument Based on the Contingency of Material Being

This argument can be called, more succinctly, "The Argument from Contingency." Before getting into it we must first make some clarifying comments about contingency. It is a term that has multiple meanings, not only within philosophy, but in ordinary usage as well. In this argument we are using "contingency" or "contingent" in what can be taken to be its most basic meaning as applied to material substances, be they animate or inanimate, and that is as referring to their tenuous hold on existence. Material substances are contingent in the sense that they bear upon themselves the indelible mark of impermanency; they are radically time-bound: they're here today and gone tomorrow, and they weren't here yesterday. During the course of their existence they are constantly changing, sometimes in beneficial, sometimes in detrimental ways; in time the changes become steadily deteriorating; eventually they lose their identity as individual substances of a specific kind. Material substances are subject to generation and corruption: they begin to be, and after a while they cease to be.

The tree outside my window is contingent, so is the squirrel sitting on a branch of that tree, so is the car parked on the street under that tree. The chair I am sitting on is contingent, so is the one sitting in that chair and writing these words. The earth, the moon, the sun, and the planets are contingent. The myriad of stars are contingent, as are the countless galaxies that their congregations make up, and so are the bashful black holes that lurk within those galaxies. Everything named above has or had a history, meaning it had a beginning and an end.

If every material substance that we can name had a beginning, then we can ask, what accounts for that beginning, for its coming into existence in the first place? We cannot say a material substance accounts for its own existence, that it somehow brought itself into existence. That makes no sense. If you say something could bring itself into existence that would involve the absurd situation where it existed before it existed so it could bring itself into existence. So we conclude that every material substance depends on something other than itself for its existence; that is one of the fundamental facts about a contingent being. Another way of expressing that fact is to say the existence of a contingent being is not self-explanatory.

The absolute dependency of contingent being on something other than itself for its very existence is clearly evident with regard to organic life. Think of that squirrel; it would not be out there on that branch were it not for its squirrel parents. In the floral realm, think of an oak tree: it clearly owes its existence to oak trees that have gone before it, prolifically producing acorns that, if squirrels didn't get to them first, grew into oak trees.

At this point in our argument we can confidently assert that all material being is contingent being. It exists, it is definitely *there*, but—this is the point we are stressing—it does not have within itself the explanation for its being there. This is not a conclusion we arrive at after a lengthy and complicated theoretical argument. We are simply trusting the reliability of our sense knowledge, and our sense knowledge provides us continuously with sound empirical evidence of the contingency of material being. The only kind of being that we can come to know from our senses is material being, and if sense knowledge were the only kind of knowledge of which we were capable, we would naturally conclude that material being is the only kind of being there is. We then would presumably all be contented materialists, dialectical or otherwise.

Let us imagine that the only kind of being that could exist is material being, which would mean that in the world we are imagining the only beings in existence are contingent beings, beings no single one of which is self-explanatory, that can account for its own existence. In that case the question is, how did they all get here? Each and every one of them is dependent for its being on a being other than itself for its existence, but the only beings it can depend on for that fundamental favor are just like itself; they all cannot bring themselves into existence, and are therefore incapable of bringing into existence anything else. So, a putative world populated only by contingent beings would in fact be empty. If there were nothing but contingent being then contingent being itself would not be possible, for contingent being is not self-explanatory.

There is obviously no doubt about the reality of contingent being. We are aswim in a universe of contingent beings; we ourselves are contingent beings. But how to account for contingent being if it cannot account for itself? There must be something other than material being in order to have an explanation for what cannot explain itself. What would that alternative mode of being be like? It would be just the opposite of material being; it would be immaterial, for if it were material it would be contingent, and that would mean it could not account for its own existence, much less for the existence of anything else. As non-contingent, its existence would not be dependent on anything other than itself. It would be the explanation (the explanation, not the cause) of its own existence. As immaterial it would be simple, that is, not composed of parts, and as we saw in Chapter Three with regard to the human soul, it therefore would be immortal.

This non-contingent, immaterial, immortal being, the complete opposite of material being, is called necessary being. Contingent being is what it is because its essence does not entail its existence, whereas it is the very definition of necessary being that its essence, the very heart of its meaning so to speak, is "to exist." Necessary being is being that cannot not exist; it is therefore eternal. It is this being that accounts for the being that cannot account for itself, material or contingent being. Without necessary being there would be no explanation for the existence of the material, contingent world in which we live, the reality of which is undeniable. This necessary being is what we commonly refer to as God. He is the Supreme Being, and as such he is one, for there can no more be two supreme beings than can an isosceles triangle have two apexes. He is all-powerful, for He brought contingent being into existence out of nothing.

Objections to the Argument

There are a number of objections that can be raised against this argument, and they must be addressed. In delineating these objections I will assume the voice of the Objector.

You have argued that there must be a being other than material being, to bring material being into existence, but in that you are presuming that material being must have had a beginning. Why do we have to presume that? Why cannot we take it as fact that matter had no beginning; it has always existed, in one form or another? For that reason there is no need to appeal to anything other than material being to explain material being; it is self-explanatory. To bolster that point, couldn't we appeal to the law of the conservation of matter or energy? It is interesting that in the examples you use to illustrate the generation and corruption of contingent being you stick to organic material being. How about inorganic being? This particular squirrel or that particular oak tree may come and go, but how about the matter, the molecules and atoms of which they are composed? They endure. We might even call them eternal. Earlier in your book you used as an example of a natural substantial change the process by which uranium passes through various stages of decay until it eventually ends up as lead. Granted that the uranium as such was contingent; it passed away. But not matter itself; it endures, though in a new form. The earliest of the ancient Greek philosophers, those who came before Socrates, seemed to have taken it for granted that matter had no beginning, it was simply always there. The great Aristotle, whom you obviously much admire, believed that the universe it-self was eternal; it had no beginning, it will have no end. Why cannot we be satisfied with these lines of reasoning? I maintain that there is no need to suppose the existence of an immaterial, necessary being to explain material being; we can say that material being is itself necessary being, because it is the only kind of being there is.

Response to Objections

These objections come from a refreshingly straightforward materialistic point of view. The nub of the various points made is the advocacy of an eternal world, or, at least, the perpetual existence of unorganized matter, having no beginning, having no end. It is beyond question that many of the ancients held this point of view, indeed it was probably the dominant point of view among them, and many astute minds subscribed to it, not only in times past but in modern times as well. The first response to be made to the thesis that matter is eternal is that it has never been demonstrated, and, if Thomas Aquinas is right, it cannot be demonstrated. Therefore, as it stands it is simply an assertion, and it can be reasonably responded to by a counter assertion: "Matter is not eternal."

But we need not stop at so unsatisfactory an impasse. Does modern science have anything to contribute to the discussion? Let us, for the sake of argument, accept that there is something to be said for the Big Bang theory which, it would seem, is acknowledged to be a viable theory by the majority of physicists, astronomers, and cosmologists today, and which, I think I am safe in assuming, the soundness of which the Objector would have no occasion to question. What is particularly interesting, and relevant to the subject we are discussing, is that very many of these scientists are materialists, and not a few are avowed, even militant, atheists. The Big Bang theory holds that the physical universe which we now inhabit had a definite beginning, some 13.72 billion years ago. It would seem, then, that modern science, in which many today put much stock (and presumably including the Objector), denies the idea of an eternal world, and in fact can, at least to its own satisfaction, offer empirical evidence to prove that the universe as we know it had a definite beginning in time.

As to the point that though the universe, as an immense display of ordered, organized matter, may not have always existed as such, at least it can be said, in deference to the law of the conservation of energy, that matter did exist in the form of molecules or atoms, but that too would be contested by advocates of the Big Bang theory. They tell us that the natural atoms which make up the Periodic Table of Elements all had a beginning in time, and some, like carbon, had to await the creation of stars before coming into existence.

The deeper commitment to philosophical materialism that undergirds and inspires the objection, a position which holds that material reality is the only reality, is one that, as I tried to show in the previous chapter, is extremely problematic. The materialist, given his repudiation of metaphysics and his thus limiting himself to the empirical mode of reasoning, is incapable of clearly articulating or cogently defending his materialism. The Objector is inviting us to assume the eternal existence of matter. Now, of course anyone is perfectly free to make that assumption, but to assume that something is the case is not to prove that it is the case.

In sum, the objections raised against the argument we have presented, proving the existence of God from the fact of the existence of contingent being, do not hold up under careful scrutiny, according to criteria the Objector himself, given his world view, would be disposed to accept.

An Argument Based on the Fact of Motion

In this argument, as in the previous one, we begin with and concentrate on what generally we know best—material being. In the first argument it was the fact of material being's contingency that was our specific point of departure; here we will focus on another basic characteristic of material being, the fact that it moves. What could be more obvious, more self-evident, than that? Material being is constantly in motion, constantly changing in one way or another. All we have to do is look around us to be aware of that, or we can just look at ourselves, for we are constantly moving, something which is patently the case with regard to bodily movements, external and internal. But consider your mental movements, your ever-changing thoughts, skipping through your mind non-stop, one after another. It is happening as you read this. Our thoughts are not only always on the move, sometimes they move in directions we would prefer they didn't. "And as to one's thoughts," St. Augustine once wrote, "who can control them?" So, motion or change does not have to be proved; it is obvious and ubiquitous.

At the very outset we call attention to a metaphysical principle which plays a key role in the argument, and which we discussed in an earlier chapter; it is stated thus: everything that moves is moved by another. The truth of that principle may not strike us as immediately obvious; in fact, it might seem to be contradicted by facts we know about the natural world. A case in point: back in Chapter Three we claimed that one of the basic identifying features of animate being is the fact that it is self-moving. If that is a true description of animate life, then it would appear that the principle does not apply universally.

How are we to respond to this problem? What at first blush might seem a contradiction to the principle in fact is not so, for if we analyze "self-moving" beings carefully, including ourselves, we see that there is always a clear distinction to be discovered between mover and moved, be that distinction within the animate being itself, or between the animate being and something external to it.

Let us first consider ourselves as self-moving, animate beings. I'm sitting here writing away and I suddenly decide it's time for a cup of coffee, so I get up, walk to the kitchen, take a cup from the cupboard, and pour myself a cup of coffee. In that prosaic little bit of domestic activity we have a series of bodily movements. How to explain them? Did my body move itself? Did my legs go into motion on their own, without my having anything to say about it? Obviously not; it was I who moved my body. More precisely, we could say my mind or my will moved my body; I made a decision to make a move and I followed through on the decision. So there was a distinction between mover (mind, will) and moved (body) which was internal to the self-moving me. But there was also a distinction between me, as moved, and something external to me that caused me to move, namely, the coffee. It was my desire to have something external to myself that prompted me to decide to get up and move to the kitchen. Almost all of our bodily movements are instigated by something external to the body. Consider the case of commercial advertising. That bustling industry devotes unremitting and ingeniously devised efforts to move people to want what they do not at the moment have or are even thinking about. The ad is intended to move us to take a certain course of action.

Consider our mental movements, such as in those cases when we change our minds about something. Unless we are being completely whimsical, we change our minds because we are moved to do so. It is *we* who decide to change our minds, yes, but the decision is instigated by extra-mental factors. Something happens to affect our mode of thinking: a serious promise made to us is broken; one evening we see an entirely new and positive side to someone we previously had a very low opinion of; we learn something which is both new and significant in a public lecture we attend; we are persuaded by a line of argument we read in an op-ed piece. In each case we are moved to change our minds about persons or issues.

The principle that whatever is moved is moved by another is most clearly manifested in the realm of inanimate material being. The seven ball moves across the surface of the pool table because it was struck by the cue ball, and the movement of the cue ball is explained by the fact that it was struck by the cue stick.

Motion is action, and our principle tells us that everything that is in action has to be activated, otherwise it will remain inactive. Motion is change, and in the chapter on the philosophy of nature we learned that the essence of every change is the transition from potency to act, from the capacity to move, say, to actual movement. Now, the mere capacity to change is not enough to initiate the change; the mere potentiality to act cannot in itself bring about the action. What is needed is something which is already "in act" in the broadest sense; something, that is, which can activate the potentiality, boost it out of its state of mere potentiality and make what once *could* be actually to be.

Each and every material being, animate or inanimate, conscious or unconscious, moves, in the final analysis, because something other than that being puts it in motion in one way or another. (Keep in mind that we are considering every possible kind of movement or change.) That's the heart of the principle we're dealing with here. The proximate or immediate explanation of the constant motion of inanimate material being is other material being, whatever form it may take. Subatomic particles like electrons jiggle away because of the physical environment in which they find themselves, in which there are, say, other motion-inducing particles. What causes an electron that is part of an atom to jump from orbit to orbit is doubtless the strong force of the nucleus. The planets of the solar system move in their precisely regular ways because of gravitational fields. Whatever is moved is moved by another.

If every material thing that moves is moved by another, by something else that is material, we are in a situation very much like the one in which we found ourselves in the first argument: there, we saw that no single contingent being is self-explanatory; here, we have moving material beings no single one of which is the explanation for its motion. Its motion is dependent on the motion of other material beings. We supposedly have a universe composed entirely of non-self-moving material beings. But if that were actually the case, then we would have no ultimate explanation for all that motion. No single moving material being can account for its own motion. We could multiply individual moving material beings ad infinitum, until there are myriads upon myriads of them, which is actually the case in our universe, but that still leaves us with no explanation for all that motion. As in the first argument, where we concluded that there must exist being other than contingent being, namely necessary being, here we conclude that there must exist being other than moving being whose movement is caused by another, otherwise there would be no explanation for all the movement in the universe, no instance of which, taken in itself, is self-explanatory. This other kind of being would be completely independent with respect to movement, for though it is the cause of movement, its capacity to do so is not explained by anything beyond itself.

In the arguments based on motion formulated by Aristotle, he called the being that was the activating source of all movement the Prime Mover or the Unmoved Mover. Why "unmoved"? Because if it moved it would be subject to something other than itself for its motion, and therefore it could not be "prime," the absolutely first and completely independent source and explanation of all motion or change. Movement involves potentiality, and that implies imperfection; the Prime Mover is pure act, the supreme activating origin of all action.

This being, which accounts for all the movement in the universe, can also be identified as the first efficient cause of that movement. Because everything that moves is moved by another, each movement, of whatever kind, is the effect of what causes it to move. Now, imagine all the myriads upon myriads of movements taking place incessantly in the universe, all being the effects of the efficient causality taking place. We might zero in on and isolate a simple case of this causality, where physical Object A bumps into physical Object B and sets it in motion. Or we might be looking at what is in fact the more likely situation, where a particular instance of motion has multiple causes. Either way, if the cause of motion is one or many, the motion of those causes of motion is explained by something other than itself or themselves, for everything that moves another is itself moved by something other than itself. So, thinking in terms of efficient causality, all we have are efficient causes of motion each and every one of which is a caused cause, that is, a cause which is able to cause only because it is itself caused. We rephrase the governing principle of the argument by saying, "every cause of motion is itself a caused-cause." That gives a universe which is chock full of the efficient causes of motion all of which are caused-causes. But if that were how things really stand, there would be no explanation for all that causality. There must exist, therefore, a cause, a being, which is the explanation for all the causality of movement that is taking place in the universe but which is itself self-explanatory, or uncaused.

Summing up the two aspects of our argument, we conclude that (1) because everything that moves is moved by another, (2) there must exist a first unmoved mover that is the explanation for all movement. This unmoved mover is the ultimate explanatory cause, hence the First Cause, of all the efficient causality of movement taking place in the physical universe. This unmoved mover or First Cause is what we know of as God.

Objections to the Argument

The principle which you make the linchpin of your argument is not as universal as you would suppose it to be. The obvious fact that the motion of a physical object can set another physical object in motion, or, thinking in psychological terms, the fact that we can be motivated in various ways to act, these facts can be easily granted. But there are some things in nature which can be considered to be genuinely self-moving, or more precisely, self-organizing. I invite you to consider the example of a single cell, a rather important one, the zygote, the initiating cell of the human body. It is in a sense autonomous. Everything it needs, all the critical information necessary for it to grow and develop, is contained within it. It is quite self-sufficient, and does not have to be "moved" by something other than itself.

I do not mean to embarrass you publicly, but surely you are aware that the fact of motion, the very subject matter of your argument, is an example of accidental, not substantial, being. Motion is not a "something," but a feature of something. This being the case, and supposing your argument to be sound, all it succeeds in explaining is the movement of things; it says nothing about the *existence* of the things that are moving.

I was somewhat amused by your cosmic scenario where there is nothing but moved movers and caused causes, on the basis of which you feel it necessary to conclude to the existence of an unmoved mover or an uncaused cause, which you claim is God. I will be accommodating up to a point and accept a universe such as you describe it. But then I ask, What's wrong with that universe such as it is? Why cannot there be nothing but moved movers, or, thinking in terms of efficient causality, why cannot we suppose, for example, that there is an infinite series of caused causes. In other words, I see no need for a Prime Mover or a First Cause.

But I am in a particularly magnanimous mood at the moment, and I am going to graciously grant you the existence of a First Cause. But now I have a very simple question to ask you: What caused the first cause?

Response to Objections

The example the Objector uses, the human zygote, which is supposedly an instance of a genuinely self-moving entity, is far from being such, if by self-moving we understand an entity which is not at all dependent on anything external to itself for its activity. We perhaps might consider it to be so if we could imagine it growing and developing in a perfect vacuum, but of course it does not. Granted, all the genetic information which will account for its adult status is internal to it right from the outset, but the potential for its growth and development can only be realized because it resides within the protective, nourishing womb of the mother. Outside of a preserving and protective environment, it would very shortly die. The womb of the mother is that which, external to the zygote, "moves" it to grow and develop.

Actually, I appreciate the Objector's calling attention to the fact that motion is an instance of accidental being, for it allows me to stress the point that no one of the metaphysical arguments presented in this chapter is to be taken as completely isolated from the others. All three are interdependent, which is not surprising, for they all have the same conclusion. In considering this second argument, then, we must not forget what we learned in the first: the necessary being, God, is the explanation for the very existence of contingent being; without necessary being there would be no contingent being. Now, in this argument we are indeed focusing on an instance of accidental being, motion, a feature of contingent being, which we already know, from the first argument, is caused to exist by necessary being. The existence of the beings that move therefore does not have to be proved in this argument, for that has already been done; here it is simply taken for granted.

I do not know if the Objector has read Chapter Two of this book, but if so did he take note of the argument we sketched there, showing that it is impossible to have an infinite number of material things? Now, "moved movers" and "caused causes" are abstract terms, but they refer to concrete material objects and, as the argument shows, it is not possible that there could be an infinite number of them. As for the possibility of an infinite series of uncaused causes, appeal to such a possibility is little more than a distraction, a way of avoiding pressing existential questions. Let us grant the existence of a supposedly infinite series. That only leaves us with the question as to where that series came from. To say, "it is just there," is neither physics nor philosophy. In any event, to deny the need for a Prime Mover or a First Cause is just another way of circumventing the issue at hand, of in effect saying that what clearly needs to be explained does not need to be explained at all.

The simple question posed by the objector, "What caused the First Cause?" turns out to be an altogether remarkable question, one that could only be asked by someone who is not at all attuned to the metaphysical mode of thinking. The absolutely first cause is a cause which, by definition, has no cause; and that is precisely why it is called "first." To ask what caused the first cause is like asking, in mathematics, what comes before one, the unit. The answer is, nothing. One, the unit, is the source and absolute commencement of all numbers, positive or negative, rational or irrational, the explanation of all fractions. If you do not accept the commanding presence of one, there is no two, no thirty, no trillion. The First Cause is the cause of all things, and has no causal antecedent.

An Argument Based on Order

In this argument, as in the previous two, we direct our attention to a particular aspect of material being, and with that aspect in mind reason our way to a conclusion which takes us beyond the realm of the material. In the first argument we began with the contingency of material being, and we concluded to the existence of God to account for that contingency; in the second argument the motion of material being was our point of departure, and we concluded to the existence of God to account for that motion; here we start with the order which is to be found in material being, and we conclude to the existence of God to account for that order. In each case our initial premise has to do with something which is self-evident: that material being is contingent, that it moves, that it is ordered.

The order of material being is self-evident. Should we want an explanation why that is so, all we would need to do is call attention to the intelligibility of material being, the fact that it can be known by us; we can come to have real understanding of various aspects of it. Order and intelligibility are inseparable. If things lacked order, if all were helter-skelter, without rhyme or reason, we would not be able to make head or tail of them; in fact, they would lack both head and tail. We can recognize disorder as disorder, and chaos as chaos, but beyond that they are impenetrable to us. We can distinguish night from day, but in the night we cannot clearly see. With regard to the order of the material realm, we take it so much for granted that we scarcely notice it, much less give it any sustained thought. Interestingly enough, it is only when we encounter disorder that we become fully conscious of its opposite, the pervasive fact of order. There is not nor could there ever be anything like a 50/50 split between order and disorder. Order is the prevailing state of affairs, the dominant and controlling reality, and disorder is nothing else but a departure from, the absence of, order.

Let us suppose, fantastically, that we were living in a totally disordered world, a world in which chaos reigned supreme. If that were the case, not only would we have no idea of order, we would not even be able to conceive such an idea, nor could we even imagine what order might be like. It would be even worse than that: I used the phrase "totally disordered world," but the phrase would have no referent. If all were disorder and chaos, no "world" would be possible. Without a world, an ordered whole, a cosmos, life would be impossible. We would not be around to contemplate the chaos.

What we call nature is simply a shorthand way of referring to the sum total of material being, the physical universe. We have nature, the physical universe, precisely because the material being that constitutes it is ordered.

We live in a universe which is ordered on the grand scale, and right down to the last subatomic particle. If that were not the case, then, as remarked just above, we would not be here to talk about it. The human body, an instance of material being we tend to be particularly interested in, especially if it happens to be our own, is a veritable symphony of order. When order prevails in our bodies we enjoy good health; sickness is simply a disruption of that order.

How might we describe order, what is it in itself, and what does it necessarily imply? First, we take note of the fact that it always involves multiplicity. To order is to give systematic arrangement to many things. The result of the ordering process is a state of affairs where many things connect with and relate to one another satisfactorily; it is a coherent and at least relatively complete whole. Consider, by way of contrast, a physical object which is simple, that is, it is not composed of parts; for example, an elementary particle like an electron. It would not make sense to speak of such an object as ordered, for here there is nothing to be ordered. An electron just is what it is, its simple and presumably contented uncomplicated self. These various considerations lead us to a working definition of order: it is the logical, harmonious arrangement of parts so as to compose a coherent, intelligible whole.

Human technology, when it is successful in its endeavors, offers us countless examples of well-ordered wholes. Take the automobile, for example: a vehicle all of whose many parts are so arranged as to compose an ordered whole that serves the practical function of transporting us comfortably and safely from Point A to Point B.

The next thing implied by order is intelligibility, and intelligibility, in turn, implies intelligence as the source and explanation of intelligibility. The inseparableness of intelligibility (the potential of things to be understood by the human mind) and intelligence is most obvious to us when we consider the products of human technology. Fords or Chevrolets do not assemble themselves, nor do they design themselves. Their multiple parts must be carefully put together according to a pre-established design, the source of which is human intelligence, otherwise there would be no vehicle to pull away from Point A, much less to arrive at Point B.

Now, comparable to the intelligence which is clearly manifest in the products of human technology, there is an intelligence which is manifest in the natural world as a whole. This is a conclusion which is founded upon the fact of the inseparableness of order and intelligence, and which is a key element of our argument. We will put the nub of our reasoning in crisp, syllogistic form:

Whatever is ordered has intelligence behind it.
But nature is ordered.
Therefore, nature has intelligence behind it.

There is yet another thing that is implied by order, and that is finality. The ordering process is always directed toward a specific end or purpose. Consider situations where we are the ordering agents; we invariably have a specific reason for initiating the ordering process. We set to work to put a messy bedroom in order, because we want a room that is neat and clean: the bed is made, the clothes are hung up in the closet, necessary dusting is done; in sum, everything is shipshape and in its proper place. When fussy Aunt Flossie visits this afternoon she won't be shocked or scandalized should she happen to have a peek at the bedroom.

The order we recognize in the physical universe is anything but static. The focus of the previous argument was precisely on matter in motion. Material being is incessantly in action, and its action is not at all haphazard; it is ordered action, always directed toward specific ends. Therein lies its intelligibility, and hence its scientific predictability.

The point of this argument which we want principally to emphasize is the fact that order necessarily implies intelligence. The two, order and intelligence, are so inextricably bound up with one another that wherever we find order we can take it as an infallible manifestation of intelligence. The explanation for the order is intelligence. Order does not come about by chance; it is not the result of serendipitous circumstances. Now, it is an incontestable fact that nature, the physical universe, the sum total of material being, is wonderfully ordered. It is that order that makes material being intelligible to us, and intelligibility is the specific sign of the presence of intellect. The human intellect, in responding to what is intelligible, is in that very act responding to the intellect that accounts for the intelligible. When we respond understandingly to a product of human technology we are responding directly to the intelligibility of that product, and indirectly to the intellect or intellects behind that intelligibility.

We will now summarize the various points made above and explicitly state the conclusion of our argument. The sum total of material being, the physical universe, is manifestly and wonderfully ordered; its myriad of parts are logically and harmoniously arranged so as to compose a coherent whole, a cosmos. The fact of ordered movement, which is everywhere evident in the universe, implies finality or purpose, which is equally everywhere evident in the universe, and that implies intelligence. End-oriented or purposeful action implies intelligence. Whatever is ordered, and precisely on account of its being ordered, is intelligible; it is inherently knowable and understandable. This too implies intelligence, for the only possible source of the intelligible is intelligence. In sum, we have a physical universe which is ordered, ubiquitously end-oriented, and intelligible, all of which implies, indeed necessitates intelligence. We therefore conclude that there exists a Supreme Intellect which is the explanation for the order of the physical universe; this Supreme Intellect is the Necessary Being of the first argument, the First Cause of the second, and to which we give the name of God.

Objections to the Argument

For the sake of greater clarity, I will attach numbers to the various objections I have to the argument. (1) The argument places more weight on the idea of order than it is capable of bearing. You see the physical universe as being marvelously ordered, down to the last iota of matter or speck of cosmic dust. You argue that order is the dominant characterizing fact of the universe, and that disorder is, so to speak, no more than a minor footnote to the main text. Things are not quite as you see them. Granted that there is order in the universe—no one would deny that—but there is disorder as well, chaos if you will. There would seem to be no way to determine precisely what is the ratio of order to disorder in the universe, but we can reasonably conjecture that there is a great deal of the latter, perhaps there is more disorder than order. Look at the spectacular photos of the far reaches of the visible universe taken by the Hubble Space Telescope. There we see massive clouds of who knows precisely what kinds of loose and disjoined matter, whirling about in what could only be called a wildly disordered way. Given the fact that there may very well be as much disorder as order in the physical universe, your argument loses its force. How to explain all that disorder? Are we to conclude the existence of an immaterial deranged intellect, a cosmic idiot of sorts?

(2) But for the sake of argument I will grant you as much order as you want, but I balk at your insistence that order implies intelligibility, especially because you want to go on from there to connect intelligibility with intellect. I will grant that we can understand whatever is ordered, and in that sense it can be said to be intelligible. But we can understand disorder as well. If we couldn't, we would not be able to identify it as such. What prevents us, then, from saying that disorder is just as intelligible as order, and if that is so then the intelligibility of order does not allow us to draw from it the grandiose conclusion that you do in your argument.

(3) Now I come to the crux of your argument, the claim that the order which you see as objectively present in the physical universe is proof that there is a cosmic intelligence behind that order. If you permit me, I will summarize the heart of your argument in the following terms: (a) The existence of order necessarily demands intelligence as the explanation for that order; (b) it is manifest that the physical universe is ordered; (c) therefore, the physical universe, as ordered, has an intelligent explanatory source, and that is God. The first proposition in the argument, the major premise, is what I contest. Dedicated student of logic that you are, you know very well that if the major premise of an argument is faulty, the whole argument grinds to a halt right there. I contend that there is not, as you maintain, a strict bond between order and intelligence. Surely, if we are talking about human artifacts, the products of human ingenuity, then there is obviously intelligence behind them—*human* intelligence. But you take that relation, between the order found in human artifacts and the intelligence behind that order, and presume that it applies on the grand scale, to nature itself. I say that it does not. We find in nature certain instances of what could be called self-ordering, or self-organizing phenomena, which, as such, do not require any appeal to intelligence to explain their ordering capacities. One need not look beyond them to find an explanation for the order they display. Now, if that can be said of phenomena of that kind, there seems to be no reason why it cannot be said of the physical universe as a whole. If you want to say that it is intelligible, fine, but its intelligibility is self-contained, it is rooted in material being itself and the multiple potentialities to be found in material being. We

need not look beyond material being for an explanation of the fact that it displays order.

(4) You claim that intelligibility is inherent in things in the physical world, specifically in things which are marked by order, arguing that intelligibility is, as it were, part and parcel of the very nature of material being. I reject that claim. On a more fundamental level, I reject the assumption on which your entire argument is based, that order itself is somehow *out there*, that, in other words, it is an objective feature of material being, and that all we need do, therefore, is simply recognize its presence. That is a very large assumption on your part, and may I politely suggest that you have it just backwards in the way you look at reality. It is not the case, as you aver, that order and intelligibility are given facts of the physical universe; rather, they are what the human intellect brings to its study of the physical universe so as to develop a reliable scientific understanding of it. In other words, order and intelligibility are concepts that originate in the human intellect, and they are the means by which we give orderly arrangement to the data provided by our senses, thereby creating a coherent context within which to deal with what otherwise would be completely incomprehensible to us.

(5) You perhaps may find me to be a friendlier critic of your argument than others might be. I am not what you would call a religious person, but I would not mind being called spiritual. I certainly am not an advocate of materialism, a position I find to be superficial and rather boring. I believe reality to be much deeper and haunting than what shallow, unreflective thought would take it to be. With that attitude, I can accept the possibility that there is a mysterious organizing force that accounts for the order to be found in the universe. I am willing to call it intelligent. I am even willing to concede that it may be immaterial, but I wonder if it would be necessary to go that far. Perhaps the very distinction between material and immaterial is not as strict and mutually exclusive as we suppose. Perhaps reality allows for the existence of something that is not clearly one or the other. However that might be, this ordering intelligence the existence of which I am suggesting would be a powerful, positive, but impersonal force that is intrinsic to the physical universe itself, not something extrinsic to and separate from it. Adopting this possibility would render unnecessary the line of reasoning followed in your argument, which concludes to the existence of a supreme, personal being, the idea of God. Now, this idea, though noble and edifying

in its way, has been the cause of much animus and divisiveness and dissension among human beings over the course of our history, all of which could be avoided if we would subscribe to what I am proposing.

Response to the Objections

I will follow the Objector's numbering in responding to the objections. In reviewing those objections, I detect not a little inconsistency in his thought. One would almost think that it was coming from three different sources: the first three from one source, the fourth from another, and the fifth from yet another. Be that as it may, I will reply to each objection as it is presented.

(1) In response to the first objection, I will start by reiterating the point stressed in my argument, that order is manifestly present throughout the universe. The universe is a thoroughly ordered system; if it were not, it would not be a universe, a cosmos. The counter-claim made by the Objector, that there is disorder in the universe, is not demonstrated, and the suggestion that disorder is equal to, or even more prevalent than order, remains only a suggestion, with no argument to back it up. Order is the foundational reality in nature, and for that fact, as I stated in the argument, we are only able to identify disorder in reference to order; if there were no order, we would have no conception at all of disorder. The positive precedes the negative and provides it with a comprehensible standing, as its opposite.

The Objector maintains that disorder is as intelligible as order, and this is proved by the fact that we can understand it. Here some important distinctions need to be made, relating to the difference between (a) the order which is to be found in the products of human invention and production, and (b) the order found in nature. With regard to the former, it is true, as the Objector maintains, that disorder can be intelligible to us, but that is so only if an important condition is met: that you know the order which is the contrary to what you recognize as disorder. For example, let us say you know nothing about auto mechanics; you are out driving one day and suddenly your car breaks down, it stops running. The car is then in a disordered state; you recognize *that* it is disordered (it won't run), but in such a case the disorder is *not* intelligible to you; you do not understand why your car does not run. The car is towed to a garage where a seasoned mechanic gives it a quick examination and immediately diagnoses the problem. To him the disordered state of your car is intelligible; he understands it, and that is because he knows what the ordered state of the car should be.

Now, let us say further that, though you don't know much about auto mechanics, you are an expert chess player. One day your cousin Lydia invites you over to have a match with the beautiful new chess set she received for her birthday. Walking into the game room, a cursory glance at the chess board tells you that everything is ready: the white pieces are lined up on the back two rows on one side of the board, and the black pieces oppositely, each piece placed neatly on an individual square. But then you take a closer look at the board and what you see is flagrant disorder. The pawns are not all in the front row as they should be, and the king, queen, rooks, and knights are not placed on their proper squares. In this case you are able to recognize disorder as disorder—it is intelligible to you—because you know the proper order for the chess pieces at the beginning of a match. You do not simply know *that* something is disordered, but how it is so. We are in a quite different situation when we discuss order and disorder as they relate to natural phenomena. I would argue that when we identify something in nature with which we are not familiar as an instance of disorder, we are in more cases than not wrong in doing so. If I claim, wrongly, that certain phenomena in nature that I am observing are disordered, it is because I do not know enough about the phenomena to say otherwise. The order is there, but I am not able to recognize it. A common cause of making mistakes of this kind is our tendency to equate order with stasis. We must be mindful of the fact that the motion of matter we observe in nature is orderly motion; it is directed toward a specific finality.

Matter, as we know, is constantly in motion (matter = *ens mobile*), and that motion is ordered because it is directed toward specific ends. The Objector calls our attention to the spectacular photos taken by the Hubble Space Telescope, and interprets what he describes as instances of massive, outer-space disorder, matter seemingly in haphazard and directionless motion. An astronomer would look at those photos and interpret them quite differently, seeing in them the dramatic process by which matter—huge clouds of gases, probably composed mainly of hydrogen and helium—is on the way to eventually becoming stars and planets, at least according to one theory proposed by cosmologists. However that might be, whenever matter in motion obeys the laws of physics it is orderly, and matter in motion always obeys the laws of physics.

If you have never watched a cricket match, the first time you do so can leave you rather puzzled. A good bit of the activity you are watching on the field, the moves made by individual players, is not intelligible to you, and that is because you do not know the rules of the game, the rules that give order to all the movements you are witnessing. Once we know the rules of a game, it makes sense to us, and we may even come to enjoy it. The situation is somewhat comparable when we study the natural world. If we are confronted with an instance of matter in motion that is completely new to us, it stands to reason that we would not find it intelligible; we see the motion, but we do not see its proper contextual setting which would inform us of its finality, the end or ends toward which the motion is heading. The fact that in any given instance we cannot immediately determine the end or resolution of matter in motion—which is especially the case if the motion is very turbulent, even explosive—provides us no basis for claiming the motion to be disordered.

(2) The second objection rejects the idea that order implies intelligibility because intelligibility in turn implies intellect. He is certainly right in recognizing that if you grant intelligibility you necessarily grant intellect, so, in order to avoid intellect, he will not grant intelligibility. So, we must start with intelligibility. To say something is intelligible is to say that it is knowable to us in terms of its essential nature. I can be said to know Object X in any meaningful sense (it is intelligible to me) if I do not simply know that it is, the fact that it exists, but I know what it is, I have some grasp of its essential nature. And the intelligibility of anything has everything to do with the fact that it is ordered. The Objector's claim that intelligibility has nothing to do with order is a bit breathtaking.

The rock bottom matter of fact is that order and intelligibility are inextricably bound up with one another. The Objector admits as much when he grants that we can understand whatever is ordered (I would state the case more strongly by saying it is only *because* something is ordered that we are able to understand it: no order, no understanding), but then he goes on to say that we understand disorder as well. To reemphasize important points made earlier: we do not understand disorder as disorder if we do not know the order from which that disorder is a departure. Order is the *sine qua non* touchstone by which disorder is identified, and it is the very foundation of intelligibility. The Objector wants to know what prevents us from saying disorder is just as intelligible as order. Nothing prevents us from saying that if we are using the term disorder properly, to refer to what we see as a departure from a known order. But if by disorder we are referring to what we do not understand, such as when, for example, we do not see the finality of certain instances of matter in motion, then the Objector's question becomes: what prevents us from saying the unintelligible is intelligible, what prevents us from saying that we know what we don't know? Strictly speaking, there is no disorder in the physical universe, but there is a great deal of human ignorance regarding that order; we easily enough detect the movement, but we do not see where it is heading.

Though he does not expatiate on this point, the Objector clearly indicates that he wants to sever intelligibility from intellect. It is an impossible task. Again, to say something is intelligible is to say that it is knowable, that it is a source of knowledge. One cannot have knowledge without a subject of that knowledge, a knower, and at the highest level that means a person possessed of an intellect. Consider again human artifacts, say Beethoven's Third Symphony, a work chock full of beautiful intelligibility. Place that in the middle, and put intellects on either side of it. On one side is the intellect of Beethoven, who created the intelligibility to be found in the symphony; on the other side is the intellect of the listener, who can appreciate and relish that intelligibility. Intellect and intelligibility are inseparable.

(3) The third objection does indeed go to the very heart of the argument. The Objector roundly rejects the claim that order necessarily implies intelligence, and offers the counter-claim that you can have the one (order) without the other (intelligence). If he is right about that, then the foundation of the argument dissolves. The Objector rejects the claim that order implies intelligence, as its necessary explanation. Now, to reject intelligence is to reject intellect, for intelligence is nothing else than what an intellect possesses. It would therefore be absurd to suggest that there could be intelligence without an intellect; that would be like saying you could have thought without a thinker.

The Objector concedes that on the level of the human we can recognize a connection between order and intelligence: when we see an artifact made by an artificer, behind the order of the artifact we see the intelligence of the artificer. There is no problem there. But the Objector claims that it is illegitimate to establish an analogy between what takes place on the human level, and what takes place in the natural world. This is a strange prohibition which he lays down, all the more strange because the Objector does not deny that there is order in nature; he only makes the claim that there are certain instances of what he describes as self-ordering or self-organizing phenomenon behind which, he maintains, we need not find intelligence, and then wonders if that state of affairs could not apply to the universe as a whole. In other words, cannot we say that the ordering activities of matter, giving rise to intelligibility, are intrinsic to matter itself, and not to be explained by an intelligence extrinsic to matter? In this he would seem to be subscribing to a kind of animism, the idea that the whole of the natural world is "alive," or as the ancient Greek philosopher Thales would have it, the gods are at work in nature, causing such things as magnetic attraction.

Because the views of the Objector are far from clear regarding several particulars in his statement, let us return to a pivotal point about which there is no ambiguity: his contention that it is not legitimate to discern intelligence behind the order we observe in nature, whereas it is altogether reasonable, indeed unavoidable, to see intelligence behind the ordered products of human making. On what basis can one say that it is illicit to draw an analogy, a fruitful comparison, between the two? In fact, there is none. That nature is ordered is indisputable. It is not irrational, reasoning analogically from what we know about human activity, to claim that there is intelligence behind the order we see everywhere in nature. We are not, by reasoning along those lines, violating the principle of contradiction. What is more, we are following a mode of thinking which human beings have commonly entertained since time immemorial. Given the general slant of his thinking, the Objector might be affected by this consideration: If it is admitted, as he does, that ordered human artifacts reflect human intelligence, and if humans are part of nature, whence comes their intelligence if there is no intelligence in nature itself?

Let us next pick up on the Objector's point that intelligibility is self-contained and rooted in material being itself. That is a point which I will concede, but if we push the point, where does it lead us? We have shown that intelligibility is inseparable from intelligence; if, then, you grant that intelligibility is "rooted in material being itself," as the Objector puts it, then you cannot escape the conclusion that intelligence is rooted in material being itself, which can be said to be the case, although with qualifications. The most obvious sign of intelligent behavior in human beings is that it is end-oriented or purposeful. We act to accomplish things. That animal behavior is intelligent in this sense is manifest, especially in the higher animals. Bees build honeycombs, birds build nests, beavers construct dams: all examples of intelligent (i.e., end-oriented) behavior. It would not be stretching the term too much to speak of the intelligent activity that takes place in the plant kingdom. Plant corn kernels in good soil, make sure they get sufficient water and are not pestered by weeds, and, barring any catastrophic interruptions, in a few months you will have a field full of seven-foot-tall corn stalks. Thus, because intelligent action is end-oriented, the ends are predictable.

We can drop down into the inorganic realm and find intelligence at work there too. We have salt on our table because we can rely on the intelligent (i.e., predictable) way in which sodium and chlorine will get together and combine. How to account for the intelligent activity that is constantly going on within the realm of inanimate material being? We have argued that intelligence is inseparable from intellect, and intellect implies consciousness. But certainly we cannot say that the actions of sodium and chlorine are conscious, that those two elements decide to get together and become common salt. So we cannot say that the activity of chemical elements is intelligent in the strict, literal sense, for that would imply the presence of intellect and that, in turn, of consciousness. And yet that activity can be described as intelligent in the non-trivial sense that it is end-oriented and that the ends are predictable. How then to explain that intelligence if it is not intrinsic in the strict, literal sense? It can only be explained by an intelligence which is extrinsic to the activity, the intelligence of a Supreme Intellect that accounts for all the ordered activity in the university.

To describe certain natural phenomena as self-ordering or self-organizing is implicitly to acknowledge that the phenomena is intelligent, in the analogical sense that it is comparable to the literally intelligent actions of agents that consciously act for the sake of an end. (The robin gathers twigs and straw to make a nest.) Because the supposedly self-ordering or self-organizing phenomena is directed toward specific ends (organized or ordered states) it can be rightly described as intelligent. But the phenomena itself obviously lacks an intellect. Therefore, there must be an intellect external to the phenomena that explains its intelligent, end-oriented activity.

(4) It is clear from this objection that the Objector is a student of the thought of the idealist philosopher Immanuel Kant. For Kant, fundamental ideas such as that of substance, of cause and effect, of the difference between the possible and the impossible, are not learned through our encounter with the physical world through sense experience. Rather, they are innate to the human mind and, as the Objector explains, serve as the means, the mental tools, by which we are enabled to lend intelligibility to the physical world. Immanuel Kant also held the view that we cannot know things in themselves, meaning that we cannot know the essential nature of things. This is tantamount to saying that things are not intrinsically intelligible; they are impenetrable to the human mind. And so our Objector, committed as he seems to be to this way of thinking, believes he has warrant for maintaining that the human mind confers intelligibility on things.

We will take seriously the possibility that this is how things actually stand, and see where that might lead us. The contention is that the essential natures of physical substances in the external world cannot be grasped by the human mind. But is the Objector justified in generalizing about the human mind in the way he is doing here? We can properly generalize about the human mind only if we depart from the fact that the only actually existing minds are individual minds. There is my mind, and your mind, and all those billions of other individual minds around the world. If, as the Objector maintains, our minds confer intelligibility on things, in effect thereby establishing their essential natures for them, there would be no common understanding of any given thing, of what objectively it is. There would be countless different meanings assigned to this or that substance, by the countless different minds doing the assigning, each with its idiosyncratic character, and we can easily imagine that many of those meanings would be in conflict with one another. One mind would look at an animal and call it a mouse; another mind would look at the same animal and call it a muskrat. But this is obviously not the situation in which we in fact find ourselves. Therefore, the human mind does not confer intelligibility on things; intelligibility is intrinsic to things, and the human mind, capable of grasping that intelligibility, can know the essential natures of things.

A comparable absurd situation would result if we were to suppose that the human mind confers order on the physical universe. What order? There would be potentially as many notions of order as there would be minds doing the conferring. Again, with this fantastic scenario there would be no agreed understanding as to the nature and structure of the universe. A science of astronomy would be impossible. The universe is beautifully ordered, and no thanks to man.

(5) This objection presents a line of argument which we encountered in the second objection, advancing the idea that the order to be found in the universe is intrinsic to the universe and not to be explained by a cause external to it. The Objector here alters the picture somewhat, and proposes that the universe's order is caused by a mysterious force, possibly but not necessarily immaterial, which seems to be somehow one and the same with the universe itself. I take the Objector to be proposing a kind of pantheism. He finds the traditional understanding of a transcendent divine being to be problematic, and believes the problem can be avoided by divinizing the universe. Pantheism, as a solution to "the problem of God," has an ancient lineage behind it, and has not a few connections with animism. It is a seductive position for the simplicity of the monism if proposes.

The duality of matter and spirit is done away with, all is one, which is to say, everything is material, including God. The Objector registers his dissatisfaction with materialism, but his pantheism is nothing else but a form of materialism, albeit "spiritual."

It is true enough that human beings have shown themselves to be anything but unanimous over the course of the centuries in what they understood to be the nature and ways of the being they call God. One could agree that the idea of God is problematic, but does that offer good reasons for abandoning it? Sometimes it is the very problematic quality of an idea that signals its substance and depth. On the natural level, ideas like freedom, rights, democracy, and truth can be highly problematic, but we do not reject them on that account. In any event, there is something buried deep in our nature which rebels against the notion that all reality is reducible to matter. Even though we may not be able precisely to specify it, we cannot rid our minds, our hearts, of the conviction that there is a "More" out there that cannot be confined to what our senses alone tell us is true.

Can the Non-existence of God Be Proved?

Before we move on to discuss the attributes of God and then the moral arguments that have been put forward to prove God's existence, it is appropriate that we acquaint ourselves with an argument that attempts to prove the non-existence of God, and give it close scrutiny. This argument has become somewhat of a standard, and for many years atheists have used it as an attack against theism. It is focused upon two ideas relating to the nature of God which are firmly held to by all believers: that God is all good, and that God is all powerful. (These, as we shall learn presently, are known as attributes of God.)

The atheist takes as his starting point the observation that evil exists in the world, something which of course no theist would deny. We will let the atheist speak for himself.

"You theists say that God is all good and all powerful, but that is impossible, and I will explain to you why it is so. If God is all good, as you claim, he would certainly do something about the evil in the world, but it is obvious that he doesn't. That means that he is not all powerful; he might want to do something about the evil in the world, but he can't. Now let's see what can be said about your other claim, that God is all powerful. If God is all powerful, so that he could in fact do something about the evil in the world if he chose to do so, but chooses not to, then the only reasonably conclusion to be drawn is that God is not all good. You must choose one or the other, but whatever choice you make leaves you in a very embarrassing position, for it flatly contradicts what theists believe about the nature of God, that he is both all good and all powerful. And this, therefore, calls into question the very existence of God."

This argument could have a certain emotional appeal to it, if looked at only superficially. Considered closely, though, it is seen to be, under the guise of being strictly logical, basically an appeal to the emotions. Such arguments can be persuasive, but that in itself is irrelevant, for an argument can be persuasive (it can lead people to believe that it is true) and yet be quite false. That is the case here. Now, the entirely wrong way to respond to an argument of this kind, that rides upon emotion, is to respond to it in emotional terms. The only approach to take is to analyze the argument from the point of view of logic. That is what we shall do here.

The principal flaw of the argument is that it commits, indeed relies totally upon, two major logical fallacies, the non sequitur fallacy and the false dilemma fallacy. Of the two, the first is the more serious, because it violates what is most basic in argument. Recall that the non sequitur fallacy is committed when there is no logical connection between the premises of an argument and its conclusion, with the result that the conclusion simply doesn't follow from the premises. What we discover subtly blended into the major argument are two minor arguments that are clearly implied but not stated explicitly. (If they were stated explicitly their illogic would be immediately evident.) Here are the two arguments:

There is evil in the world.
Therefore, God is not all powerful.
There is evil in the world.
Therefore, God is not all good.

What we have in those arguments are two textbook cases of the non sequitur fallacy. In each, there is simply no logical connection between the first statement and the second. Consequently, the second statement, though it begins with "Therefore," does not at all follow from the first.

The other fallacy with which the argument is burdened is the false dilemma fallacy, which you may remember from Chapter One. This fallacy is committed when one is presented with two propositions, A and B, which are to be accepted as if they were mutually exclusive; in other words, it is a situation where the very nature of A is such that it excludes B, and the very nature of B is such that it excludes A, when this in fact is not the case. Consider an argument which follows along the lines of the one we are analyzing. Jerry is in the Navy and Jerry is from New Jersey. If Jerry is in the Navy, then he cannot be from New Jersey; on the other hand, if Jerry is from New Jersey, then he cannot be in the Navy. We can clearly see the fallaciousness of this argument. It is proposing a strict either/or situation when in fact none exists. Jerry's being in the Navy does not preclude his being from New Jersey, nor does his being from New Jersey preclude his being in the Navy. The one is completely compatible with the other. It would be an entirely different situation if we were to say, Jerry is a married man and Jerry is a bachelor, in that here one statement clearly precludes the other.

In the argument proposed by the atheist, the fact that God is all good does not preclude the fact that he is all powerful, nor does the fact that he is all powerful preclude the fact that he is all good. The two are entirely compatible, and there is no contradiction in taking them to be such. It is obvious, then, that the atheist is trying to foist upon us, by his fallacious reasoning, a non-existent contradiction. Shining the spotlight on its fallacious reasoning exposes the logical incoherence of the argument, showing that it offers no support for the claims it is making.

We might be so concentrated on the false dilemma fallacy which plays a major role in the argument that we may not give sufficient attention to the totally gratuitous and unwarranted assertion the atheist is making when he confidently claims that God does nothing about the evil in the world. On what basis does he make that claim? What evidence does he offer to back up his assertion? He has none to offer. He is ignorant of the fact that God's providential care of the world is continuously countering the world's evil; not directly, through spectacular miraculous interventions (though that can sometimes happen), but indirectly, through what St. Thomas describes as God's mediate providence. This is the divine plan by which God exercises his providential governance of the world through the action of his creatures, who are thus co-operators in that governance. Only someone who is willfully blind can deny that genuine good is being done everywhere in the world, and that this has always been the case, whatever the general state of the world at any one time might be. The immediate source of this good is the work of good men and women; its ultimate source is God.

The atheist incorporates another insinuation into the argument—something strongly implied but not stated explicitly—which, when brought out into the open, reveals a second example of the non sequitur fallacy. I will put it in syllogistic form.

If evil exists, then God doesn't.
But evil exists.
Therefore, God does not exist.

This is of course the conclusion toward which the entire argument is directed. The flawed nature of this particular line of reasoning may be obvious enough, but it is important to make clear the major logical problems which it involves. This is a hypothetical or conditional argument. An argument of this type is sound if, in its major premise, the first statement in the argument, there is a necessary connection between the statement's antecedent ("If evil exists") and its consequence ("then God doesn't"). In other words, in order for the argument to be valid it would have to be true that if evil exists it *necessarily* follows that God does not exist. But there is no such connection between the antecedent and the consequent, and thus the consequent is a non sequitur, for it does not follow from the antecedent. For that reason the whole argument collapses and its conclusion is false.

Some atheists have appealed to their materialistic philosophy to provide them with a basis for proving the non-existence of God, but their attempts along those lines have been unavailing. If the general position they take is put in the form of a syllogistic argument, the radical weakness of that position is made apparent. Here is the argument:

Material being is the only being that exists.
"God" is not a material being.
Therefore, "God" does not exist.

I put the term God in quotation marks to indicate how the atheist regards it, as an empty term without any referent. What are we to make of the above argument? From our logic we know that the premises of an argument must be self-evidently true. The first statement in this argument, the major premise, is anything but self-evident, and therefore what follows it can simply be ignored.

For an argument that attempts to prove that the only reality is material reality to have any standing at all, it cannot simply claim that to be the case. It must be proved. We are still waiting for an argument that even comes close to doing so. As I argued in an earlier chapter, the materialist, because of his single-minded commitment to his philosophy, by his unwillingness, or perhaps his inability, to abandon an exclusively empirical mode of reasoning, is prevented from being able even to formulate such an argument. The methodology to which materialism chooses to limit itself cannot provide one with the intellectual wherewithal to prove the supremacy of materialism.

In recent decades we have witnessed, through the publication of several books, a splashy outbreak of the public proclamation of atheism. In reviewing current atheistic literature what is particularly striking is that it is pervasively negative in content and tone. The reader is served up a heavy diet of the woes and wrongs of theism, but considerably less, in fact very little at all, having to do with the wonders and rightness of atheism. The books are often dour and pessimistic, although it is reasonable to assume that they were not intended to be such. What is especially conspicuous for its absence in this literature are any really substantive arguments on behalf of atheism. If the books are meant to gain converts to the position advocated by their authors, it is difficult to see how they can have much success in that regard. Perhaps they believe that their strategy of putting theism in the worst possible light will somehow have the effect of making atheism, by comparison, look like the better option. But this is only to succumb to another fallacy, which I will call the good guy vs. bad guy fallacy. It works this way: If I devote all my efforts in showing that your side is populated by nothing but bad guys (where "bad guys" can be understood as bad ideas), then that is to be taken as meaning that my side is full of nothing but good guys (i.e., good ideas). Non sequitur.

The Attributes of God

Natural theology, after it demonstrates the existence of God, then goes on to attempt to determine, relying on human reason alone, what can be said about the nature of God. There are a number of what have traditionally been called the attributes of God; Thomas Aquinas, in his monumental *Summa Theologiae,* treats at length eight such attributes. Here I will discuss but three of them, briefly outlining the arguments that are offered to elucidate them.

The Simplicity of God. A simple being is one without any composition; it is not made up of parts. Complexity of any kind is foreign to its nature. It is evident, then, that it is impossible that a simple being could be material, for a material being, by definition, is composed of parts.

Some eminent thinkers have thought otherwise, however. The seventeenth-century philosopher, Thomas Hobbes, reflecting the thought of the ancient Greek philosopher Epicurus, argued that God was corporeal, but the matter of which he was made was of a very refined kind. The Dutch philosopher Baruch Spinoza, also of the seventeenth century, adopted a pantheistic position and taught that God was simply one and the same with the physical universe. *Deus sive Natura* was his watchword, "God or Nature"; two words, but they refer to a single reality, one can be exchanged for the other. We can see the radical inadequacy of these materialistic notions of the divine essence if we recall what we know about the nature of material being. Material being is constantly changing (*ens mobile*), and the essence of change is the transition from potency to act. Now, potency is an imperfection in the sense that it implies a lack of something. (X is in potency with respect to Y because it is lacking Y.) Now, there can be no potency in God because he is lacking in nothing. A being lacking in nothing is a perfect being, and such a being does not change for, if we were to allow that a perfect being could change, the only way he could change would be for the worse.

If we put these various considerations together, that God is not material, therefore does not change, therefore is without potency, therefore lacks nothing, we have some specific ideas as to what we mean by the simplicity of God. But more needs to be said. Because God is immaterial he is not composed in that fundamental way as are all material beings, of matter and form. But we learned that there is a composition even more fundamental than that, between essence and existence, between *what* a being is and *that* it is. Is God composed of essence and existence, and, if so, does not that count against his simplicity? God is absolutely unique in that in him essence and existence are one and the same. The implications of this are profound. For every other being that exists in the universe there is a difference between its nature, what it is, and its existence. That means that it is not of the very nature of that being to exist, for if its nature were otherwise, it would be impossible for that being not to exist; it would be eternal. (If essence and existence were one and the same in us, we would be eternal.) With God, because in him essence and existence are identical, it is in fact of his very nature to exist, and therefore he is eternal. God is the one for whom it is impossible not to exist. We may say that the deepest "meaning" of God is "to be."

The simplicity of God implies another of his attributes, his immutability or changelessness which, as noted above, points to his perfection, for mutability or change is fueled by a lack or deficiency, and there is no lack or deficiency in God. We saw that there is no potency in God. Apropos of the distinction between act and potency, that leads to the conclusion that in God there is only act, so we say that he is pure act, *Actus Purus*.

The Infinity of God. God is infinite, meaning that there are no bounds or limitations to him; there is nothing above him or beyond him, nothing external to him that in any way curbs or restricts his pure act, from which we conclude to the omnipotence of God. Another way of describing the infinity of God is to say that he expresses, in his being, unqualified existential completeness. In considering the infinity of God we need to be careful not to confuse it with mathematical infinity, which represents a fascinating example of permanent incompleteness. Mathematical infinity is the persistent and irresoluble indefinite. An irrational number goes on forever, vainly pursuing a closure that will never come. The mathematical infinite is a purely quantitative reality, which means that it is an instance of accidental, not substantial, being. Numbers are qualities of the human mind. The infinity of God is substantial, not accidental; it is actual, not potential. In God there is not, as in mathematics, an incessant progression *toward* some culminating realization that is never reached (*ad infinitum*), for in him all is complete, beginning and ending are one; he is the *Alpha* and the *Omega*.

We can offer what are perhaps some helpful conceptualizations of the infinity of God, but we can never come to anything like an understanding of it, for the simple reason that the human mind is finite and thus cannot fully embrace, cannot encompass, the infinite. We can use the word, but we cannot fathom its depths.

The Unity of God. There are two ways of thinking about the unity of God: first, in terms of God himself; second, in terms of God in relation to what is other than himself. God is one in terms of himself in the sense that he is undivided; he is one in relation to what is other than himself in that there is only one God. He is, in himself, the Supreme Unity, the Absolute One. What was said above about the simplicity of God is applicable here, and bears repeating: God is in no way composed. Though we may speak of the essence and existence of God these are but logical distinctions (i.e., they exist only in the human mind, not in God). There is no duality in God, for in Him essence and existence are one. Nor is there any distinction between act and potency in him, and so the unity of the divine essence is given emphatic expression by saying that he is Pure Act.

There is another argument for the unity of God which I will briefly sketch. It is based on the unity of the universe. We have argued previously that the universe is an ordered whole, a cosmos. Though immensely complex, composed as it is of myriads upon myriads of individual physical substances, be they minuscule or enormous in size, they constitute a unit, albeit a unit whose dimensions boggle the mind. A unit is best described as a coherent whole; now, the most logical source to be supposed for the existence of a coherent whole is a single, unified source. We argue, then, that the unity of the universe is a reflection, a concrete manifestation, however imperfect, of the unity of God. Apropos of a distinction introduced earlier, we say that the unity of God is substantial and absolute, whereas the unity of the universe is accidental and finite.

There is only one God. Given a proper grasp of the nature of God, of what we mean by "God," polytheism is a contradiction in terms. The uniqueness of God follows from the fact that in him nature (what he is) and existence (that he is) are one, and this stands in marked contrast to what is the case with us human beings, or with any other created beings, i.e., those that do not owe their existence to themselves. God is his nature; his nature is summed up and expressed in the single being that is himself. This cannot be said of Socrates; we cannot say that Socrates is human nature. He *has* a human nature; it is something he shares with all other human beings. We say, "all men are equal," meaning that no single human being, male or female, is more or less human than any other human being. Socrates is part of humanity, not coextensive with it. With God it is precisely the opposite: His unity is coextensive with divinity; divinity is exclusively God's. Humanity is not exclusive to Socrates or to any of the rest of us.

The perfection of God is an attribute which is implied by the other attributes treated in this section. To say that any being is perfect is to say that it is complete, that it lacks nothing. God is infinitely perfect, by which we mean that there are no limits to his perfection, and that underscores his uniqueness, the fact that there is only one God. There cannot be two infinitely perfect beings. To claim otherwise would be roughly like saying, to use an image I availed myself of earlier, that there could be two topmost points to an isosceles triangle; if that were so, it would cease to be what it is, a triangle, and become a pentagon.

But let us suppose, for the sake of argument, that there are two Gods, two infinitely perfect or supreme beings. If there are two Gods there would have to be something by which one could be distinguished from the other.

But what would we point to in order to do that? Again, we are assuming that there are two infinitely perfect beings, two supreme beings. But that means, both being perfect in every respect, neither lacking in anything whatsoever, they would have to be absolutely identical, and that would mean there is no way to distinguish them, and therefore we have no basis for calling them "two"; "they" are one and the same. Conclusion: there is only one God.

In order to see if we can avoid that conclusion let us take a different tack and say that both of these beings share a common nature, which we might designate as "infinite being," or "supreme being," or simply "divine." But that, rather than solving the problem only exacerbates it, for if we were to suppose the existence of two Gods sharing a single nature, this would necessarily imply: (1) there is something apart from and superior to them, i.e., their divinity (just as humanity is apart from and superior to Socrates), and therefore neither would be the exclusively divine being (just as Socrates is not the exclusively human being); (2) because the divine nature is something they share, and not exclusive to either of them, the divinity of neither one of them is explained by the simple fact of their existence. So, because divinity is exclusive to neither of them, they must owe their divinity to something other than themselves, which leads to the conclusions that (a) there is something above and beyond them, and therefore (b) they are not supreme beings. General conclusion from the above considerations: there is only one God.

The Moral Arguments for the Existence of God

What are called the moral arguments for the existence of God, unlike the metaphysical arguments—three of which we have presented in previous pages—are not demonstrative: they are probable arguments and do not claim that they prove the existence of God conclusively. Depending on how they are constructed and developed, they can be said to be either weakly or strongly persuasive. A moral argument is not to be regarded as necessarily a bad argument; though not conclusive, it nonetheless can be significantly compelling. Again, whether or not it is such depends very much on the quality of the evidence it puts forward and how it is handled. We may not be completely convinced by a moral argument, but it can be provocative enough to give us something to think seriously about. If it is a good argument, we would be disinclined to reject it out of hand. There is no exact count of the moral arguments; suffice it to say that there are many of them, and entirely new ones are regularly being formulated. Here I will limit myself to the discussion of three of the most popular of those arguments.

An Argument Based upon Moral Consciousness

There is no adult human being of sound mind who does not have, and who is not guided in his behavior by, a keen sense of the distinction between right and wrong. Differences certainly arise among people when it comes down to identifying what qualifies as being either right or wrong regarding specific matters and in particular situations, but no one denies or ignores the distinction itself. Everyone acknowledges that in the moral order there is a real difference between the good and the bad, however one might define the two. What Sal regards as good, Sally regards as bad, but both admit there is a good and a bad. However, the differences in this respect should not be exaggerated, for they are not as radical and mutually exclusive as they are sometimes supposed to be. Surveying the basic patterns of moral thinking throughout human history, what is most striking are not the differences but the commonalities. There is more agreement than disagreement regarding basic moral principles.

There are a number of prominent constants, pervasive and abiding moral principles—call them moral absolutes—that are operatively present throughout the ages and which are found in every culture. They are the governing standards by which human beings, since time immemorial, have structured their individual and social lives. For example, no matter what the age or the culture, it has always been understood, beyond dispute, to be wrong to wantonly take another person's life, to steal another's property, to lie.

These basic moral constants are rooted in human consciousness; they are what constitute us as moral agents, but they do not seem to be the products of human invention. They do not have the character of something that we have imposed upon ourselves, as if they were no more than practical expedients created for the purpose of establishing social order, thus putting them in the same category as our civil laws. There is the commanding fact of their universality, of their being trans-temporal and trans-cultural. We take them to be representative of an objective moral order, comparable to the objective physical order; just as there are physical laws that govern the physical realm and apply to all of us as physical beings, so there are moral laws that govern the moral realm and apply to all of us as moral beings.

The question is, then, what is the source, the ultimate explanation, of these moral constants, these basic moral principles (stealing is wrong, lying is wrong, etc.), which taken together could be said to constitute a universal moral law, a set of moral standards which are common to all human beings and which can be shown to have been applicable in all times and all cultures? We contend that the source transcends human nature, and that source is God.

There have been some who, taking a Romantic view of humankind, would contest this. The philosopher Jean Jacques Rousseau seemed to believe that human beings were naturally good, that they were born not only free but without any moral blemish; if they subsequently became corrupted it was on account of civilization. But if human beings are naturally good, how did it happen that they managed to establish a morally corrupting civilization? The philosopher Thomas Hobbes, another philosopher we have met earlier, took a considerably less sanguine view of humankind, arguing that if people were allowed to behave without strict governmental restrictions, curbing their natural, pernicious propensities, they would be at one another's throats. Hobbes's view is an extreme one, to be sure, but it nevertheless seems to corroborate the general impression one gets by reading human history. Rousseau takes too sanguine an attitude toward the present state of human nature, Hobbes a too pessimistic one. Human nature is essentially good, but it has been wounded. We are capable of making steady progress along the road of moral righteousness, but we limp as we stride.

There is another objection to the argument, of modern vintage. It begins by conceding that there may have been certain basic moral principles that were for a long time universally abided by, but, the objection goes, those days are lost and gone forever. Today moral relativism reigns supreme. It is now up to each individual, following his or her conscience, to determine what is morally right or wrong. According to this view, there are no moral absolutes that can be said to apply universally. We live in a world of moral babble, of ethical incoherence.

In response to this objection one might first observe, in passing, that if, as claimed, "there are no moral absolutes," it is hard to construe that statement as anything other than a moral absolute. More to the point, though, the factual accuracy of the present state of moral affairs as just described is very much open to question. Granted, there has been a pronounced and widespread loosening up of moral standards in this country, beginning with the decade of the 1960s, but if we would simply take into account our daily experiences, in which we are commonly dealing with a number of different people in a variety of situations, do we actually believe that we are helplessly and dangerously awash in a turbulent sea of moral relativism, and that therefore we need to be ever on the alert and super sensitive to the possibility that this salesperson or that newspaper columnist is lying to us? That scarcely seems to be the case.

A little basic logic would come in handy here. Granting the prevalence of moral relativism, the presence in contemporary society of a rather widespread denial of universal moral standards, does that prove that there are no such standards? No, it only shows that there are a lot of people today who, for whatever variety of reasons, ignore those standards and freely choose not to abide by them. Ignoring a law does not erase it from the books.

With all the foregoing considerations in mind, we contend that there is a universal moral law, universal in the sense that it applies to human beings just as such; we contend that this law is transcendent, in the sense that, while it applies to humans its source is not human; and we reiterate the conclusion stated above: the source of this law is a universal lawgiver, and that is God. In sum, the existence of a universal moral order, and of a shared consciousness of and deference toward that order on the part of all human beings, stand as proofs of God's existence.

An Argument Based on the Universal Acknowledgment of the Transcendent

Atheism has always been a minority position. Every age would seem to have had its representatives, and some of them have been prominent and outspoken personages, and not a few of them have been very articulate. Some of the most articulate among them have been philosophers; one thinks immediately of Friedrich Nietzsche, who has become somewhat of a hero for those who take a dim view of theism. The son and grandson of Lutheran pastors, Nietzsche was definitely no friend of religion, and waxed positively wrathful when it came to the subject of Christianity in particular. However, many of his readers and admirers do not seem to register his ambivalent attitude toward "the death of God" proclaimed by his spokesman Zarathustra.

Looking at the big picture, we find that the full sweep of human history provides no evidence that there has ever been an entire society, a whole people or nation, which was naturally atheistic, that is, where atheism was an organic feature of its culture. In modern times there have been nations which have been declared officially atheistic by their rulers, but in every case this was an imposed atheism, maintained with whatever degree of conviction only by a governing elite who made up but a small portion of the total population, and was not freely subscribed to by the large majority upon whom it was imposed. Poland when it was under Communist rule is a classic case in point. Cultural anthropologists, in their study of so-called primitive peoples, have found in every culture not simply the presence but the dominance of what can generally be described as a religious consciousness, reflecting a belief in a reality that transcends the natural order.

There has been, since the eighteenth century, a decided increase in overt atheism in Western culture, a phenomenon which goes a long way toward explaining the progressive secularization that has been taking place in recent decades, most pronouncedly in European societies. A significant number of the intelligentsia, and many scientists, would declare themselves to be atheists or agnostics. We have witnessed lately the emergence of a cadre of militant atheists who write books, give lectures, and generally receive a good deal of attention from the mass media. Some of these men come across as veritable missionaries of atheism, whose earnest proselytizing is presumably fueled by the conviction that benighted believers need to be converted to un-belief so that they might then qualify as fully-fledged rational creatures. But taking it all in all, the contemporary scene, as far as atheism is concerned, is far from clear. From the fact that there are now atheists who are boldly declamatory in expressing their views, we cannot conclude that they are the spokesmen for the majority. Not a few people, especially among the intellectual elite, claim that, while not religious, they are nonetheless "spiritual," by which they seem to mean that, at the very least, they are not crude materialists and have an acute sense of the transcendent.

The basic premise on which this argument is based is this: humankind is naturally religious. The overwhelming majority of the human race—one could simply say the human race, period—throughout the course of its history, in all of the cultures by which it has been represented, has consistently shown itself to be religious. What does it mean to be religious? Religion manifests itself in a wide variety of ways, and all people have been and are religious in specifically identifiable ways, such as Christian, Jewish, Hindu, or Muslim. All men of all times have displayed, typically as a dominant and centralizing aspect of their lives, what I call a basic religious sense, identified by four fundamental features: (1) It is non-materialistic, and involves a belief in a spiritual realm and spiritual beings. (2) The spiritual realm transcends, is superior to the natural, material realm; it is supernatural. (3) The spiritual beings which are believed in: (a) are personal; (b) are good; (c) govern and benevolently care for human beings; (d) are themselves governed by a supreme spiritual being (e.g., "the Great Spirit"). (4) Human beings are not purely material, but have spiritual souls that survive the death of the body, which is attested to by the elaborate funeral rites to be found in every culture.

What are we to make of all this? Some atheists have argued that the basic religious sense is nothing but a persistent illusion which has been delaying the progress of the human race for far too long, and that it is now high time that we all finally grow up as a people and rid ourselves of this debilitating nuisance. All things considered, it is difficult to decide which is the more remarkable: the religious sense itself or the atheists' response to it. If the religious sense of humankind is nothing but an illusion, then, given its pervasiveness and the powerful tenacity it has exhibited throughout the ages, surviving all the profound, mind-challenging changes the human race has been through since the beginning, especially in modern times, it would have to be recognized as arguably the most colossal phenomenon the world has known, and scarcely something to be trivialized by dismissive labeling.

And what are we to say of all the extraordinary people of every age, indeed the towering geniuses, who have been devoutly religious, including some of the major figures in the history of science (e.g., Copernicus, Kepler,

Galileo, Newton). Are these people to be condescendingly regarded as some-how victims of arrested development, intellectually and emotionally imma-ture, who had the misfortune not to have lived in our highly enlightened age? One may say that the scientists I mention above all lived in an age in which Christianity was still a significant factor in Western culture, and that their religiousness was no more than a product of the social milieu of which they were a part. That would be a hard view to accept for one who is ac-quainted with what these gentlemen had written about God and theological matters. Newton spent the last several years of his life, not principally work-ing in physics or mathematics, but poring over the Bible, which provided him with the knowledge he needed to predict the end of the world.

To glibly dismiss the religious sense as no more than a grand mistake needs to be recognized, among other things, as a prominent case of intel-lectual shiftiness, a studied refusal to reflect seriously on a monumental fact of human history.

The strength, universality, and tenacity of man's religious sense argues against the claim that it is based on illusion; it would be irresponsible to brush it aside cavalierly as if it were a major but nonetheless mindless quirk of human history. Quite to the contrary, the evidence compels us to con-clude that the overwhelming majority of human beings have not been beset by illusory ideas over the entire course of the race's history: our basic reli-gious sense serves as proof for the existence of God.

An Argument Based on Beauty

Is there any human being who is so obtuse, so thoroughly insensitive, that he does not respond positively to beauty? One would not want to think so. What is it about beauty that so captivates us, demands our complete atten-tion? It will not be ignored, cannot be dismissed as inconsequential. It defies precise definition, yet we never fail to recognize it. It has countless inter-preters, yet their efforts are unnecessary, for beauty speaks for itself, and al-ways eloquently.

If we think about beauty in terms of the effects it has on us, three things stand out: it is arresting; it is provocative; it is transporting.

Beauty is arresting, it has a way of putting the brakes on the humdrum motions of the moment. A college professor walks out of a classroom building at the end of the day, making his way toward the parking lot and his car. His head is swimming with good and bad thoughts about a lecture he has just given; his eyes are on but not really seeing the gravel pathway along which he is walking. He suddenly looks up and beholds splashed across the western sky a spectacular sunset. (He is going to say later, often, it was the most spectacular sunset he had ever seen.) At that moment he did not say to himself, "I am going to stop and stare at this sunset," he just did, quite involuntarily; he had been arrested by beauty. He stood there, half mesmerized, drinking in all the details, taking note of the peculiar distribution of the clouds, their positions, configurations, coloration. The picture before him was dynamic, not static, continuously changing, but slowly, subtly, seductively. Patterns would overlap patterns, overlay them, replace them, forming new patterns. He was especially entranced by the colors. Some were standard and he could readily identify them—red, orange, rose, pink—others he had no names for, and he wondered if the most skilled painter, the most state-of-the-art camera, could capture them, do them justice. You have to be right here, right now, he thought, to appreciate this, to properly assimilate this, drink it in, get tipsy from it. Was he standing there a couple of minutes, five, more? He wasn't quite sure and it seemed it didn't quite matter. There was something about the experience that had little to do with time. He shook his head and walked on; he had to get home for supper.

Beauty can have that kind of arresting effect on us, sometimes literally stopping us in our tracks, interrupting our routine, emptying the mind of the prosaic and filling it with a rush of unexpected poetry, giving us a kind of pleasure that seems somehow to instruct as well as to sooth. The calmness that can all of a sudden settle upon us when we have an encounter with beauty may be of short duration, but it penetrates deeply, makes a permanent mark on the memory.

Beauty can be powerfully provocative, sometimes positively disturbing, and if the disturbance can be called painful it is of the healing type, an aesthetic surgery of sorts. The unrest it can provoke is resolvable. The "thing of beauty" is right before us, being registered by our senses, concretely realized as something quite specific—a sunset, a work of art, a person—and yet, somehow, it is more than just *there*; it seems to point beyond itself, intimating that it is not entirely self-explanatory, that it has a fully explanatory source in something more complete, more compelling, more satisfying.

This intimation can be quite vague, and yet persistent for all that; it is not an explicit, perfectly clear declaration, but a subtle, circuitous suggestion. Beauty captivates us, but, paradoxically, not to confine us. It has a freeing quality; it opens our minds and hearts to new realms of possibility. It lures us to itself, but only to lead us to something beyond itself.

Beauty is transporting. It can take us out of ourselves, remove us from the quotidian here and now and introduce us to a state of novel tranquility. We experience a quiet peace, a peace pregnant with meaning, but we would be hard-pressed to specify that meaning with any kind of exactness. An experience of this sort is almost always momentary: it can be gone before we fully realize its presence, but the memory of it is tenacious. What was happening? It was something inspired, provoked, by beauty; it was an especially intense experience resulting from an encounter with a specific thing of beauty; Chopin's First Piano Concerto let us say, and yet, while very much rooted in that thing of beauty, it somehow carried us beyond it. To what? Plato taught that when we respond to beauty, in nature, in art, in persons, we are responding to material beings whose beauty, though real enough, is not entirely complete and self-contained. These things of beauty are beautiful by participation; they share in, represent, and reflect Beauty itself, which is a substantial reality, immaterial and eternal. This Beauty is not merely a sublime instance of beauty, but the very essence of beauty, the source and explanation of everything that we call beautiful in the material world; it thus has a status that could be called divine. So, Plato would say, when I recognize and am gratified by something that is truly beautiful, what I am really recognizing, though I may not be cognizant of the fact, is Beauty itself. I am in touch with the divine, the transcendent, albeit indirectly so. Plato came very close to expressing the truth of the matter.

Why is beauty arresting? Because the deeper meaning it has to convey to us forces us to suspend our normal, commonplace way of thinking, the regular horizontal flow of our thoughts, and to think in new and startling ways, to give a vertical direction to our thoughts and feelings.

Why is beauty provocative? Because it points to something which is beyond itself, not to a Platonic Idea, to the immaterial and eternal substance he called Beauty, but rather to God, the cause of all being, the ultimate source and explanation of the beauty we see and hear all around us. Thus we can say, not that God is beautiful, for that would put him in a category external to himself, but that he is one and the same with beauty, just as he is one and the same with truth and goodness. We can rightly say that beauty is another name for God.

Why is beauty transporting? Why does it have the capacity, however rarely and briefly, to make time stand still and lift us out of ourselves? Because it is coaxing us toward a moment of singular illumination, when we see that the innermost meaning of beauty is that its source is the beauty who is God.

The conclusion of our argument, succinctly put, is that the mere fact of beauty, given the effects it has upon us, can be offered as a proof for the existence of God.

Some Retrospective Reflections

The several arguments directed toward proving the existence of God that were provided in this chapter are representative of the central occupation of natural theology. The arguments were of two kinds, metaphysical and moral. Those called metaphysical are demonstrative; that is, their purpose is to prove in the strict sense. If the premises of the argument are true, if its structure is sound (i.e., valid), then the conclusion, "God exists," follows necessarily. The moral arguments have the same conclusion, but it does not follow necessarily because it is not the end product of formal deductive reasoning. On that account the conclusions are regarded as probable; they may not convince, but they could be persuasive, depending on the basis or point of departure of a particular argument, how it is constructed, and how it is developed.

An argument may be generally described as compelling or persuasive. It can be called compelling if it convinces, if someone who reads the argument accepts its conclusion without hesitation, has no doubts that the conclusion is true. Now to consider a different situation, we may come across an argument that, having read it carefully, find it to be quite impressive in many respects, but we are reluctant to give unqualified assent to its conclusion. However, we do not reject it out of hand, for we see that its conclusion is strongly supported, and could probably be true. In a case like that, we would call the argument persuasive. With compelling arguments, it is usually a clear matter of yes or no; with persuasive arguments it is more a matter of maybe, of an argument being more or less persuasive, depending on the strength of the backing for its conclusion. In any event, however we judge the quality of an argument, that judgment must have a solid objective basis, and that basis can be nothing else than the argument itself.

That means that our analysis and judgment of arguments very much depends—everything entirely depends—on the quality of our knowledge of the arguments. Any argument which deals with important and serious subject matter of whatever kind, presuming it to be a sound argument (it does not violate any of the rules of logic), is going to make special demands on us; we have to meet it actively, often more than half-way, give it our full attention, encounter it with an attitude of mind which combines critical astuteness with an unprejudiced open-minded receptivity. All this is especially called for when it comes to the metaphysical arguments that natural theology presents to us; they are not as immediately accessible as are the moral arguments, and that is because metaphysics itself is a demanding science which requires disciplined thinking and patient perseverance of those who would seriously pursue it.

Regarding the arguments in which natural theology specializes, those dedicated to the ambitious task of proving the existence of God, we are called upon to think along lines which, I think it safe to say, most people in our now quite secularized world are not much, if at all, familiar with. This would require our becoming somewhat "unworldly" in our thinking, shedding the vacuous clichés and facile mental formulas which are the marks of a tired modernity.

An important point needs to be stressed, regarding the arguments which are the regular fare of natural theology. A metaphysical argument for the existence of God, if successful, proves that God exists; it does not bring about religious faith. Here the limitations of philosophy must be clearly stated. No philosophical argument, regardless of how carefully constructed and clearly articulated, can, of itself, be the efficient cause which brings about the act of faith, and the reason for that is quite simple; faith is a gift, and God is the giver.

But what those arguments can do, and this is what natural theology intends that they do, is to serve as what Thomas Aquinas called the preambles of faith, which can be loosely described as all matters, including arguments for God's existence, that can have the effect of leading up to and preparing for the faith.

But more can be said about how natural theology can profitably be related to faith, specifically with regard to its centrally important intellectual aspect. The initial act of faith by which one comes to believe, accepts the gift, is an act of intellectual assent. As such, it is the altogether normal, perfectly natural, response of a rational creature. The will is of course involved, inseparably so, in this singularly important human act, but the movement of the will follows upon, or perhaps we can say accompanies, the illuminating assent of the intellect. The point of that little review is simply to stress the vital conjunction of faith and reason. Because we believe as rational creatures, our faith, if it is to remain vibrant, must be the continuing subject of our reasoning attention; we think, and think much, about what we believe.

In describing the nature of natural theology at the beginning of the chapter we specified how our science was similar to sacred theology and how it differed from it. The similarity between the two lay in the fact that they both had the same basic subject matter: God and everything that relates to God. The significant difference between the two is that natural theology approaches its subject matter from a natural point of view, relying on human reason alone, whereas sacred theology, while of course also employing human reason, does so in treating its subject matter as appreciably expanded and enriched by divine revelation. Now, given this significant difference between the two sciences, sacred theology can contribute immeasurably more to religious faith than can natural theology. Even so, natural theology, while staying within its proper bounds, and simply by fully living up to its proper purposes as a science, has much it can contribute to the Christian faith simply by standing as a continuing, active witness to the importance of the relation between faith and reason. Natural theology is, as a science, an organized, systematic way of thinking about God and all that relates to matters divine, and for that reason can serve as stimulus and sustenance to faith. We noted earlier in the book the distinction St. Thomas makes between reason and "right reason" (*recta ratio*). It is right reason, reason that is uncorrupted by sin, which is not only entirely compatible with faith, but is that without which faith can become a dead letter. We naturally reason about faith because we believe as rational creatures; we think much about, meditate upon, what we believe because if we were not to do so we would not be responding to the inclinations and invitations of our proper nature.

Recall that natural theology is part of metaphysics, is in fact its culmination. Recall also that one of the names that Aristotle explicitly assigned to what today we call metaphysics was "theology." He believed that not just metaphysics but all philosophy, if it is done rightly, fulfilling its proper tasks, should end up with God. Why did he believe that? Because what philosophy should be all about is searching for and discovering first principles, those fundamental truths that are the explanatory underpinnings of reality itself. And what is God? God is the Absolute First Principle, which is to say that God is the ultimate and complete explanation for all that is, for the sum total of existence.

In the Introduction to this book I invited my readers to become philosophical, that is, to give serious, thoughtful, critical consideration, as they moved from chapter to chapter, to assimilating the content, and adopting the governing principles and ways of reasoning, typical of the Aristotelian-Thomistic philosophical tradition. Does that mean that I would want you all to become philosophers? Yes it does, but I would want you to become philosophers in the only meaningful and worthwhile way of doing so. Becoming a philosopher doesn't mean that you should get professional degrees in philosophy; that is not necessary, and often it can prove to be a positive hindrance. I would want you to become true philosophers, which means that you take the etymology of the word with passionate literalness. A true philosopher is simply, and devotedly, a lover and persistent pursuer of wisdom. A true philosopher is an everlastingly faithful lover of truth.

THE END